FRENCHIE

ISBN 13 (paper): 978-1-959569-10-7

http://ulpress.org
University of Louisiana at Lafayette Press
P.O. Box 43558
Lafayette, LA 70504-3558

This book was generously supported by the Franco-American Benevolent Society of Lafayette, Louisiana.

Printed in the United States

Library of Congress Cataloging-in-Publication Data

Names: Theriot, Jason P., 1975- author.
Title: Frenchie : the story of the French-speaking Cajuns of World War II / Jason P. Theriot.
Other titles: Story of the French-speaking Cajuns of World War II
Description: Lafayette, LA : University of Louisiana at Lafayette Press, 2024. | Includes bibliographical references.
Identifiers: LCCN 2023049632 | ISBN 9781959569107 (paperback)
Subjects: LCSH: World War, 1939-1945--Participation, Cajuns. | World War, 1939-1945--Military intelligence--United States. | Translating and interpreting--United States--History--20th century. | Cajuns--Europe--History--20th century. | Cajuns--Pacific Area--History--20th century. | Cajuns--Africa, North--History--20th century. | World War, 1939-1945--Africa, North. | World War, 1939-1945--Europe. | World War, 1939-1945--Pacific Area. | World War, 1939-1945--Secret service. | Soldiers--Louisiana--History--20th century.
Classification: LCC D810.C14 T44 2024 | DDC 940.53089/410763--dc23/eng/20240130
LC record available at https://lccn.loc.gov/2023049632

FRENCHIE

THE STORY OF THE FRENCH-SPEAKING CAJUNS OF WORLD WAR II

Jason P. Theriot

2024
University of Louisiana at Lafayette Press

TABLE OF CONTENTS

ARKANSAS
LOUISIANA
Shreveport
Monroe
N
MISSISSIPPI
Alexandria
TEXAS
Baton Rouge
(ACADIANA)
Lake Charles
Lafayette
ATTAKAPAS
New Orleans
GULF OF MEXICO
Map by Shane K. Bernard

PREFACE

In March 2019, I received a call from a friend, Brenda Comeaux Trahan, who invited me to travel to Moncton, New Brunswick, for the *Congrès mondial acadien* that August. She wanted me to tag along with her group, Louisiane-Acadie, and share the stories of the French-speaking Cajuns of World War II. Like many who had supported my research efforts from the beginning, Brenda understood the links between the Cajuns of that great generation and our Acadian past. That generation was the last to grow up speaking French as their first language. She also had a hunch, as I had, that the Cajuns and Acadians of World War II shared a unique experience because of their language. Although I had not worked on or given public lectures about my "Cajuns in World War II" project for many years, the prospect of traveling with a distinguished group to the land of my Acadian ancestors seemed intriguing. It was definitely on my bucket list.

Before I accepted the invite, I quickly pulled up Google Earth and plotted the driving distance between Moncton and Aulac, New Brunswick, on the border with Nova Scotia, in a region known as Beaubassin. My Acadian ancestors—Joseph Terrio and his wife, Magdeline Bourgeois—came from that region, and I, like many others, have had a long fascination with my Acadian past. According to sources, they lived in an area north of Aulac in a valley that overlooked fertile growing fields—once a salt marsh that the Acadians had reclaimed to grow hay and other crops.[1] This would have been their last known settlement in 1755 before the expulsion, now known as *Le Grand Dérangement*, began. A traumatic event ultimately brought the couple—and hundreds of other refugees from Beaubassin—to south Louisiana ten years later. According to the map, the driving distance from Moncton to this general location in the Beaubassin valley was twenty-five miles. My response to Brenda was swift and without hesitation: count me in!

Thus began Phase 3—the final phase—of my nearly twenty-five-year-long project to document the stories of Cajuns in World War II. The experience

I had on that trip to Acadie, and the reception I received from Cajuns and Acadians alike, greatly influenced the research and writing effort behind what is now *Frenchie: The Story of the French-Speaking Cajuns of World War II.*

The journey to this point has been long, consuming nearly all my adult life. I have always been fascinated with World War II. As a kid, movies like *The Dirty Dozen* and *The Longest Day* as well as picture books in my stepfather's collection first drew my attention to the subject. For my last course at Louisiana State University in 1998, I took a World War II correspondence class, which required extensive reading and a deep dive into the literature. I bought my first World War II book, Stephen Ambrose's *D-Day, June 6, 1944: The Climactic Battle of World War II* and read it twice before I bought another. I visited The National D-Day Museum (now The National WWII Museum) in New Orleans the year it opened in 2000. From then on, I became a voracious reader of all things related to World War II. Somewhere along that book-reading marathon, I came up with an idea to interview my grandfathers and a few of their friends, using their stories to write my own short book on their World War II experiences. Why not? I had a journalism degree and had honed my writing skills during those college years. After moving to Houston, Texas, with a night-shift job at Fox Sports, I had time during the day to work on this new hobby book project.

When I initially contacted my grandfather, Hewitt Theriot, about the idea for this project, he wholeheartedly agreed to participate. However, we both expressed hesitations about finding enough veterans to interview. He seemed to think that not many people his age would be willing to tell their stories. Yet during my first "research trip" to Louisiana, I found an interesting book at Books Along the Teche, a bookstore in New Iberia, that set the foundation for this project. It was the *Honor Roll of Iberia Parish World War II Veterans*, an alphabetized "Honor Roll Yearbook" with photographs and brief biographies of more than 1,400 World War II veterans (mostly white males) from the area I grew up in and published shortly after the war. I left the book with my grandfather to peruse, and upon returning to Louisiana the following weekend, he informed me: "Jason, I have good news and bad news. The good news is I read the book and found at least fifty people we can interview starting today. The bad news is that I only got through the B's." Enlightened by the thought of launching this worthwhile endeavor with so many veterans still living in my birthplace—Iberia Parish—yet overwhelmed by the enormous challenge ahead, we set out to capture and record the stories and

Jason Theriot and Hewitt Theriot, cir. 2002

memories of as many veterans from the area as we could. We called it the "To Honor Our Veterans" oral history project.

Nearly five years later, I had conducted (with my grandfather as a tagalong) more than a hundred interviews with veterans from across the Acadiana region, written and self-published a three-volume book series, given dozens of lectures, and sat for interviews on TV and radio to discuss the project. From the interviewees I learned that war is uncomfortable, monotonous, and often dreadfully painful; it robs our young of their innocence, rips apart families and communities, and leaves profound emotional and physical scars. In the case of World War II, the collective experiences of millions of Americans brought the nation closer together. The Cajuns who served—in whatever capacity—felt drawn to the patriotic cause. Moreover, speaking with these veterans, most of whom were born in the early 1920s, taught me the importance of my Cajun-Acadian heritage, which was, sadly, not a subject covered in school. I simply had no reference point. Gaining knowledge from community elders gave me that reference point. And, not surprisingly, I quickly became drawn to Cajun-Acadian history as well.

One of the lessons learned from that oral history project, and subsequent others, is that the "big questions" sometimes do not reveal themselves until way down the road. Such was the case with the To Honor Our Veterans project. Initially, I set out to uncover what Cajuns specifically contributed to the war effort. I found that they participated in virtually every front, from building the warships at home to fighting in the trenches. A year or two into the research, I also began to discover that many Cajuns played unique wartime roles because the vast majority of them spoke French. As such, scores of these Cajuns used their vital language skills in a variety of military jobs, from interpreters in North Africa to secret agents working behind enemy lines with the French Resistance. "Frenchies," as most American GIs called their French-speaking Cajun comrades, became highly valued by American field commanders in need of soldiers to translate. For many Cajuns, their upbringing provided them with the skills needed to survive in a combat environment, where living off the land, for example, became a necessity. Many excelled in leadership roles and received subsequent military accolades and promotions. Even on the home front, in the shipbuilding industry, hundreds—potentially thousands—of women from south Louisiana flocked into the welding and riveting schools to learn to build the ships and military machines in Gulf Coast factories. Many women, like Effie Logan and Irma Darphin, served as nurses in combat zones overseas. Like the young men, Cajun women joined the war effort in droves. They too felt a patriotic duty to wear a uniform, tend to the injured, and work in the shipyards. Their collective contributions, while not unlike other American ethnic groups during the war, were documented for posterity.

Nevertheless, that first project did not dig deep into an understanding of the ways in which the war impacted the Cajuns themselves. This proved to be a more challenging question. As part of my master's thesis at the University of Houston, I decided to pick up where I left off. I began interviewing veterans again in 2006, but with a different purpose in mind. I wanted to know how the war experience changed the Cajuns who had taken part, in particular those who used their French-language skills overseas. Did it change the way they viewed their culture and heritage? A deep dive into two sets of wartime letters, found in the Joel L. Fletcher papers at the University of Louisiana at Lafayette (UL Lafayette) and the *L'Echo du Teche* church bulletins originally printed in Breaux Bridge, revealed something new, if not astonishing. Young Cajuns from that generation seemed to have experienced a cultural awakening. For the next year, I conducted another extensive round of oral history interviews to ask new questions from many of the same veterans. From this work, I produced a thesis, "Cajuns in World War II, 1940–1947." I had two copies of the manuscript printed and bound, one for the university library and one for my bookshelf. And there it sat for the next fifteen years, awaiting some reason to push it forward.

During that time, I grew busy doing other things, and although I would occasionally receive phone calls from old veterans or give a talk now and again, the story of the Cajuns of World War II, from my perspective, appeared to have been sufficiently covered by myself and other scholars. There didn't seem to be any new interest in pursuing the project further. All that changed after spending a week emersed in Acadian culture during the 2019 *Congrès mondial acadien*.

On the plane ride home, sitting next to my wife and me was Matt Mick of CODOFIL, the Council for the Development of French in Louisiana. Our paths had crossed during the busy week at the festival, but he had not seen my presentation, nor did he know the full story of "Frenchie." With a five-hour flight ahead of us and my laptop in hand, I gave him the full account. He was captivated and explained that not enough people in his CODOFIL circle, much less the broader public, knew the details of this story. How could we fix that? For one, I thought of making these stories more accessible with a podcast series. I had previously discussed this idea with Chris Segura and Josh Caffery at the Center for Louisiana Studies at UL Lafayette a few months prior, but the concept needed some direction, partners, funding, and, most importantly, a spark. With help from Warren Perrin and the Acadian Museum in Erath, and with a generous grant from Louisiana Endowment for the Humanities (LEH), the "Frenchie Podcast" came alive in 2021.

But what about dusting off that thesis to write another book? And could I find any living veterans to add to this compelling story? Two important contacts helped launch that effort. I reached out to Dave McNamara, a feature reporter and videographer in New Orleans who hosted a program on Fox 8 titled "Heart of Louisiana." I met him at The National WWII Museum for an on-camera interview. A week later, we met again in Abbeville at the home of my good friend Robert LeBlanc, a legendary military veteran who served with the Office of Strategic Services (OSS). McNamara filmed my interview with LeBlanc about his wartime activities with a special forces unit that worked directly with the French Resistance behind enemy lines following the Normandy invasion in 1944. The feature story, "Frenchie," aired in the New Orleans region in early 2020.

Around the same time, I reached out to another old contact, George Morris, a career reporter and editor with the *Advocate* in Baton Rouge. He wrote a feature story about the Frenchie project that ran in the Sunday edition of the paper in November 2019. At the end of the article, he added a simple line: "If anyone has information about the French-speaking Cajuns of World War II, contact Jason Theriot directly." Over the next few weeks, I received more than two hundred individual messages—emails, texts, letters, and phone calls—from people who had a story to share about their family member who was known as "Frenchie" or who used their French language in some capacity during the war. Most were secondhand stories that had been passed down. Several individuals had wartime letters, journals, and even a few recorded interviews to share. As news spread through various channels, I discovered several war veterans still living, and they were eager to tell their stories. But Father Time was knocking on their doorstep.

And so, with a renewed focus, a new set of veterans to interview, and a running start, I mapped out a project plan and went to work. Over the course of the next three years, I interviewed another eight veterans, all of whom were nearing one hundred years of age. I revisited the wartime letters mentioned previously and mined those sources more extensively. The new availability of online newspaper archives provided a near-endless supply of fascinating short entries about French-speaking Cajuns during the war. It developed into a valuable tool for tracking hundreds of individuals and their military activities across the globe. Gradually, the primary source material began to pile up.

Jason Theriot and Norris Morvant, "Cajun-Acadian WWII Commemoration," The National WWII Museum, 2022, photo by Frank Aymami

During this new research effort, I had the opportunity to promote the Frenchie project with appearances on several radio shows and podcast episodes. All the while, I continued to host and produce my own podcast, with a generous grant from CODOFIL, the Atchafalaya National Heritage Area, and others, that featured stories from the French-speaking veterans themselves. In a landmark event in April 2022, The National WWII Museum in New Orleans formally recognized the contributions of French-speaking Cajuns *and* Acadians who served in World War II. This commemoration and recognition, in partnership with the Consulate General of Canada to the United States (southwest region) and the museum, had been long over do.

With the 2024 *Congrès mondial acadien* in Nova Scotia and the eightieth anniversary of D-Day on the horizon, and with only a handful of these Cajun Frenchies still living, the preparation of the manuscript began in earnest. This book, *Frenchie*, pays a final tribute to them and the generation of French-speaking Cajuns who participated in the most pivotal global event of the twentieth century.

Jason P. Theriot
August 29, 2023

INTRODUCTION

"Il fait chaud à Suez."
"Les dés sont sur le tapis."[1]

The night before Allied forces landed at Normandy in a massive collaborative effort known as D-Day, coded radio messages such as these sent from London launched an underground army of French Resistance fighters into action. They cut German communications, blew up bridges, and sabotaged enemy columns all through the twilight hours and well into the ensuing days after June 6, 1944. When the Allied forces stormed the Normandy beaches, tens of thousands of American soldiers were thrust into an epic battle against a well-entrenched German army in France. The GIs had been preparing for this momentous invasion for months. They had weapons and maps, and carried plenty of cigarettes and chocolate bars to trade with the French people whom they encountered. Yet few were prepared to meet the challenges posed by the language barrier once they arrived on French soil. As the fighting waged on for weeks and months and the American liberators made their way throughout the French countryside, US military commanders came to rely on "Frenchies" to serve as interpreters with the local population.

"Frenchie" was the name given to the young Cajun soldiers from Louisiana who, like their Acadian ancestors, grew up speaking French as their first language.[2] The bilingual Cajuns, who learned English in school, represented the largest group of French-speaking Americans in the military, and their linguistic abilities proved invaluable to military operations around the world. Ironically, this same generation experienced ethnic discrimination growing up in a state-sanctioned English-only school system that sought to do away with their native language. Cajun boys and girls of the World War II generation were often punished for speaking French at school; many grew up ashamed of their language and culture. Society tended to view the Cajun French dialect as a handicap and the people who spoke it, lower-class citizens. All that change during the Second World War when these same Cajuns arrived in French-speaking territories, like North Africa and Europe, where their linguistic ability became a vital resource. When the military needed bilingual interpreters, they called on Frenchies to bridge the language gap. This had a profound impact of their sense of a Cajun identity. What emerged from this unique wartime experience was a long-lost pride in their heritage.

"Throughout the war it became common knowledge, especially in France, that if you wanted somebody to communicate with the French people, or the French army, find yourself a Frenchie from Louisiana," said Robert LeBlanc, a retired brigadier general who worked closely with the French underground as a member of the special forces in World War II.[3] Cajun Frenchies gathered critical intelligence on enemy whereabouts, road hazards, and battlefield conditions. They talked freely to local leaders and provided liaisons with French Resistance groups. With an unhindered ability to communicate with the native people, a Frenchie could find certain desirable items throughout the countryside, such as food, fresh water, and liquor to share with his comrades. Cajuns befriended French families and were invited guests in their homes. Some became lifelong friends with these French people; a few even married French girls. The language benefit extended across Europe, throughout the Mediterranean campaign, and even certain areas of the Pacific Theater. Everywhere the French-speaking Cajuns went, they seemed to be in high demand for their particular linguistic aptitudes and other skills acquired from their rural upbringing. For the Cajuns, the nickname "Frenchie" became a term of endearment, and they carried it like a badge of honor.

For so many ethnic groups that made up American society, the entrance of the United States into the war following the Japanese attack on Pearl Harbor served as a powerful unifying force for a common national goal. The war solidified the Americanization process that sought to generate a homogenized Anglo-American culture from the nation's ethnically diverse melting pot. Joining the American war effort was the "in thing to do," regardless of one's background. In this respect, the Cajuns were no different from other groups. This entire generation of Cajuns, born during the Progressive Era of the early 1920s, enlisted *en masse* alongside millions of other proud young Americans eager to serve their country.

Yet something else happened to this particular group as the war went on; the experience in French-speaking areas and association with other French-speaking people (including other Cajuns) reconnected them to their francophone heritage, of which many felt ashamed growing up. Those who had the opportunity to use their bilingual skills on the battlefield, in villages, or with other soldiers in chance meetings felt accepted, appreciated, and valued. They became aware of their unique cultural differences. Lo and behold, that backward and broken dialect they were told to disregard suddenly had merit and purpose, and it changed the way they viewed their own culture.

This study, which began years ago as an oral history project, evolved into a sort of wartime memoir with a focus on Cajun use of the French language and other group qualities displayed during their military service. As the interviews and other sources, primarily newspaper articles and wartime letters, began to coalesce, a number of themes emerged. First, there seemed to be a need to correct certain misperceptions that had stereotyped all Cajuns of that period as ignorant swamp-dwellers who had little interest in joining the rest of the advancing mainstream society. This was certainly not the case for the majority of those Cajuns who went off to war in the early 1940s. They were bilingual and better educated than any previous generation of Cajuns, and they desired to be a part of the modern American experience. Nevertheless, it's important to understand how society at large, especially travel writers and outside observers, portrayed the Cajun people and their lifestyle leading up to the war. Second, this study demonstrates how their inherited traits, thought to be a burden, actually proved to be an asset. It gave them purpose in the military, chiefly within the broader francophone world. Similarly, their native language and related cultural ties—often depicted in their writing—worked as a bonding agent that brought Cajuns serving overseas closer together through commonalities and cultural exchange. Last, through this realization and boost in self-worth, Cajuns came to view their heritage as a mark of distinction.

The source material for this project, taken as a whole, indicates that Cajuns of World War II adopted many of the same positive cultural elements that defined modern Cajun culture of the later twentieth century. How could it be that a group so slandered and prejudiced for their ethnic differences suddenly embraced those differences? To what degree did the wartime experience of Cajuns contribute to the formation and maintenance of a group identity? As more and more examples emerged, the need for some cross-disciplinary analysis and definitions to help frame this study became apparent.

Although written from a historical lens, this work is the study of a subset of a particular ethnic group and its experiences during a specific, short, but monumental, time frame: the 1940s. As such, there are a few general terms and concepts borrowed from the field of ethnic studies to explain, from a social scientist's view, what happened to these people in the mid-twentieth century. Group identity formation is the process by which people with similar values and customs develop a shared sense of belonging that distinguishes their group from others. As this formation occurs over time, people within the group actively seek to perpetuate that identity through practice and recognition of those unique attributes. This is referred to as boundary maintenance, whereby people in an ethnic group take steps, consciously or not, to safeguard and reinforce their cultural identity. The term *ascription*, which can be positive or negative, refers to how particular qualities are attributed to a specific ethnic group by those from within and from outside of that community of people. Ascription plays a critical part in shaping a cultural identity, and ethnic groups have tended to shift the emphasis of some practices to adapt to change. Cultural exchange is simply a way in which people of a particular ethnic group express among each other their commonalities that make up recognizable cultural elements: language, religion, music, etc. As the reader will see, the wartime experiences of Cajuns, and the cultural changes they endured, are not easily pigeonholed, but some general understanding of and appreciation for identity formation and boundary maintenance can be gleaned from this representative sample.

It is important to note that this work focuses on a specific demographic and does not attempt to encapsulate the entirety of Cajun society as it existed in the 1940s. This is the story of mostly young Cajun men between the ages of seventeen and twenty-one who served in the military overseas. This work does not analyze the war's impacts on Cajuns on the home front, nor does it incorporate experiences of other French-speaking groups from Louisiana, such as Creoles of African heritage.[4] For the sake of a historical-cultural comparison, however, the book includes a separate, condensed section (see Appendix) on the wartime experiences of the Acadians soldiers from New Brunswick and Nova Scotia, based on the traditional scholarly narrative and a handful of interviews conducted with Acadian veterans by the author in Canada in 2022.

The Cajuns who went off to war in the early 1940s were typically born in the early 1920s. They were raised in relatively poor rural farming and bayou communities in what is today recognized as Acadiana—the Cajun homeland—a twenty-two-parish region that encompasses much of the southern part of the state, except for metropolitan areas east of the Mississippi River (Baton Rouge and New Orleans, for example, are not considered part of Acadiana). They came from large Catholic families with extended relatives living nearby. Few of them had ever ventured outside of their tight-knit communities, although some had attended in-state college. They learned to speak English in school and were fairly bilingual by the time they entered military service. Most had Acadian surnames, and it can be assumed that the vast majority had some Acadian ancestry in their pedigree, although few at that age had a full understanding of their ancestral past. It should be noted that by the 1930s and 1940s, the term "Cajun" had evolved to incorporate a segment of the white, French-speaking, lower-class population of Louisiana, regardless of last name or any direct Acadian relation.[5] And not all who fit that classification identified as Cajun.

It is clear from the source material that Cajuns who served in World War II actively pursued group formation and maintenance. For these young service members traveling abroad, speaking Cajun French became a mark of one's distinctive association within the group. Cajuns didn't shy away from or discount their culture; they relished in it. Their bilingual abilities, previously thought to be useless, distinguished them. Military commanders and platoon leaders caught on to this valuable skill set in short order, hence the ubiquitous nickname "Frenchie" given to Cajuns throughout the armed forces. Off the battlefield, and at every given opportunity, Cajuns flocked to each other like magnets. These meetings, whether prearranged through letters or chance run-ins, always spurred conversation in their native language—a sure sign of "boundary maintenance."

A rather instrumental change in Cajuns' self-evaluation occurred during this wartime period. The generation that fought in the war had grown up with a negative ascription attached to their culture. In very few cases had Cajun people been given opportunities to perform outside of their own sphere. As legendary Marine pilot Jefferson DeBlanc often metaphorically stated, "We were loaded like a two-bit cap pistol fired nine times," meaning Cajuns were heavily burdened with, and disadvantaged by, cultural baggage—a stigma—when they entered the military.[6] Yet their world travels exposed them to vast new enterprises and different cultures. Wartime participation and proficiencies in certain skill areas validated their natural aptitudes as rugged individualists reared on farms and in marshes, swamps, and bayous with their forefathers. They were the ideal archetype for Uncle Sam's military. "They can shoot straight, they can handle a knife, they're good physical specimens and they love a scrape," noted Captain Robert Mouton, who led a Marine Corps recruiting campaign into south Louisiana at the start of the war. "If that doesn't make good Marine material then *moi, je suis fou*."[7] When given the opportunity, Cajun soldiers excelled, despite being marginalized at the war's outset.

Stigma

For much of the groups' long history leading up to World War II, Cajuns experienced cultural denigration that cast a dark shadow over their heritage. Their detractors—Anglo-Americans, upwardly mobile French Creoles, and outside commentators—tended to belittle Cajuns as unsophisticated rural peasants who lived a meager existence on the fringe of society and spoke a nearly unrecognizable, if not corrupted, version of French mixed with broken English. This stigma had been attached to Cajuns and perpetuated for generations. Those Cajuns raised in the 1920s and 1930s had to contend with this overt discrimination while being subjected to the state-approved removal of the "local" French language spoken in school and forced learning of English—often using cruel methods. Cajuns who went off to war in the 1940s thus had this stigma firmly ingrained in their identity and psyche.

World War II veteran Harry Jackson, whose family identified as *cadien* before the war, started school at five years old at St. Cecilia Catholic School in Broussard, where nuns served as teachers. "I think out of twenty-eight, there was either twenty-six or twenty-seven of us that didn't speak a word of English," he said. "Not one word of English. And boy, they were strict." Jackson learned English quickly and was fully bilingual by the time he reached eighth grade, when he decided to take "standard French," which had been introduced into high school by the late 1930s. Jackson, who had spoken Cajun French since birth, assumed this would be an easy elective. "I ought to be able to fly through that," he thought. "After two weeks, Tante Melancon, who was the French teacher, she called me on the side: 'Harry, I'm going to make a good suggestion to you. Go take another subject. You'll never be able to pass this French course at all.' That real French is a tough subject!"[8]

James Marlow, staff reporter for the Associated Press, traveled to south Louisiana—"a strange land where past surrounds present"—in 1939 and described, as he saw it, the peculiar society still clinging to old customs and struggling to adapt. He interviewed a high school teacher in New Iberia who said, "A lot of the Cajun children, when they come to school, deny they know a word of French. Their parents speak French, but the children are

Jason Theriot interviewing Harry Jackson, 2002

ashamed of being consider Cajun." The reporter quoted historian Lyle Saxon, who claimed that of the estimated 100,000 (likely underestimated) Cajuns in Louisiana, "many of them are still poor, a lot of jokes have been written about them, and they are still called 'country gee-gees.'"[9]

Another Associated Press story, carried across national newspapers in 1940, reported on the Cajun trappers and fisherfolk from the Bayou Lafourche area who came to the town of Lafitte to register under the newly implemented Selective Service Act, "which few fully understood." These Cajuns, "picturesque descendants of early French Canadian exiles like the fabled Evangeline . . . live a remote, almost primitive life. . . . Many of them even today speak only a patois based on French." The article suggests these rugged-looking men, many in their later years, were highly illiterate, only able to place an "x" on the government document as a substitute for a formal signature. In stereotypical fashion, the reporter picked out, poked fun of, and quoted one of the more colorful characters, a "Patriot Martin, distinguished for his ability to stand on his head in a pirogue." This older Cajun, turned down for military service due to his age, apparently had this response: "Dey wouldn't take me in de las' war, cuz I was too wide dis way and too short dat way. Now I can trow up one of my wife's biscuits, shoot de flour out of it and leave de bakin' powder and dey still don't want me. What kinda of defense you call dat?"[10] Regardless of the good-natured humor of this story—or whether the reporter was being purposely fooled by this jovial Cajun prankster—the widespread coverage of the ignorant marsh-dweller only personified the "typical Cajun" from Louisiana.

Cajuns of the Teche, a short film released in 1942 in theaters across the country, depicted the "pirogue-pushing Cajuns of the Bayou Country." The Columbia Pictures movie featured the nostalgic customs and traditions of the Acadians (bonnet-wearing quilt makers, for example) with a waterway tour of the Cajuns' homesteads and fishing grounds in the flooded swamps. "There are many Cajuns who make their homes in the great swamp," said the narrator, in a poised, rhythmic tone typical of the period. "It's an unusual way to live, with trees for gardens, waterways for roads, and boats for houses, but some of us prefer it." The *Atlanta Constitution* carried a similar story of the Bayou Cajuns—"the most primitive of the French"—as portrayed by Vena Aguillard, a French-speaking Baptist missionary originally from Acadia Parish, sent to the Morgan City area in the late 1930s to spread the gospel. Miss Aguillard, once associated with Cajuns, now a "cultured, educated American" who traveled the country, gave her perspective on the people of the swamps. The newspaper summed up her views: "They are all satisfied to sit on the banks of the streams in their little shacks in their scanty clothing, eating their rice and gumbo, sipping their liquors."[11]

A researcher from the Federal Writers' Project who did work in the region in 1939 described Cajun people as "simple, uneducated, uncultured, yet intrinsically genuine and lovable people."[12] Even their traditional cooking and music could not escape the stereotype of a culture stuck in the past. "In this day of modern transportation when delivery trucks bring bread to the front door daily, the Cajun mother of from eight to ten children prefers to make her bread outdoors. Her attitude toward bakery bread is that 'bought bread is good, but it takes the real homemade style to fill you up satisfying.'"[13] A book review on *Louisiana Folk Songs*, a collection of traditional French ballads, published in 1940, had this to say: "They are simple folk, preoccupied with the realities of a none-too-prosperous existence. One would call them earthy."[14]

Writing from Fort Benning, Georgia, in late 1942, *Times-Picayune* reporter Alex Melancon, who identified as a Cajun, provided insightful analysis on the use of the complex term "Cajun," especially for those writers seeking to cover—and sensationalize—the groups' lifestyle and peculiar habits. Other eager journalists wanted to know: should the French people way down south be called Cajun? "Not unless you want your popularity to sink to zero," he said. "For among the bayou folks, 'Cajun' is a touchy word for anybody to use—anybody who isn't a Cajun, that is." Melancon's comments, though by no means universal, suggests that Cajuns viewed the delicate term as inappropriate for others to use, but not themselves. Cajuns will "bristle with ire if anyone else so much as tries to call us Cajuns," he exaggerated, even though the term had gained a broader popular significance among the group. But on the outside, others still generally applied the label to the illiterate lower-class French of south Louisiana. "How stupid!" is manifest by "how Cajun!" he said. And "how backward and behind the times," is expressed as "*C'est si Cajun*."[15]

Harnett Kane's *The Bayous of Louisiana*, published in 1943, for all its fanfare and publicity in Louisiana and abroad, barely mentions the word *Cajun*. He referred to the French-speaking people he encountered, from Bayou Teche to Bayou Terrebonne and down to Bayou Lafourche, as Acadians. And like most writers of the time, his work focused on the groups' simple habits, trademark traditions, and deep connection to—and subsistence living from—their natural surroundings. He does, however, provide his quick take on the use of the term *Cajun* in the book's introductory chapter: "In many cases an Acadian may use the word in speaking of another and to another in conversation, but woe to the outsider who tosses it about. To quote a common Louisiana saying it is the kind of word with which one accompanies a smile, and friendly one at that. Too often it has been used by others as a term of disparagement, with a superior smirk. The word has acquired strong social implications."[16] Despite the tangled use and appropriation of the Cajun label, Kane recognized that some, even professionals, proudly claim a connection to it. His bestseller, while meant to shed light on colorful Cajun characters in their flowering paradise along the bayous and swamps, perpetuated, perhaps unintentionally, the stereotype. "In spite of the way in which the world about them changes," he told an audience on his book tour, "the Cajuns maintain their old customs and traditions, and live in the swampy Bayou Country much as they did when they first settled there."[17]

When it came to saving lives of marooned mariners along the Gulf Coast, however, the media outwardly praised Cajuns for being just that—Cajuns. Recruited by the military to guard and patrol the coastal marshlands during the early stages of the Second World War, these hardy outdoorsmen, "swamp-wise Cajuns," pulled dozens of shipwrecked crewmembers out of the barren marsh after their ships were sunk by German U-Boats lurking just off Louisiana's coast. "In their rustic pirogues, homemade motorboats, giant marsh buggies and by horseback they roam the swampland on patrol" in search of stranded Americans, the *Dallas Morning News* reported. Glorified as the "Louisiana Swamp Angels," these Cajuns conducted their campaign with "primitive courage and ingenuity."[18] Yet, it was through their military service in the war that Cajuns ultimately gained notoriety and replaced that stigma with self-respect.

The experience and testimonials of those Cajuns of World War II featured in this study cast doubt on those stereotypes and simplistic views. The so-called "country bumpkins" and "backward peasants" who went off to war soon found out that their language was indeed not backward and their culture not inferior. To be sure, plenty of young Cajuns were illiterate, some of whom did grow up in the wetlands, especially during the seasonal forays with their family trapping muskrat in the marsh, picking moss in the swamp, or swabbing the deck on the back of a shrimp boat. Yet many more of them graduated from high school, and they were all, for the most part, bilingual by the time they went to war. They still spoke with an accent, in one form or another, and no doubt struggled with pronouncing the "th" words—the proverbial "dis, dat, and da udder ting" that many Cajuns still employ in their natural speech today. Because of this, they were picked on and singled out at training camps and on military maneuvers, an experience that must have stirred up some painful scars from their past, especially when called the pejorative "coonass."[19] No one in the military paid much attention to the knowledge that Cajuns in Louisiana had of the French language at the start of the war. Once they landed ashore in French-speaking territories, however, that all changed. As Robert LeBlanc stated, "We proved them wrong."[20]

Framework

Scholars and writers of Acadian-Cajun history have studied this group for at least a century, with the bulk of the research produced in the last decades of the twentieth century. Most of the works analyze the evolution of the group's socio-cultural development, its ethnic makeup, and its folklore, from the arrival of the Acadians in Louisiana in the late 1760s to the Cajun

Renaissance movement in the 1970s—and all points in between. Aside from a handful of published works, most notably Shane K. Bernard's *The Cajuns: Americanization of a People*, the corpus of study tends to gloss over the pivotal period of the 1940s. This is not surprising considering the limits of primary source material available to researchers prior to the digital archival age and the fact that most "storytellers" from that generation kept their stories quiet until the last few decades. This study, while historical in nature, lends itself to and relies upon the litany of Cajun ethnohistory—a multi-disciplinary approach that combines the study of history, culture, and ethnicity. For help in framing these ideas, a few leading works that speak directly to this specific topic have been consulted as a guidepost.

Historian Shane Bernard first explored the war's impact on Cajuns to explain how the group experienced the Americanization process in the twentieth century. The war served as a transformative event that opened the once isolated French-speaking Cajuns to mainstream American culture and began the demise of the monolithic, native French language spoken in south Louisiana. Through impeccable research, qualitative analysis, and archival data, Bernard charted a path to an otherwise deep void of mid-twentieth-century Cajun history. The notion that Cajuns entered the war as Cajuns and came back from the war as Americans is quintessential to the Americanization process. "Proud of their wartime contributions," Bernard wrote, "they came home staunch patriots, defenders of the American way of life. They had at long last become part of the national melting pot."[21] Yet even Bernard's heretofore stand-alone work dedicates only a chapter of material (twenty pages) to the Cajun experience during the Second World War. *Frenchie* seeks to build upon Bernard's text with a deeper dive into the underpinnings of their unique experiences and emerging identity awareness through their commonly shared experiences.

James Dorman's *A People Called Cajuns* (1983) offers a concise ethnohistory of the Cajuns. It's detailed description and analysis of the process of ethnic group formation and maintenance makes it a foundational work on Cajun ethnic studies. He posits that for much of their history, the Cajuns essentially hid from their heritage, embarrassed by their cultural differences and lower socioeconomic status. "To be a monolingual French-speaking Cajun was to be something undesirable and degraded even in one's own eyes or in those of one's children, who now came to be taught that speaking Cajun French was somehow 'bad,'" he wrote.[22] Removal—and persecution—of all French from public schools beginning in the 1920s, just when the young Cajuns of World War II first entered school, led to "negative value attachment to the individual's ethnic identity."[23] This is critical to understanding the social stigma that Cajuns who entered the service in the early 1940s still carried with them into basic training and thence overseas. By Dorman's account, that stigma prevailed through the war and even into the post-war years, which ultimately led to the nadir of the culture by the mid-1950s. In Dorman's view, the returning Cajun GIs "undermined their ethnic uniqueness simply by virtue of contact with others so different."[24] If these soldiers were able to maintain a sense of identity, "albeit marked by overtones of self-denigration," as Dorman asserts, what then explains the desire to embrace their cultural traits and the overabundance of cultural exchange and positive ascriptive writings expressed among so many Cajuns in the service?[25]

Blue Collar Bayou, another seminal work on ethnohistory, explains Cajun identity in more detail and how Cajuns came to be seen as a distinct American ethnic group. Through an ethnographic approach and use of statistical data (surveys and census records), authors Jacques M. Henry and Carl L. Bankston III poke and prod into the complex social structure and the paradox of Cajun ethnicity over time. Although the focus is on the development of a working-class Cajun society that emerged in the second half of the twentieth century (primarily through employment in the oil industry), *Blue Collar Bayou* provides a useful framework for understanding what happened to Cajun people up to the 1940s and during the post-war era. Until mid-century, Cajuns were largely defined by origin and language. Gradually, Cajuns more closely identified with other ethnic elements, such as cuisine, music, and joyful living—and apparently working in the oil field. "Contemporary Cajun ethnicity may be based less and less on speaking French," they wrote, "but this does not mean that Cajunness is becoming baseless."[26] Their collaborative research shows that the ethnic markers so critical to the Cajun's identity continued to develop in the post-war years despite a shift in language preference at home. The study gives special attention to the history and use of the term "Cajun," which they assert did not engender a positive connotation among the Cajuns until the 1960s. This study, on the contrary, suggests that the Cajun self-concept took on new meaning with the deployment of thousands of Cajuns overseas during the war, especially in French-speaking areas. That collective experience lent itself to an awakening of sorts in which Cajuns discovered themselves and their own brand of Cajunness.

Drawing on these seminal works, as well as many others, the complicated picture of Cajun people of the early twentieth century comes into sharper focus. It's clear that the World War II generation represents a link between the stereotypical illiterate Cajun peasants of the past and the celebrated Cajun society that we think of today—with many twists and turns along the way. They were the genesis for much of the social, cultural, and economic changes that occurred during the last century. In Louisiana, they were also the generation that, for various reasons, chose not to raise their children to speak French at home. Nevertheless, as the readers will see, the signs of ethnic identity awareness and affirmation radiate throughout these book chapters, as Cajuns went from one corner of the globe to the other and left an account, through letters and interviews, of their thoughts, emotions, and experiences.

Note on Sources

The literature and research material gathered for this project stemmed from multiple sources, including libraries, newspaper archives, and individual collections. In addition, hundreds of hours of oral testimony and subsequent transcripts, personal memoirs, papers, and military documents supplied an array of primary source material for this work. While the interviews took place decades after the war, the letters and newspaper clippings originated from the 1940s. These materials constitute a snapshot of history and offer personal narratives in real time, whereas the oral history interviews provide abundant anecdotal evidence of the veterans reflecting on past experiences.

The *L'Echo du Teche* wartime newsletter produced out of Breaux Bridge is a proverbial gold mine of valuable firsthand accounts of Cajuns in World War II. This mimeographed bimonthly newsletter was first issued in March 1942 and sponsored by local churches and civic leaders from the surrounding communities. These newsletters, mailed to all the "boys and girls" in uniform, served as a bulletin board of information about their military adventures and hometown news.[27] "Wonderful piece of work you people are doing," wrote Harry Periou in 1943. "Brings joy and pride to a Cajun's heart."[28] James Domengeaux praised the newsletter idea: "The preparation of this very newsy publication is most worthy and admirable, and all those connected with it deserves the highest praise."[29] Delta Devillier, a member of the Women's Auxiliary Corp, wrote, "I received *L' Echo* during the week and was more than glad to receive it. Whenever I get the paper, I sit in bed and read it, and when the girls say, don't talk to 'Frenchy' (that's my name here), she is reading her church paper."[30] Writing from a communications school in California, Francis Tauzin said, "I met a Cajun from New Orleans named Hebert; he was the only one with whom I could hold a French conversation, and now that he is gone, I sorely miss him."[31]

The onset of culture shock for those young Cajuns featured in *L'Echo du Teche*, who had never left home before, came quickly. As they bounced from one training camp to another, and then shipped off overseas to England and French North Africa, their worlds changed. Staying connected with each other through newsletters and chance run-ins with other French speakers was a godsend. While in New Jersey, local boy Harve Pellerin met up with another Breaux Bridge native, Claude Romero—and, as occurred countless times throughout the war, the Cajuns always reverted to their native language. The staff of the *L'Echo du Teche* picked up on this phenomenon early in the war effort: "Well folks, don't ever let the boys and girls at school say or even think that the French they learn or speak in good little Breaux Bridge, is of no value when one is away from home; here's an example which proves the contrary; a few words in our own dear French brought together two Breaux Bridge boys before they were to leave and perhaps never meet again."[32]

In addition to letters, *L'Echo du Teche* ran current event stories and editorials written by clergy members from St. Bernard Catholic Church; some were written in French, which struck a chord with many Cajun readers serving abroad. Jessie Mae Schalaida, a 1942 graduate of Southwestern Louisiana Institute (SLI, now UL Lafayette), wrote from Camp Lejeune in North Carolina. "The Catholics here are well taken care of. There is a lovely chapel with services at hours which will make it possible for most of us to attend. . . . I was especially interested in the articles 'On Peace Terms' and 'La Marine Francaisse l'Honneur.' Being able to read French makes up in some way for no longer hearing it spoken every day."[33] For the young Cajuns who traveled the world and experienced military life, war, and a longing for home, *L'Echo du Teche* comforted them along the way.

Throughout the war, the president of SLI, Joel Fletcher, sent out a regular bulletin titled *Vermilion News* that combined numerous letters from service people who regularly wrote back to him about their experiences in far-off places. The "Men in Service" letters in the Joel L. Fletcher presidential papers at UL Lafayette provide a rich cache of correspondence from former students who identified as Cajun or espoused the virtues associated with being Cajun.

The letters, some of which were reprinted in local newspapers, became a lifeline for those stationed in obscure places and foreign lands who yearned for a connection to their culture. "Words cannot describe the thrill that your letters and the 'Vermilions' [*sic*] gave us boys in the service," Ramond Collins from Opelousas wrote to Joel Fletcher. "It seems as if I am surrounded by that cajun[34] atmosphere again."[35] Murphy Fontenot, writing from California, noted, "I remain just another Cajun who hasn't spoken a word of La. French for many, many months."[36] Harry Baudoin, writing from the Aleutian Islands off Alaska, signed off on a letter to Fletcher: "Je Me [*sic*] porto bien, merci; et vous? Just another Cajun from the Bayou Country!"[37]

Joel Fletcher, who had a long career as an educator and president of SLI, had an affinity for the French-speaking people of Acadian descent. He wrote:

> It has been my privilege to teach the children of the French-speaking people of Louisiana for 25 years and I know them as few persons of English descent do. Without exception I have found them to be loyal, patriotic citizens of this, their motherland. There are no families which have more willingly given their sons and daughters to the service, and no people serving in the armed forces of this nation who have made finer records in this and every war since the American Revolution than these people of French descent.[38]

His wartime newsletter provided a platform for Cajuns to express their ethnicity and share in a collective cultural exchange.

Local community newspapers across south Louisiana ran weekly columns featuring stories of, and letters from, Cajuns serving abroad. Some read like a personal diary entry, others are short and sweet. Stephen Benton Sr. of Carencro was assigned to a grave detail in France. "I also served as the first cook and the only French interpreter for the company," he wrote home. "My fellow troopmates nicknamed me Frenchy."[39] Alden Soriez of lower Vermilion Parish, writing from the Army Air Corp training center at Maxwell Field, said Alabama was by no means a soldier's paradise. "The Alabama heat is terrible and the Cajun hospitality of south Louisiana is being missed very much by this Cajun."[40]

With so many letters coming in, the newspaper columns often paraphrased the content, featuring only short sound bites. Roy Fuselier from St. Martinville, who served in a tank destroyer battalion, was mentioned in the *Teche News* after writing from Germany in the winter of 1945: "Roy says he is feeling great, but it's too damn cold over there for a Louisiana Cajun."[41] From the *Eunice News*: "Weldon Fruge of Eunice, who after 30 days of dodging bullets and shrapnel as a rifleman, finally was pulled off the line to serve as interpreter."[42] The *Clarion-News* in Opelousas carried this interesting tidbit from one of its hometown soldiers, a French interpreter in Europe: "French families in the neighborhood of this Ninth Air Force Service Command base who like to invite Yanks to their homes are probably grateful to Private Howard St. Cyr for teaching the boys of his chemical company the rudiments, at least, of conversational French."[43]

The overabundant references to Cajuns as translators or interpreters in newspapers are insightful but contain some limitations. More often than not, the excerpts simply state their roles in that communicative capacity and do not digress into further detail about that individual's activities abroad. For example, the Alexandria *Town Talk* mentioned that Ferdinand Duhon received a Bronze Star for his actions in Europe: "Acting as interpreter for his reconnaissance unit, he volunteered on many occasions to go on dangerous patrols when his knowledge of the French language was invaluable, often enabling his troop to by-pass destroyed bridges and enemy strong points."[44] The Jennings *Daily News* ran this one-liner: "Sergeant [Alcide] Hebert is a French interpreter and has been in Africa, France, and now Germany."[45] The Lafayette *Daily Advertiser* reported that John Dugas from Coteau Holmes was wounded in Belgium while fighting "in a special recon unit serving as liaison between his armored regiment and the French underground," but provided no further details.[46] These countless short entries leave the reader to ponder just what these GIs did as interpreters, how the exchanges occurred, how often, and what information was gleaned from communicating with foreign allies.

Americans first caught a glimpse of these Cajun interpreters in action with the drama series *Combat!*, released in 1962. This popular TV show portrayed an actual American infantry platoon fighting in Europe during World War II. The character "Caje," the squad's radio operator, was depicted as a French-speaking Cajun GI who served as an interpreter for the unit and spoke to local French people. Although the actor selected for that role was from Quebec and did not speak Cajun French, the series did capture the essence of that role and the importance of having French speakers among the ranks.

The real-life stories of Cajun interpreters in World War II first received broad appeal in Louisiana with the 2008 release of Pat Mire's documentary,

Mon Cher Camarade. Mire, an award-winning filmmaker whose father was a French interpreter, relied on personal memoirs and interviews with several French-speaking Cajuns who served in the war as members of the special forces or as regular infantry who translated for their unit in France. "Cajun translators were as important to the American war effort as the much acclaimed Native American 'Code Talkers,'" noted historian Carl Brasseaux on the film's release, "Yet, the Cajun translators' contributions have been entirely ignored."[47]

Oral histories of war veterans, first generated by Forrest Pogue, a US Army historian who interviewed GIs following the invasion of Normandy, reached its zenith decades later with Studs Terkel's *The Good War: An Oral History of World War II* (1984), followed by Stephen Ambrose's *D-Day, June 6, 1944: The Climactic Battle of World War II* (1994). The "skilled elicitation of memoirs," as one oral historian described the methodology, has been used in scholarly research for decades to find answers to key questions only available through human experience and memory.[48] Oral history serves as an additional primary source to collect data, often filling a gap in the written record that might otherwise be lost to history. As interviewing relies heavily on an individual's memory of past events, generating useful historical content from this proven research method is always subjective—and subjected to that person's mental capacity, age, and biases. The same could be said for the person conducting the interview.

Jason Theriot interviewing Lee Bernard, 2020

The bulk of the interview material for this project originated from the author's oral history collection of World War II veterans conducted from 2001 to 2006. A second phase of interviews, recorded from 2019 to 2022, specifically targeted those Cajun veterans who utilized their native French in some capacity during the war.

Over the years, a number of other interviews, conducted mostly by family members of veterans, availed themselves for use in this project. Robin Meche Kube's set of five interviews with French-speaking Cajuns from St. Landry Parish became the basis of the first scholarly article published on this topic. According to Kube, these Cajuns who grew up speaking French "never regarded their linguistic ability as an asset. On the contrary, it was often a liability. . . . Outside of South Louisiana, their accent and difficulty with English caused Anglo-American's to label them as different. This perception and the negative reaction that it often elicited limited Cajuns' potential for advancement not only in the opinions of 'the Americans,' but also in their minds." Yet the Cajuns Kube interviewed had a unique experience during the war as interpreters. "They returned home with shoulders a little higher and a different view of their language and themselves," she writes.[49]

There are undoubtedly recorded interviews in personal family collections tucked away in dusty trunks or boxes in a drawer awaiting discovery. Moreover, there are of course an inexhaustible number of personal stories passed down over the last three generations that have become a part of individual family lore. These stories hold significance both for family members as well as local communities. I received countless emails, letters, and other correspondence from family members who shared interesting stories of their "Frenchies." Without additional documentation or other methods to corroborate a story, most of those secondhand accounts were generally woven into the broader narrative and therefore not attributed to a source.

There are other noteworthy limitations to the source material used for this book. Most of the historical data come from individuals who lived in the deeply rooted Cajun communities of southwestern Louisiana, with a heavy concentration in Lafayette, Vermilion, Iberia, and St. Martin Parishes. Representation from the southeast region, from Houma to Bayou Lafourche, for example, and as far west as Lake Charles and Cameron, is noticeably lacking. This is simply the result of a deficiency in and accessibility of historical material. What is more, the dearth of digitized archival material obtained from using search terms, like "Cajun," suggests a dichotomy of views on cultural association and identity between French speakers in the southeastern part of the state versus those in the southwest. With the sizable French-speaking population in the southeast region, Cajuns from this area most assuredly used their bilingual skills during the war. Yet the lack of source material from this region, which no doubt contributed thousands of French-speaking GIs to the war effort, makes that historical connection all the more elusive.

To be sure, this study on Cajuns of World War II is not exhaustive. As in all historical research projects, the researcher knowingly or unknowingly leaves potentially valuable source material behind. For those eager to pursue this topic further, here is a short list of untapped collections: hundreds of hand-written letters from World War II veterans in the "Town Talk Scrapbook" archived at Nicholls State University Special Collections; a newly discovered collection of 600-800 interviews conducted by high school students in Kaplan with members of the World War II generation archived at the Center for Louisiana Studies in Lafayette; dozens of interviews recorded with Cajuns of World War II as part of The National WWII Museum's oral history collection; and thousands of pages of digitized newspapers that did not contain specific search terms such as "Cajun" or "French came in handy." A study of the Cajuns who went to college or otherwise benefited from the GI Bill of Rights (more formally called the Serviceman's Readjustment Act of 1944) after the war would be a worthwhile topic to pursue. "South and Southern Children," SLI President Joel Fletcher once stated about the GI Bill, "have never had an opportunity like this one. Let us see that it is used to the fullest extent." From the last year of the war to the 1947–48 academic year, enrollment at SLI nearly tripled.[50]

Because of the abundance of personal testimony, in letters and interviews, this work takes a wholly qualitative or narrative approach. When confronted with the question of how many Cajuns served in the war or how many served as interpreters, the best (and only) point of reference to start with is Shane Bernard's book, *The Cajuns*. Bernard extrapolated data from census records to come up with a number—24,500—of native-born Cajuns who served in World War II.[51] That number, however, does not account for the Cajuns with non-Acadian surnames who served. He looked at how many respondents to the longform version of the 1990 US Census (known as Public Use Microdata Samples, or PUMS) identified themselves both as "Acadian" in ancestry and as World War II veterans; then, he plugged that data into a formula to estimate how many Cajuns might have served in the war in general. Sticking with Bernard's figure, and assuming the national averages of total enlistees (14 million) who served in Europe (60 percent), it's safe to say that at least half or more of those Cajuns estimated by Bernard served in Europe as well. A vast majority of them no doubt served in France or in places where their French language could be beneficial. To say that a few hundred Cajuns served the role of "Frenchie" in World War II is likely an understatement.

Of course, not all Cajuns who served in the war served as interpreters. And not all Cajuns had contact with other francophones, or indeed with other Cajuns. Especially for those sailors who remained at sea for months, if not years, or those stationed for long durations across the country, the opportunity to express themselves in their native language or participate in traditional customs would have been limited. For these Cajuns, or for those who did not leave behind any written or oral testimony about their experiences, we cannot speak to their experiences.

Taken as a whole, the sample size of source material presented here paints a picture of Cajuns quite different from that of the prevailing literature and attitudes at the time. While a formal education eluded a large percentage of the young Cajun population leading up to the war, especially for those raised in isolated areas or on farms, most Cajuns of the 1940s had a least an eighth-grade education. Many graduated from high school, and plenty went on to college, primarily to SLI, prior to military service. Some could read and write in French. The Cajuns who went off to war thought deeply about their culture and made it a point to emphasize those shared traits that they associated with being Cajun. These ideas set them apart from other groups and set their beloved "Cajun Country" apart from other places around the world. It's through the lens of these letters and interviews that we begin to see the formation of a new identity—yes, proud Americans, but also proud Cajuns.

Robert LeBlanc, a highly decorated veteran who possessed one of the more impressive resumes of any Cajun in the war, published a memoir and was interviewed numerous times over the last two decades. When asked to reflect on how the war impacted Cajuns, LeBlanc spoke with confidence and authority on this compelling topic: "It seemed as though people had the idea that we Cajuns in south Louisiana were from a different country, because they treated us as though we were peasants; we were the ignoramus boys from the swamps, and that we didn't know too much about life. However, in the competitive nature of the military, it became necessary for us to demonstrate to

Jason Theriot interviewing Robert LeBlanc, 2020, photo by Dave McNamara

these people outside of this area that we were very competent Americans who could definitely do anything they could do. Even though our English was not the best English in the world, we could still accomplish everything they could accomplish and then some."[52]

The Cajuns of south Louisiana who had come of age during World War II had a once-in-a-lifetime opportunity to showcase their talents on the world stage. Until then, neither Cajuns nor their detractors thought highly of their language abilities or their way of life. They had inherited a stigma and shame attached to their upbringing and marginalized social status, which their parents and grandparents endured and accepted. Yet this generation of Cajuns also inherited skills that made valuable contributions during the war. For the first time in the groups' long history, their Cajun French language skill was no longer a source of ridicule but a necessity. The wartime experience released a feeling of pride in their heritage that had been bottled up for generations. This cultural revival, often attributed to the late 1960s and 1970s, has its roots in the 1940s with the "Frenchies" of World War II.

CHAPTER 1
FRENCHIE GOES TO NORTH AFRICA

"Let me tell you that I am prouder of my French now than I have ever been; and do I use it!"

—Andrew "Pim" Angelle, North Africa, 1943

In November 1942, nearly a year after the United States entered World War II, American military forces launched a large-scale offensive in North Africa—a region deeply influenced by French culture and colonial rule. It was in French North Africa where these Cajun "Frenchies" first became highly sought-after as homegrown French interpreters. Many of these Cajuns who participated in the Mediterranean campaign (1942 to 1944) had years of extensive training as members of local National Guard units. Several hundred joined the Louisiana National Guard in the years prior to America's entry into the war. As the new army prepared for potential operations overseas, military planners realized that deploying soldiers with French language abilities would be an asset to communicating with the local French-speaking population. An entire battalion of Louisiana soldiers (five companies, roughly five hundred men), mostly Cajuns, served as military police in places like Oran, Morocco, Tunisia, and Rome. Numerous interviews and wartime letters testify to the personal experiences of French-speaking Cajun soldiers who realized, for the first time, the value of their native language and heritage. As the North African campaign unfolded and later led to the invasion of Italy and southern France, the advantage of having access to a pool of bilingual GIs became widely known among military commanders.

Cajun National Guard

With war raging in Europe and Asia in 1940, and the United States still neutral, the American government put in place the necessary changes and policies to prepare for a global military conflict. The Selective Service Act of 1940 set in motion the nation's race to military preparedness. The institution of a peacetime draft, the creation of military training camps, and the calling up of the reserved armed forces signaled the beginning of the end of the isolationist mentality in the United States. Enlistment in state National Guard units soared. The new recruits from Louisiana, Cajuns among them, went through extensive training at various army camps. Cajun soldiers in the Louisiana National Guard had the benefit of almost two years of infantry training prior to deployment overseas. They participated in the Louisiana Maneuvers and related training experiences. The company-sized local units (composed of 115 to 130 men) that stretched from Lake Charles to Houma represented perhaps the largest concentration of French-speaking soldiers anywhere in the country.

As war inched closer, President Franklin Roosevelt said to Congress, "The security of the nation demands that this component of our Army [National Guard] be brought to the highest possible state of training efficiency more rapidly than its present program permits."[1] Four months later, on November 25, 1940, by way of executive order, the 156th Infantry Regiment of the Louisiana National Guard, Thirty-First "Dixie Division," received induction into federal service at its headquarters at Jackson Barracks, New Orleans. Across the state, two thousand young guardsmen packed their bags and left their hometowns for one year of infantry training at Camp Blanding, Florida—an unfinished training camp in the swamps near Gainesville. Among this group were several hundred Cajuns from south Louisiana, most from community-based infantry companies; Company E from Jeanerette, Company F from Breaux Bridge, Company G from New Iberia, and Company H from Lafayette (along with the smaller Headquarters Company out of New Orleans) made up the Second Battalion. Other Louisiana National Guard Companies established in predominantly French-speaking communities included Jennings, Morgan City, Houma, Crowley, and Lake Charles.[2] The Cajun population comprised the bulk of these local units. For example, Acadian surnames accounted for about 40 percent of Company K's roster (based in Jennings), including a dozen recruits with the last name Broussard. These roster lists mirrored the names found fighting with Acadian militia units that served in previous wars. Nowhere else in America did the US military recruit more French-speaking soldiers than from the Louisiana National Guard.

ARMISTICE DAY
D-A-N-C-E
Sponsored by Stanley Martin Post,
American Legion
— In Honor Of —
Company 'H', 156th Infantry
Louisiana National Guards
MONDAY NIGHT, NOV. 11
AMERICAN LEGION HOME
LAFAYETTE
9:00 P. M. 'Till — ??
Music By
RED LABAUVE
And His Collegians
Gentlemen 50c — Ladies Free
Proceeds for Benefit of Mess Fund of Company "H" Which is to Leave Soon For Florida for Training

Armistice Day Dance in honor of Company H (Lafayette),
The Daily Advertiser, *1940*

During the post-Depression era, few programs offered more benefits to underprivileged Cajuns than the National Guard. They enlisted in the ranks for a number of reasons—most importantly, a monthly paycheck. Homer Comeaux of New Iberia grew up in a poor family with eleven brothers and sisters. He thought that by joining the Guard, his parents would have one less mouth to feed. "My momma and daddy was so poor and they had so many children that I figured they wouldn't mind one of them off their back. . . .

I didn't have the most education, but I believed in my country and I fought for my country. And I would go back and fight for it again."[3] Addy Melancon from Breaux Bridge received $13 a month. "That was a lot of money back then," he said. "Money was hard to get in those days. When you made a dollar a day cutting sugarcane or something, that was big money."[4]

Some of the young men enlisted to be with friends; others sought adventure. Warren Hebert from Jeanerette and R. J. "Chink" Broussard from New Iberia wanted to fight in the ring. They were amateur boxers who joined the army boxing circuit that toured throughout North Africa and Europe entertaining the troops. Ernest Broussard, a farm boy from Iowa, Louisiana, joined the 108th Calvary Unit, K Company. His unit did not have enough horses for all the guardsmen, so he actually brought his own horse to weekend training maneuvers before the unit was federalized. "It all started with a love of horses," he wrote in his journal from his military service. "Once a month usually on Sunday afternoons we'd drill on horseback, brush, groom, and clean their hooves, didn't have enough horses for everyone so sometimes I'd bring my own." According to his wartime journal, Company K's horses were shipped to Camp Blanding along with the cavalrymen.[5] Eventually, they received motorcycles to replace the horses.

Company K from Jennings on horseback, cir. 1939, courtesy of the Broussard family

Company K on motorcycles, Camp Blanding, 1942, courtesy of the Broussard family

For many, the Guard came to represent a family away from home. At a time of scarce jobs and few opportunities during and after high school, these young men joined a group that offered them comradery, discipline, training, and a modest paycheck. For those who joined in November 1940, they anticipated a twelve-month training period. Few expected to spend years serving overseas in places like North Africa, Italy, and France.

Many of the Cajuns in these companies grew up in rural areas and spent time hunting and trapping in the woods and marshes. They knew how to cook, clean, and handle themselves in the outdoors with guns, even at a young age. A majority grew up speaking French and learned English much later through secondary education. They went to Catholic Mass on Sundays and placed emphasis on family values. The Guard provided an opportunity for these Cajun soldiers who shared so many cultural similarities to bond together for the defense of their community and country. Joining the Guard was *the* thing to do.

For instance, the Breaux Bridge unit, Company F, recorded perfect attendance at regular weekend training sessions throughout the late 1930s and into 1940. Simon Castille, who commanded the Breaux Bridge company at the time, noted that recruiting young Cajun boys for the Guard was easy. "We had a waiting list, sometimes with as high as twenty-five men on it," he acknowledged. "Membership was handed down from father to son." As Lieutenant Bender Scarpero explained, "It was a community project, the center of civic and social activities. Not to be *un homme de la Garde Nationale* was unthinkable!"[6] The Cajun National Guardsmen conducted training maneuvers in north Louisiana before they were called up to the regular army, roughly a year before the attack on Pearl Harbor. Their distinctive language and cultural habits did not go unnoticed by military commanders who led these first full-scale maneuvers. A reporter writing from the war games at Camp Beauregard in early 1940 noted that while the Oklahoma and Arizona have Native American speakers among their ranks, and the Texas National Guard have several Hispanic recruits who spoke Spanish, the guard units from south Louisiana have their own language specialists—"Cajun" Frenchmen. "If Uncle Sam ever goes into actual war," the reporter noted, "the enemy is going to have trouble learning his 'signals' even if he does tap the communication lines."[7] Many Cajuns who participated in the Louisiana Maneuvers would ultimately serve as interpreters in overseas campaigns. Until that time came, however, their unusual dialect remained a curiosity to most and a source of ridicule by others.

In late December 1940, the young enlistees of the 156th Infantry Regiment boarded a train in Baton Rouge for a four-day journey to Camp Blanding, Florida. This would be their main training facility for the year. But the site had not yet been built up for troops. The geography consisted mostly of wooded areas and swamps that had to be cleared out and made livable. When they arrived, the soldiers found that little preparation had been allocated for their twelve months of training. With barracks half completed, the men lived in six-man tents. The army built only one latrine to accommodate the hundreds of men. Thick vegetation, sand, and overgrown forest inundated the surrounding fields and training grounds. "It was nothing but a jungle of palmetto shrubs," said one guardsman.[8] "More or less a swamp," stated another.[9] At the beginning, they ate outside together and cooked their food over a wood fire. For the young Cajuns and country boys (ages eighteen to twenty) from south Louisiana who practically lived off the land, Camp Blanding must have felt a bit like home, despite the inconveniences.

Upon arrival at the camp, the army issued the troops World War I uniforms, 1920s weapons, and outdated equipment. Instead of the M1 Garand rifles that would be used later in the war, in training the soldiers used the

Louisiana National Guard, Company G, Fourth Platoon, Camp Blanding, 1941, courtesy of the Nugent family

Camp Blanding Postcard, 1941, courtesy of the Broussard family

1903 Springfield bolt-action rifle. In those early months, live ammunition was limited, but there were plenty of shovels, pickaxes, and related construction equipment to keep the men busy at the new training camp. As time went on, and the condition of the facilities improved, the men received updated weaponry, including modern rifles, pistols, and anti-tank guns.

At Camp Blanding, physical and military training consumed most of the day, including a multi-mile march every morning. By July, the training intensified. James Melancon from Breaux Bridge wrote, "We are in fine shape, we proved this when we marched 120 miles last week, and we are equipped to perfection."[10] The men drilled and did calisthenics every day. They ran obstacle courses and practiced shooting rifles on the target range. They learned military courtesies and how to throw grenades. And they learned how to clean and field-strip a rifle. The more realistic combat training took place during full-scale maneuvers, including the Louisiana Maneuvers at Fort Polk and Camp Beauregard in north Louisiana.[11] The Cajun soldiers trained hard and thus advanced their skills in basic military craft; many became noncommissioned officers, and several advanced to officer candidate school.

Addy Melancon was one of them. He joined Company F (Breaux Bridge) in late 1940 at seventeen years old alongside his older brother, Adley. Addy was not old enough to join the outfit, so he lied about his age. "Well, we went to camp, and my brother, who was fifteen months older than me, joined, but I had lied one year so that made us three months apart. Colonel Castille called us in one day. He said, 'I know your daddy and mama are good people, but how they made y'all three months apart, I don't know.' So I told him, I said 'Colonel, I lied about my age.' I said, 'You can get me out.' 'No, no,' he said, 'I have to have 135 people to go to Camp Blanding. If I let you go, I got to find somebody to replace you. Let's forget about the age.' And that's how I ended up at Camp Blanding."[12]

Like the rest of the recruits in the Breaux Bridge company, Melancon grew up in a French-speaking home. "Nobody spoke English at all," he said. "Nobody knew a thing about English, none. All my mama's brothers and sisters didn't know a damn word in English. They all spoke French. Then we got in school. . . . Mama and Daddy couldn't speak English, but they could understand you, and what little I knew came from that. But when I went to school, I spoke French. I got punished because I was speaking French instead of English. We had a little country school right here about a mile from here,

Beauregard Grade School. We went there till the third grade, and the fourth grade we went to Cecilia by bus." He remembered getting whipped across the hands with a ruler by the teachers as punishment for speaking French on the school grounds. "She was a mean bitch," he said. "Oh, you had to be careful what you said in class and what you did out of class, because she was going to beat the hell out of you. That was that country teacher."[13]

The little Florida town of Starke, where Camp Blanding was located, reminded Melancon of his birthplace: "One thing nice, Camp Blanding is on a lake, Silver Dollar Lake. Every company had a certain area that was your beach for us to swim in, so that was something nice about the camp, but otherwise, Starke was a little town like Breaux Bridge and had 15,000 people when you went to town. You got in a restaurant; you had to sit down and wait for two or three hours before you could get served. So we didn't go to town at all."[14]

By all accounts, the Cajuns enjoyed their experience at Camp Blanding. Between exercising, drill, and maintaining the facilities, Cajun troops found ways to relax and entertain themselves. They created a beach on Lake Kingsley. The men cleared away the trees and stumps around the lake, hauled in white sand to replace the mud-covered shoreline, and spent hot afternoons and weekends swimming in crystal-clear water. Some wrote letters home; others played cards and gambled. A group of Cajuns, known as the "Nickel Gang," often sneaked off behind the tents to play a round of poker or shoot a game of craps. Homer Comeaux, a member of the gang, was a prankster: "At Camp Blanding when we played cards, we would sometimes speak French to each other. We would like to catch two or three of them that didn't speak French so we would take their money."[15] As the story goes, these half a dozen hard-nosed Cajuns ventured to town on weekends with only a nickel in their pockets to have a good time, and they somehow managed to get fiery drunk in the process. "The day we collected our money, half of 'em were broke fifteen minutes later, shooting craps," Melancon recalled. "I was lucky; I won most of the time. I used to send the money back home because I knew Mama and Daddy needed some."[16]

The boys from south Louisiana brought with them to Florida much of their distinct culture. Group cohesion, particularly at the company level, allowed these men to practice their folkways freely. Musical instruments, joke-telling, games, and conversations in Cajun French were commonplace at Camp Blanding. Some of the officers—Simon Castille of the Breaux

Cajuns from Company G, Camp Blanding, 1941, courtesy of the Nugent family

Bridge company in particular—still gave drill orders in French. "Get the hell in step," he would call out to the soldiers in French to get their attention. Addy Melancon linguistically demonstrated Colonel Castille's frequent use of French in close-order drill. "The company commander would say, '*En arrière ou en avant.*' That means back up or go forward. '*Mets ton arme contre ton épaule et baisse-la*' meant, 'Put your gun up to your shoulder and snap it down.' I don't remember exactly how it is, but they all had a command of French because very few of them could speak English. . . . We stayed in step, I guarantee you. He believed in making a soldier out of you, whatever it took."[17] According to Melancon, when the troops transferred to Camp Bowie, Texas, Colonel Castille would often forget that he was supposed to give orders in English. "He'd turn around and give us an order in French and then march away."[18] But it came natural for the guardsmen to speak to each other in their native language while in training camp, even among English-speaking soldiers and officers. As soldiers in the US Army, these Cajun were becoming more Americanized, yet they continued to maintain much of their traditional customs.

As luck would have it, the Cajuns at Camp Blanding shared training grounds with a group of troops from Maine, many of whom also spoke French.

Louisiana National Guard, rifle range, Camp Blanding, 1941, courtesy of the Nugent family

Louisiana National Guard, rifle platoon, Camp Blanding, 1941, courtesy of the Nugent family

Louisiana National Guard, mortar section, Camp Blanding, 1941, courtesy of the Nugent family

This unique occasion, perhaps unprecedented in wartime, brought together Louisiana French and New England French. "The Louisiana French, many of them descendants of the Acadians, did not believe that the New England French could talk their language," a reporter for the *Boston Globe* said. Milton Crochet from the 156th Infantry visited with the guys from Company B, 103rd Infantry Regiment from Rumford, Maine, to see if any French speakers were among them. "After 1st Sergt. Armand Soucy fired a little French at him and then introduced him to the rest of the company, more than two-thirds of them of French-Acadian ancestry, and they all talked the same language, Corp. Crochet was convinced. This may be the start of a beautiful relation," the story continued. "There is apparently about the same difference between Yankee French and Louisiana French that there is in the English accents of the two places, and it is much the same kind of difference."[19]

For twelve months at Camp Blanding and on subsequent maneuvers, the Cajuns of the Louisiana National Guard found ways to integrate their cultural norms into their American military training camp experience. They regularly spoke the French *patois* to each other (and apparently with Frenchmen from Maine), but not everyone appreciated or accepted the Cajuns' way of communicating; some complained. Addy Melancon related a story that occurred in training: "We used to assemble at night at the PX, drink beer, and shoot the bull amongst each other but in French, and the guy handling the PX . . . he thought we were criticizing him, and he quit serving us beer one night. So, we went back, we took [Colonel] Castille. Castille went over there, told that guy, 'By tomorrow morning, you lose your job unless you can feed these people what they want to [be fed], whether they speak French or English or Spanish.' And that guy served us well after that. That's one thing about Castille, he was strict but fair."[20]

The men brought their cooking techniques and Cajun cuisine with them to training as well. Al Nugent, one of the few non-Cajuns in the Second Battalion, recalled, "You talk about the Cajun influence, that's where we really felt the Cajun influence was in the cooking. They didn't cook just exactly the way the army instructed them to cook; they cooked the way they knew how to do it."[21] Typical meals at the Cajun mess halls included bouillabaisse, étouffée, court-bouillon, crawfish bisque, gumbo, and jambalaya with plenty of onions, peppers, sauces, seasoning, and, of course, rice. "Usually, they take about 500 pounds of rice with them to camp, and serve it with every noon meal," one article noted.[22]

Local reporters picked up on the Cajun soldiers' habits and proclivities, particularly when it came to cooking. The unabashed French-speaking Company F (Breaux Bridge) received national media attention in the early stages of the war. An article appeared in *L'Echo du Teche*, the town's church bulletin, as a reprint from a national magazine story. Its genuine description of the Cajun National Guard and their popular culinary skills bares full reproduction:

> Since the late days of November 1940, the officer candidate has served in a colorful unit, one as different as the Free French, as highly publicized as the commandos. To compile all the stories about this outfit would require too much space, so just a few high spots can be hit in this limited account. Here are a few samples from the hectic past: Company F, 156th Infantry was composed of National Guardsmen

> from the Bayou Country of Louisiana. As French as Paris, as independent as their own swamp country, the men decided to issue orders in their native tongue. In fact, many could not speak English. In this way, matters proceeded calmly for quite a while. Then one day a flock of selectees were sent into Company F. There stood the newcomers, boys from Mississippi and Alabama, listening with hanging jaws to close-order drill commands in the French language. Some of the selectees had been involved in the military before, thought they could carry out commands perfectly. But the best of drill sergeants fall far short of mutilating orders when compared to those French-speaking sergeants. Final outcome of the affair was the assignment of an interpreter by Division HQ. Then there was the matter of cooking. Those Bayou lads like their food seasoned—know how to make ordinary rice resemble a rare old country food. Shrimp by the barrel, rice by the sack and seasoning by the case arrived from home. A small area of Camp Blanding, Fla, took on the atmosphere of Southern Louisiana. Men and officers from neighboring units took to 'accidentally' being in the area when mealtime arrived. Came a day when Dudley Haddock, *Colliers* correspondent, was told of the fantastic Army mess. He accepted an invitation to try a meal and was lost. A couple of months later the writer's magazine devoted an article to the culinary skill of the chefs who prepared the food for Company F. As a last incident, a story accompanies the unit that it hasn't been confirmed by Sergeant Fred Patin. According to an article appearing in the Dixie 31st Division Newspaper, the regiment was on parade and the command, "In cadence count" was given. Company F out shouted all the others. They were asked why the sudden enthusiasm. "Why," said the Top-Kick "You said Cajun count." In case that needs clarifying, the term "Cajun" is a term applied to inhabitants of the Louisiana lowlands.[23]

While covering the highly publicized Louisiana Maneuvers, reporters often poked fun at the Cajuns' unique sense of humor and quirks. "Locally the real heroes were the 'Cajun' soldiers," said one reporter. "They were the pride and glory of the 'Cajun' Country and stories abounded about them. One regaled with great relish throughout the Third Army, which prides itself on military discipline, was about a young Cajun recruit who failed to salute his colonel. The colonel stopped him and said, 'How long have you been in the army?' 'Two months,' was the pleasant answer, 'and you?'"[24]

Back at Camp Blanding, the Cajun troops' use of French became commonplace. French was so pervasive among the bayou ranks that commanders requested general orders to be written and displayed in English *and* French. An article titled "Medium French for the 156th Regiment" in the 31st Division newsletter carried this story about the unorthodox method of communicating instructions to the Cajuns in uniform. "These are printed in French up in the 156th Infantry regiment, for the benefit of the French-speaking selectees. The French they used was 'neither school-book, Parisian nor cajun,' said Lt. Colonel Frank P. Stubbs, in charge of training the regiment. 'We tried to strike a happy medium that the majority could understand,' he said."[25]

The Japanese attack on Pearl Harbor on December 7, 1941, immediately elevated military preparedness across the country. Within days of the attack and the subsequent declaration of war, the army sent the Louisiana National Guard, whose yearlong tour had been extended through the month of December, to defend the Atlantic Coast in South Carolina. Homer Comeaux recalled an immediate change in orders: "We were supposed to come back within a year, but they kept us there longer. We figured something was wrong. They wanted to keep us there to train us for one more month. I didn't have a lot of education, but I had enough sense to know that they were keeping us around for a reason. Within that month the war broke out and they sent us to South Carolina to guard the coast."[26] Ernest Broussard from the Jennings company recalled the abrupt shift in plans. "All [discharge] papers went into the waste basket," he wrote in his diary, "and the ones that were gone were called back."[27] Three guardsmen from New Iberia, Oswald Ronsonet, Ed Broussard, and John Mestayer posed in their pajamas for a group photograph taken that morning. Little did they know that the United States had just entered World War II and within a few years they would be in combat overseas.[28] Lennard Martin, from Arnaudville, remembered hearing the news of the Pearl Harbor attack back at Camp Blanding: "It was Sunday; we were all sitting around a tent having fun, drinking beer, playing music, all of a sudden this came over. And this was Sunday. . . . Tuesday morning we moved out."[29]

A month later, writing from Stoney Field, South Carolina, Lazard Landry, a Cajun from Delcambre, stated, "No one knows how long we will be here. . . . We are guarding for anything which may be attempted by the

Guardsmen from Company G, Camp Blanding, December 7, 1941, courtesy of the Nugent family

enemies on the East Coast. We are ready and on the alert at all times—ready to go into action any moment of the day."[30]

As was typical, Cajuns made the best of the new situation and quickly adapted their customs and routine to their new surroundings. The *Charleston News* picked up on the Cajuns' distinctive ways and colorful history. One reporter remarked that the Carolina coast had been invaded by a group of soldiers who talked differently, but cooked delicious meals: "A 'Foreign Legion' has come to Charleston in the French-speaking soldiers from the Louisiana bayous, now stationed at Stoney Field. But, these 'freest French', while not precisely English and not exactly French, they are absolutely American. Their forefathers were driven out of Acadia along with Evangeline of Longfellow fame, and came down to settle under the giant moss-hung oaks that shadow the lazy-moving Bayou Teche. . . . A former commander of this group, the courteous Major Simon Castille, explains that most of these men were born on rice, sugar-cane, or cotton plantations and spent most of their days outdoors farming, or hunting and fishing."[31]

"When first taken into the army," the *Charleston News* continued, "this band of French-speaking soldiers were first given instructions in French, and then in English. Many, of course, had learned English in the parochial schools, but they often dropped back into their French Creole patois when they got together. The creole chefs at Stoney Field have been having a fine time since they arrived here making their famous crawfish bisque and chicken oyster gumbo. Not without due cause is this company's mess; one of the most popular at the [Stoney] field, and one that draws the most visitors."[32] Sergeants Castille, Dore, and Melancon—all from Breaux Bridge—ran the mess hall and prepared the meals. During the interview with the crew, one of the chefs began singing a popular folk song in French, for which the reporter recorded: "*Je passai devant la porte, Je criai bye bye la belle, Il n'y a personne que me reponde.*" This translated into: "I passed in front of the door. I cried out

Louisiana National Guard at Camp Bowie, 1942, courtesy of the Nugent family

bye bye, my dear! But there was no one to answer me." One of the lieutenants interviewed for the story responded: "The men in this outfit are noted as the best fighters, the best cooks, and the best lovers in the army!"[33]

A month or so later, the Cajun militia made its way back to Camp Blanding before being shipped off for advanced infantry training at Camp Bowie, Texas. Once there, they shared the camp with other guard units from Texas, Oklahoma, and New York. Naturally, the cultural differences between the groups created some tension.

At Bowie, the Second Battalion received several new recruits who were not from Bayou Country. The army also assigned an English-speaking captain to lead the Frenchmen in drill and training exercises. Lennard Martin recalled some of the animosity that surfaced due to cultural clashes at the Texas training camp. "We had some draftees that came in from all over, all over the country who could not speak French. But basically, 90 percent of the boys that were in that battalion spoke French. . . . We had gotten a captain. I think he was from maybe Baton Rouge or somewhere, that came in the outfit and he didn't want us to speak French anymore. That was kind of hard to take. Anybody who was a sergeant or corporal or whatever rank you held. If he caught you speaking French, he'd bust you down to private. We'd hide in the latrine and everywhere to speak French. Several of us wanted to transfer out of the company because of him."[34]

The men from the Breaux Bridge unit—some of whom could not speak much English—took offense to the criticism and language restrictions. Addy Melancon recalled a fiery backlash from the unit's commander, Colonel Castille. "When we met together with our Frenchmen, we'd speak French and these guys would go report us to the company commander, 'Them damn Frenchmen, all they're going to do is speak French, no English.' So Castille told them, he said, 'If you don't want to speak French to them, get the hell out of the way. They talk what they want.' And that was it. So the guys from New York left it alone."

Ed Broussard, who didn't learn English until the first grade, served with the New Iberia company. While his unit was mostly bilingual, the feisty Breaux Bridge company was not. "In the Breaux Bridge company, Company F, they spoke French a lot, and they were ridiculed—of course the [outsiders] were not familiar with our culture. They spoke French and poor English. There were some fights in town."[35] Addy Melancon recalled that the Anglo-American guardsmen often used ethnic slurs to call out the Cajuns. "A bunch of coonasses from Louisiana. That's what we were known [as], at Camp Bowie. But that's all right," he affirmed. "We called them worse names than that. So fights started. We had a few fights on account of that."[36] Homer Comeaux, also from New Iberia, praised his brethren from up the Bayou Teche, but noted that gradually the Cajuns had to accept the English-speaking protocols of the US military. "They were good people from Breaux Bridge and St. Martinville, and they helped the war out a whole lot. Just like us, they wouldn't back up. Them Cajuns wouldn't back up for nothing. . . . Ninety-nine percent of us [spoke French]. Some of our orders in the beginning were in French, but they got away from that because they had to teach us in English. They wanted us to speak French, but not to train as Frenchmen, because we had learned the American rules."[37] Lennard Martin concurred: "Some of the guys, there was a little, probably . . . they resented us. I guess they felt that we were, when we'd speak together, they thought maybe we were speaking about them, you know. Criticizing and we did that. Just a habit we had of speaking French. Hard to break."[38]

Through it all, these Cajun soldiers maintained tight unit cohesion and strict military discipline. They had been molded into hardened, expert infantrymen. They were tough and carried a chip on their shoulders. Their cultural differences stood out—but instead of conforming, they persisted in their Cajun ways. It's important to note that these same Cajuns were ridiculed and punished in school for speaking French as kids. They had to learn English the hard way. As they matured, they began, willingly, to assimilate into a broader American culture. Joining the local National Guard and participating in training with many other non-Cajuns in the US Army brought to the surface their cultural distinctiveness. And they relished in it, despite continued ridicule for being different. Soon, they would get an opportunity to showcase their talents in overseas campaigns. And it wouldn't take long for military leaders to see the value in these French-speaking Cajuns.

After more than two years of extensive training in various camps around the country, the unit was sent overseas and stationed in England. The entire 156th Infantry Regiment shipped out of New York in late 1942 on the *Orentos Barros* troop transport ship. Once in England, they were summarily split up by battalion and sent to various military outposts to serve as security detail. Most units from the Louisiana National Guard stayed in England until the invasion of Normandy a year and a half later. But the army had other plans for the predominantly French-speaking Cajuns from the Second Battalion. Following the successful, though hard-fought, invasion of North

Africa by Allied forces in November 1942, military commanders did something unusual. They detached the Second Battalion from the regiment and sent the four companies from the Bayou Teche valley to North Africa to serve as military police. According to Shelby Stanton's *World War II Order of Battle*, the reason for the Cajuns' special assignment to North Africa was because of their "French linguistic abilities."[39]

Operation Torch

On November 8, 1942, the Allies launched Operation Torch, the first major campaign against German-occupied territory in the Mediterranean theater. The campaign began with three simultaneous amphibious invasions along the coast of North Africa at Casablanca, Morocco, and in Oran and Algiers, Algeria. The assault succeeded in liberating North Africa from German control, but only after months of intense fighting and bloodshed. The French culture and cities in the region offered a unique opportunity for many Cajuns to use their bilingual talents. Upon arrival in Oran, the French-speaking National Guard soldiers of the Second Battalion—redesignated the 202nd Infantry Battalion—performed escort guard duties as military police. They provided security on army bases, airfields, and supply depots in the rear echelons. They guarded prisoner-of-war camps and port facilities. They rode on trains to protect troops and supplies. The Cajuns directed traffic, broke up fights, and arrested belligerent GIs. The Cajuns from the National Guard, and from other military units, had the benefit of speaking the language of the local people. Many ultimately served as interpreters in various capacities. They wrote letters home expressing their complete surprise and enthusiasm about communicating with the local French population and the Allied troops in the campaign. This was their first encounter with another francophone culture, and the experience made a lasting impression on the Cajuns. Although thousands of miles away from Cajun Country, North Africa felt a bit like home.

"We did a variety of things," said Lennard Martin, who went with the group to North Africa. "And any time that they needed somebody to interpret, they'd called on somebody from the unit. They took all the French-speaking guys and put us all together. We went into North Africa, [and] everywhere we went, most of the people spoke French and all that. And we stayed as a separate battalion well into 1944. I think it's just because our French heritage this was done. That was probably the primary reason for that."[40]

Breaux Bridge National Guardsman Alton Green, Military Police, North Africa, cir. 1943, courtesy of Scott Landry

As soon as they arrived in North Africa, Cajun soldiers, including those from the Guard units, began writing letters back home. These letters provide a captivating glimpse on how the Cajuns viewed their experiences in a faraway land and how their French came in handy, both socially and militarily. They appreciated their bilingual abilities and praised the merits of being "Cajun"—a label that, for at least a few generations

Abbeville National Guardsman Lazard Landry, Military Police, North Africa, cir. 1943, courtesy of the Landry family

before the war, carried with it derogatory and shameful undertones. Alphonse Angelle, from Breaux Bridge, noted that he was getting along fine with the French girls. "There must be lots of boys from home who are in North Africa now, and I hope that I can meet up with some of them soon. Boy, if there are any 'Cajuns' when we meet, won't we chew the rag?"[41] His brother, Andrew "Pim" Angelle, penned a letter in May 1943 that said, "Let me tell you that I am prouder of my French now than I have ever been; and do I use it? When I go to town, I have lots of fun; I ask the French people questions in English, and they do all kinds of signs trying to make me understand, then before leaving them I start rattling my ole Cajun stuff, and they just stand there gaping as if to say, well it's impossible that I can talk French so well. Of course, when I see a nice-looking squaw, naturally I don't talk English to her, but get on the good side, you know."[42]

Zerben Badeaux had similar thoughts on the benefits of speaking French: "I never thought that I would use French in the Navy, but there are many French women in North Africa, so that I get to talk French quite often."[43] Writing to his mother in Ville Platte, another local boy said, "The girls here all speak French, so my thanks to you for making me speak it always. I am the only one in my company who talks their language, so now I have it all over the other fellows."[44] Percy Hebert noted: "I am in a French-speaking country and we are very friendly with the people here."[45] Rodney Young from Church Point said "having some knowledge of French is certainly an asset over here. I have met several French families who are most hospitable."[46]

The arrival in North Africa of hundreds of French-speaking Louisiana National Guardsmen caught the attention of many. In early 1943, a Cajun soldier named Francis Johnson wrote a letter to his hometown priest about meeting up with his friends from Company F in French North Africa:

> I will write you a few words on the customs of the population at the location where I am. The great majority of inhabitants are French, are very correct, very hospitable, and very likeable. There is also evidently many Arabs. They are dressed in a strange way, sometimes with a big white, wool cap on their head a fez or even a piece of white sheet wrapped on their skull. They speak a language incomprehensible and have strange ways. Arabian women never go out; you can never see their face. They wear a big, white sheet on their body and resemble traveling ghosts. Since the three months that I've been

> here, I have not had the joy of finding someone from my country. But since yesterday, I met several of my comrades from Cecilia and Breaux Bridge. I am extremely excited, since this reminds me of [my] town, my family. There has been more than two years that I have not seen my friends and I did not expect to see them this soon.[47]

In the ensuing months, the US military recognized the potential benefits of utilizing these French-speaking Cajuns in areas of communications. Several GIs transferred out of the Guard detail to serve as interpreters. Lee Roy Molbert of Cecilia was one. He wrote several letters home in 1943 specifically referencing his joy in having the ability to speak to the locals. He felt right at home among the French-speaking people. He commented that many people there spoke French and that it was a pleasure to go to church and hear French sermons. Another letter, reprinted in the local church bulletin in Breaux Bridge, noted that Molbert was transferred from Company F and "is now an interpreter in North Africa, which work he likes very much."[48] Percy Johnson, also from Breaux Bridge, did the same. He heard that the army needed French-speaking soldiers to work at the Mediterranean Base Headquarters and was able to transfer to that office. As a clerk, he purchased supplies from the French locals and assisted French telephone operators in translating incoming calls.[49] Lafayette native John Pellessier served twenty-one months in the Mediterranean campaign as a technician on a bomber crew. He acted as interpreter for his echelon when it moved by train from Oran to Casablanca, as he spoke French fluently. "I met many refugees from France," he said. "Believe me, they were genially glad to see so many Americans."[50] Lloyd "Pete" Rogers from Patterson was an interpreter as well. "I have two nicknames. One is Pete, and I got that [in Louisiana]. The other is Frenchie, I got that during the war years. I interpreted in Africa because the Arabs spoke French, and the ones that were educated, because the French nuns taught there, and we got along quite famously in the desert."[51]

Bernice LeJeune, although not in the Louisiana National Guard, had a similar experience in North Africa and later in Italy. LeJeune, a French-speaking Cajun from Church Point, had a tenth-grade education, and although he could read and write English, he was not fluent in the language when he entered the military. "I learned to speak English in large part in the army," he confessed.[52] He volunteered for the army in 1941. During the initial interview to join the army, when asked about his qualifications, LeJeune explained that he spoke two languages, English and French. The examiner, upon noticing LeJeune's place of birth, his last name, and his accent, said that his dialect—Cajun French—would be of no benefit to the army. This was not unusual, as the military had not yet placed a high priority on linguistics. What is more, the Cajun French dialect carried with it a stigma that many considered to be a backward language. "I didn't feel discriminated against," said LeJeune, "but I felt that this fellow could have given me more of a chance. I should have told him that my mother taught me to read and write basic French."

Nevertheless, the army sent LeJeune to several training camps throughout the country. He wound up assigned to a special artillery unit based in Chicago. A year and a half later, following the Allied invasion of North Africa, the army transferred LeJeune to a military police unit. In early 1943, his unit landed in Casablanca. Shortly after arriving, LeJeune had the opportunity to utilize his bilingual skills to settle a dispute between the Americans and the French over some stolen merchandise. As a result of that incident, the army immediately reassigned LeJeune as an interpreter for an American lieutenant in charge of the liaisons between the American and French forces. "As we were leaving the area, I received what I thought was a nice compliment from the French officer," LeJeune recalled. "He wanted to know where I had learned to speak English. To which I answered, '*En Louisiane, à la Pointe de l'Eglise* [in Church Point, Louisiana].'"

The North African experience brought to light the importance of communication among foreign allies. If the Americans and the French were going to work together, they had to have people, like LeJeune, who could bridge the language gap. "Most of the problems between the French and the Americans were with misunderstanding each other," he said. "Because I could speak French, this lieutenant used me as an interpreter and that kept me from the front line. When the French had a problem, they would come to him, and I would interpret for him. My French came in handy, and I never left his side."[53]

As the American forces moved farther east across North Africa, they encountered more French-speaking people. Oran, a large port city in Algeria, had a significant French population and a fairly large number of French troops. "I made good use of my French while I was there," LeJeune said. During his time in North Africa, he became good friends with a young French soldier, and he even had a French girlfriend. "The Cajuns had it made where they were," he said, speaking of those Cajuns who served in the Mediterranean campaign. "They thought we were French!"[54]

Another Cajun, Menton Chouest Jr. of Golden Meadow, wrote home about his experience in North Africa and how army commanders recognized his talents. A local newspaper featured his story. "Louisiana bayou French goes over very well with the natives of North Africa," the article said, "but Germans understand tanks better than Cajun French." The article noted that American officers in North Africa heard Chouest trying his Louisiana French on the native people and pulled him out of the tanks to serve as interpreter with the rating of staff sergeant. He later gave up that rank for a chance to get back with his tank crew. His unit made the Anzio invasion on the Italian coast in 1944 and later rolled into Rome.[55]

Sidney LeBlanc, from Vermilion Parish, learned that his native French had a distinct connection to an ancient past in North Africa. "I learned that we in Abbeville speak very good French," he said. "Our group had to train some French soldiers, and as the officer in charge knew I spoke French, I was picked to help. When I was introduced to the French officer, I spoke to him in his native tongue and later was surprised to see he and another officer with their heads together gesturing toward me. Finally, he came over and asked me where I had learned to speak. He said for an American I had an unusual accent. I told him we all spoke French at home and he then told me that the French I spoke was the 17th century French that had been forgotten in France."[56]

Throughout the war, staff members and clergymen at the St. Bernard Catholic Church in Breaux Bridge often wrote articles for the church bulletin—*L'Echo du Teche*—in French. The intent was to connect with French-speaking service members overseas, to recognize the value of the French language, and to lend support for the nation's French allies. One of the first such articles appeared in mid-1943, shortly after the church community began receiving letters from Cajun boys serving in French-speaking regions overseas. Reverend Monsignor P. A. Borel penned a remarkable letter—"A Few Words in French"—to parishioners, at home and abroad, expressing the importance of perpetuating the French language and heritage in south Louisiana:

> More than ever, we should use every means at our disposition to hasten the hour of the final victory. We all know that union of purpose is strength. The American saying, "United we stand, Divided we fall" is truer than usual.

> In our last issue, I saluted with great pleasure the meeting of the American and French armies on the battle fields of Africa. With the same satisfaction I will soon salute the joyful reunion with the French. Among them is the leadership of Generals Giraud and de Gaulle.
>
> For the first time today since the creation of Echo from the Têche, I introduce in these columns words in French. I consider that there is a new link of unity, especially since the landing of our troops in Africa. The U.S. government is working at reorganizing all of the French forces in order to free the motherland. The use of the same language, everywhere it is possible, is certainly an excellent way to facilitate the exchange of ideas and to achieve the task.
>
> Already several of our soldiers from Louisiana, especially those from the banks of the Bayou Têche, are in daily contact with people who speak only French. What a big advantage for our young guys to be able to express themselves in the same language. They are called to render only great service.
>
> Those who are in Tunisia, Algeria, Morocco or in the Islands of New Caledonia, etc., now appreciate the language that they spoke at home.
>
> Who knows, maybe the day will come when many will land in France itself. I want that our Echo from the Têche serve the men as a letter of introduction. They will be able to show the French, freed at last from the yoke of the oppressor, these few lines that come from home, and together with those from France that they will read, will give them a warm welcome.[57]

The letters in French, received by the soldiers overseas, prompted an enthusiastic response. Marcel Hebert writing from the Mediterranean region in November 1943 commented on the bulletin's French sections: "My friends and I await each issue with eagerness. Since many of my friends and I were sent to North Africa as French interpreters, we greatly enjoy the French articles."[58] Harry Periou wrote a short note praising the bulletin: "Brings joy and pride to a Cajun's heart."[59] Lester Trosclair said, "What I enjoyed reading very much is the articles you wrote in French. That is the only time I get a chance to read French. I always read your French article first."[60] Whitney LeBlanc's experience in a French-speaking foreign land made such an impression on him that he felt compelled to write a letter home *in French.*

> A lot of us are in these countries, or in occupation in which the French is required. . . . Personally, I have many occasions to put my French to use. Which? With a few words of thanks. Thank you very much for having introduced a few words in French in *L'Echo.* I greet this column with the greatest pleasure. As you have remarked, many of us are in countries, or in occupations in which the French language is "prerequisite." So, when we can point to these French pieces in our newspapers, we have made friends—as it is said in English, "we have broken the ice." We can show them that Americans show goodwill to all, and wish evil among no one. Everyone must live. Certainly, the other "servicemen" can tell you the same thing. Personally, I have many occasions to put my French to use. Quite often as a reason of me knowing French, I pass many beautiful places, and beautiful hours/times. So I say, please, continue this column. I am sure that all the others will say the same![61]

With so many French-speaking Cajuns from south Louisiana serving and living in French Algiers, W. V. Dupre, a former student at SLI, wrote, "For a time N.A. [North Africa] was just like Lafayette. We had the old National Guard composed of Cajuns from Lafayette, Carencro, Breaux Bridge, and New Iberia and all the Teche countryside. . . . I enjoyed a few good cups of coffee and good meals with them." He said there were other boys in his outpost from Crowley, Eunice, and Church Point, and they held an old-fashioned barbecue in honor of their baseball team. "We barbecued a pig and had beaucoup beer! Laugh if you will, but that 150# [pound] beast cost us $160. Nice price, wasn't it? We had a swell time."[62] Kenneth Frances of Carencro found his knowledge of French useful in military and social settings. Because of his language abilities, he made many friends and received more dinner invitations than he was able to accept.[63] Clarence Landry of Lafayette served as a wire chief in a telephone communication section. He landed in North Africa in November 1942 with the invasion forces. "Due to his knowledge of French," a local newspaper reported, "he was soon acting as interpreter for his unit in acquiring telephone facilities, or bargaining with the Arabs to get enough eggs to appease his buddies' hunger." Landry had graduated from

SLI in 1940 and served in several overseas campaigns in communications.[64] Writing home for the first time in several years, Maxie Roberts described his long journey with his fellow MPs from Company F. "From England, we went to Africa and landed at Oran. We next went to French Morocco, where we were interpreters for the American railroad. That was one of my jobs."[65]

Several other Cajuns served with the Army Air Corps in North Africa and utilized their French-speaking abilities. Sam Delcambre, a B-24 waist-gunner from Loreauville, flew with the US Army Air Corps out of Page Field, Fort Myers, Florida. From the moment his crew arrived in Florida, they flew coastal patrol missions searching for enemy submarines. From September 1942 to February 1943, Delcambre and his B-24 crew aboard *Jerk's Natural* took their experience in hunting German U-boats to the Mediterranean. From airfields in Tunisia, his unit bombed German and Italian shipping and harbors. Delcambre got a taste of home when French soldiers, camped near his barracks in Tobruk, Libya, often visited with the Cajun and had conversations in French. "I was lucky that I was born and raised in this part of the country and taught a little bit of French from my parents," Delcambre said. "I was never called any names, except a typewriter error misspelled my name; they spelled it DELCAMBRO—some people called me 'Delcambro the dago.'"[66]

Abbeville native Emery Toups, who worked as a mechanic on P-39s with the Army Air Corps in North Africa, met a lot of French people while in the service in these French-dominated cities. He recalled that once the local French people in Casablanca found out he spoke French they invited him to dinner. "They talk the same French we do," Toups said. "They couldn't believe that I was an American. My language, it helped me out."[67] As the Allies moved farther east into North Africa, his unit moved with them, setting up new forward airfields for the planes to launch air support missions. He ultimately ended up in Corsica, Sardinia, and Sicily, where his French continued to be useful in communicating with locals. He spent nine months in Pisa, Italy, and learned to speak a little Italian.

Charles LeBlanc from Thibodaux became a hero by using Cajun French. While working in air traffic control at an airfield in North Africa, he responded to a distress call from a French bomber crew preparing to land their B-26 bomber. According to the story, an emergency call came through—in French—stating that the nose wheel on the plane malfunctioned on the landing approach. "That's when LeBlanc swung into action

LEFT: *Charles LeBlanc, cir. 1944, courtesy of the LeBlanc family*

BELOW: *Charles LeBlanc Discharge Papers, courtesy of the LeBlanc family*

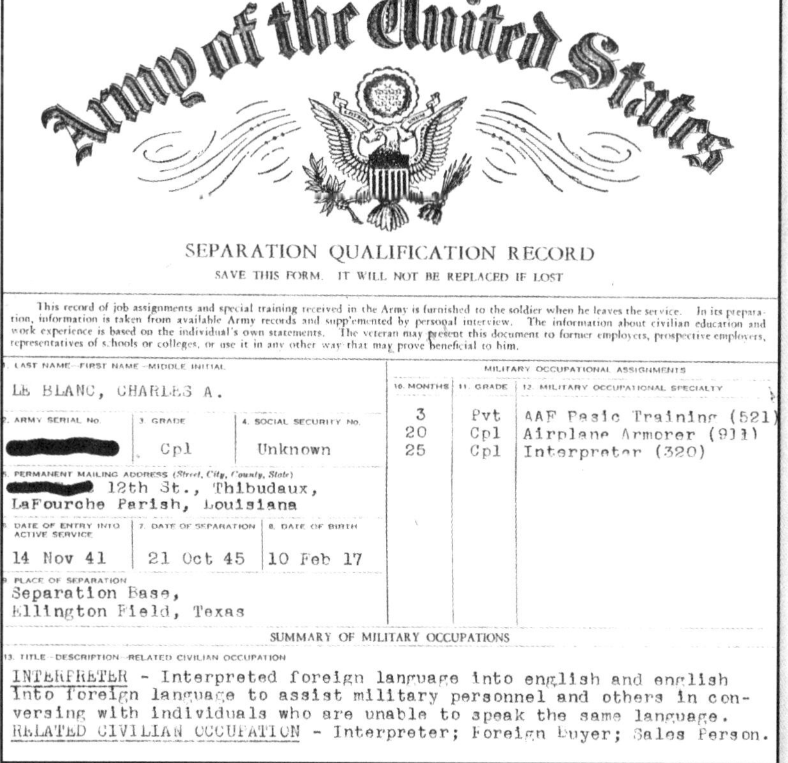

Army of the United States

SEPARATION QUALIFICATION RECORD

SAVE THIS FORM. IT WILL NOT BE REPLACED IF LOST

This record of job assignments and special training received in the Army is furnished to the soldier when he leaves the service. In its preparation, information is taken from available Army records and supplemented by personal interview. The information about civilian education and work experience is based on the individual's own statements. The veteran may present this document to former employers, prospective employers, representatives of schools or colleges, or use it in any other way that may prove beneficial to him.

1. LAST NAME—FIRST NAME—MIDDLE INITIAL
LE BLANC, CHARLES A.

2. ARMY SERIAL No.	3. GRADE	4. SOCIAL SECURITY No.
[illegible]	Cpl	Unknown

5. PERMANENT MAILING ADDRESS (Street, City, County, State)
[illegible] 12th St., Thibudaux,
LaFourche Parish, Louisiana

6. DATE OF ENTRY INTO ACTIVE SERVICE	7. DATE OF SEPARATION	8. DATE OF BIRTH
14 Nov 41	21 Oct 45	10 Feb 17

9. PLACE OF SEPARATION
Separation Base,
Ellington Field, Texas

MILITARY OCCUPATIONAL ASSIGNMENTS

10. MONTHS	11. GRADE	12. MILITARY OCCUPATIONAL SPECIALTY
3	Pvt	AAF Basic Training (521)
20	Cpl	Airplane Armorer (911)
25	Cpl	Interpreter (320)

SUMMARY OF MILITARY OCCUPATIONS

13. TITLE—DESCRIPTION—RELATED CIVILIAN OCCUPATION

INTERPRETER - Interpreted foreign language into english and english into foreign language to assist military personnel and others in conversing with individuals who are unable to speak the same language.
RELATED CIVILIAN OCCUPATION - Interpreter; Foreign Buyer; Sales Person.

with his invaluable linguistic talents, picked up in a French-speaking home in Louisiana," the article said. He was given technical instructions from several officers who rushed to the tower. "LeBlanc relayed the message to the French pilot, after transposing the instructions, given to him in English, into good, understandable French." As ground crews quickly prepped for emergency landing for the circling airplane, LeBlanc radioed to the French pilot, "*Écoutez, il faut avoir* . . ." Let your tail down first, he told them. The pilot followed his instructions and safely landed the plane. "Charley breathed a sigh of relief," the story concluded. "It was the best job of interpreting he had ever done."[68]

Louis Courtade, a Cajun from the small town of Brusly in West Baton Rouge, had a similar experience in the navy. During his seventeen months stationed in Morocco, he procured a job as an air traffic controller talking to French pilots because of his language ability. In November 1943, he wrote a letter to his mother and described his unique experiences in the French-speaking territories of North Africa. He spent several weeks in radio maintenance at an air base outside Casablanca. He then attended a B-24 bomber school and prepared to join a bomber squadron as a radio operator. That's when a call came in with an opportunity to use his bilingual skills as an air traffic controller. "Because I could speak French, I was sent down here to Agadir to land French planes. I now work in the land towers . . . talking through a microphone to planes. Not bad, eh? Ha! Ha!"[69]

Some of the French locals actually accepted these French-speaking American soldiers, such as Ames Dore and Francis Broussard of Breaux Bridge, as members of their extended family. In a letter to Dore's mother, a French girl from North Africa named Martinez Mireille referred to the Cajun GI as her "big brother" and wrote, "He is very gentile and very brave for us, and we love [him] very much."[70] Adsuar Antoine, also of North Africa, whose son had left home to fight for France, noted in a letter to Broussard's mother that "we consider [Francis] like one of our sons."[71]

> We write to you to let you know that we have been acquainted with your son, Francis, whom we consider like one of our own sons, since we too have a son who is the same age as yours and at the moment is also a soldier for the liberation of our country, France. Your son comes to the house almost every night; this pleases us greatly; we have a domino party all while chatting about different things, and

> from time to time we raise our glasses to the health of our two united nations, and to the Allies, also to the health of our two families. About Francis, you can be at peace regarding his behavior, for he is very reasonable, polite, and respectful. Finally we likewise say that it is thanks to the arrival of the Americans that we have been freed from Boche [German] slavery, for we started to feel it weighing; they took all that we had, and left us nothing; we began to have empty stomachs, be poorly shod and poorly dressed. Now, at last we can breathe more at ease. With our allies we will liberate France and all the countries under the Boche boot. I experienced war from 1914–1918—on the side of American soldiers having come in 1917; I went three times to the front, and twice was evacuated, and we brought back victory with General Pershing's soldiers. Long live America, France, and the Allies![72]

The mother of Clarence Guidry received a similar letter in French from North African residents, with whom their son, Clarence had been visiting. He spent Christmas Day with them, and they were very glad to have him, especially since he could speak French.[73] Percy Dupuis wrote that he had a swell time for the holidays and ate Christmas and New Year's dinner at a Frenchman's house in North Africa: "They are nice people; I go there more often than I stay in camp."[74]

Some expressed surprise in being emersed in a foreign francophone community. "I was sent to Algiers in Africa, and I still can't believe that I am so far away," Anton Dupuis wrote. "I've often acted as interpreter for the boys, and it seems strange to be in a land where they speak as everyone does at home."[75]

C. L. Marcantel from Elton was an interpreter for the prisoners captured in North Africa. He also acted as interpreter for officers who could not speak French. He found that his knowledge of Cajun French was a big help in shopping and getting around North Africa. While there, he learned to read and write French and to speak a different French dialect. With twenty-one months overseas, Marcantel had, like so many other Cajuns, discovered the value of his heritage.[76]

The *L'Echo du Teche* newsletter from July 1944 included a short report from Allied Force Headquarters, Mediterranean Theater, where a few dozen Cajun military police and interpreters had been stationed. "*Parlez vous français*? To this question, asked countless of times a day, in this North

PARLEZ-VOUS FRANCAIS? (From Allied Forces Headquarters, Mediterranean Theatre). "To this question, asked countless of times a day, in this North African city, at least, 70% of this military police company can say, 'Mais oui.' The Army knew what it was doing when it selected the men of this outfit to do duty where particular talents could be utilized. Among those from St. Martinville stationed here are: PFC Percy J. Gardemal, Pvt. Russelle T. Burch, PFC Jason Durio, Cpl. Alfred Melancon. From Breaux Bridge are: PFC Clevens J. Boudreaux, Sgt. Maurice Breaux, S/Sgt. Woodrow Broussard, Sgt. Antoine H. Champagne, PFC Maurell Champagne, Cpl. Ames Dore, PFC Ovide J. Dugas, PFC Percy Dupuis, Sgt. George Faucheaux, Sgt. David Guidry, PFC Paul D. Guidry, Sgt. Amilcar Hebert, S/Sgt John B. Hebert, PFC Joseph N. Hebert, Cpl. Edwin J. Huval, Sgt. Alton T. Latiolais, PVt. Gusas LeBlanc, S/Sgt. Howard J. Patin, Cpl. Maurice Perez, Cpl. Luke Robert, Pvt. Maxie Robert, PFC Clarence Stoute, S/Sgt. Wade Tauzin, PFC Raoul Trosclair, S/Sgt. Milton Wiltz, Sgt. Alfred Zeringue, S/Sgt. Aurelian Zimmerman, and PFC Sidney Blanchard. Working in a French-speaking country, their knowledge of the language is tremendously helpful in the pursuit of their duties, and has proved helpful to the French authorities in many instances in their dealings with the Americans." (The foregoing was sent to us by Mrs. Noe Robert.)

L'Echo du Teche *letter, cir. 1943, St. Martin Parish Library*

African city, at least 70% of this military policy company can say, '*Mais oui.*' The Army knew what it was doing when it selected the men of this outfit to do duty where particular talents could be utilized. Working in a French-speaking country, their knowledge of the language is tremendously helpful in the pursuit of their duties, and has proved helpful to the French authorities in many instances in their dealings with the Americans."[77] Of the original Cajun National Guardsmen, at least three—Joseph Faucheaux, Earl Landry, and Francis Broussard—worked in the Allied Force Headquarters as interpreters and reported to Lieutenant General McNarney's command for all American troops in the Mediterranean theater.[78]

By the close of the North African campaign in 1944, the Cajuns from the original Second Battalion, Louisiana National Guard, had managed to stay together for four years in the army. They traveled around the country and around the world as an intact military fighting unit, but it was their language skills that kept most off the front lines. With their bilingual proficiencies and toughness, Cajun Frenchies made their mark on America's first major campaign overseas.

Beyond North Africa

When the German stronghold of Tunisia fell to the Allied forces in May 1943, American troops prepared to invade the island of Sicily and Corsica before launching major operations in Italy and southern France. Just before being assigned to combat duties in Italy, the MPs from the Louisiana National Guard received new orders. The army once again fragmented the battalion of Cajun Guardsmen, separating them into nine smaller combat military police companies—Sixty-Sixth through the Seventy-Fifth MPs—to serve all throughout the Mediterranean. This group of as many as one hundred joined many other French-speaking Cajuns throughout the Sicily, Italy, and southern France campaigns. Once again, their bilingual skills proved useful in military operations. Their experiences have been recounted in letters, memoirs, and interviews.

Robert Gerami, originally a cook with Company E (Jeanerette), was in the group that went to Italy shortly after the Allies invaded. "We were split up and they made us MPs; half of us went to Italy, some went to Sicily. In Italy I was sent to the police department to be an interpreter. I'm Italian, so I could speak Italian. I was raised with the French people and my wife was French, so I could speak a little French, too. They took me out of the kitchen to work as an interpreter."[79] Homer Comeaux, assigned to the Seventieth MPs, served as a strongman of the law under Gerald Wattigny, former commander of Company G who became provost marshal in Rome. Wattigny assigned Comeaux and other Cajun MPs to hunt for and arrest German and Italian officers hiding out in the city and surrounding countryside. "Those Cajun soldiers were tough. We all fought hard for our country. We believed in the cause, and I would go back and fight for it again," Comeaux stated.[80] The men never lost their *esprit de corps* during their many transitions and reassignments, and they never lost the identity as Cajun National Guardsmen. "We were designated MPs," said Alfred Zeringue of Breaux Bridge, "but we always considered ourselves Company F."[81]

Pierre Laiche from St. James Parish had a very interesting experience as a Frenchie in Italy during the war. He was first assigned to a French unit as a liaisons officer and served with them from Italy all the way north through southern France and to the Rhine River. Laiche kept a journal chronicling his wartime experience. He landed in North Africa with an artillery unit attached to the First Infantry Division. He ultimately became a combat liaison officer and represented the commanding general of a French field artillery brigade at the headquarters of the French army. Captain Laiche translated orders and interpreted conversations. "Following heavy fighting in and around Italy," his discharge papers recounted, "he was reassigned to an executive officer in the 431st F. A. Group HW on Aug. 1, 1944 and went to Southern France. He traveled around with his brigade but served as liaison officer with the French in support of their advance. His unit stayed under French command for 14 months."[82]

In Laiche's journal, it is apparent that he spent more time with French officers than with Americans. He participated in many dinners with high-ranking French and American officers, no doubt serving as a translator. He often traveled into French towns to gather information and locate places for the units to stay and for officers' quarters. In an entry dated April 23, 1945, he wrote: "I was sent to Bordeaux with Major Roe to try to establish a provisional rest camp for the Brigade personnel. We arrived early in the morning and contacted French military authorities who immediately assigned us rooms in the Royal Bastogne Hotel."[83] Laiche's story of serving within a French military unit as an interpreter is one of just a handful that have been documented.

Many Cajun soldiers who fought in the North Africa campaign received military honors for utilizing their language skills. Louis Cormier was

Campagnes pour la libération de la France

(Juin - Décembre 1944)

Décision N° 782

Le Général de Gaulle,

Président du Gouvernement Provisoire de la République Française.

Cite à l'Ordre DE L'ARMEE :

Le Capitaine Pierre J. LAICHE 13° Brigade d'Artillerie de Campagne Américaine Mle 01173343

" Pour services exceptionnels de Guerre rendus au " cours des opérations de libération de la France."

Cette Citation comporte l'attribution de la Croix de Guerre avec Palme

Le Général d'Armée JUIN
Chef d'État-Major Général de la Défense Nationale,

PARIS, le 31 Mai 1945

A. Juin

ÉTAT-MAJOR GÉNÉRAL DE LA DÉFENSE NATIONALE

Signé : de GAULLE

Pierre Laiche's citation from the French Military, 1944, courtesy of the Laiche family

awarded a Bronze Star for his role as a French interpreter in military combat in Italy. Born in Rayne, he landed with the invasion troops in Algeria, North Africa, and took part in the Tunisian, Sicilian, and Italian campaigns. He was chief of a gun section in an anti-aircraft artillery battalion and served twenty-nine months overseas. When a French unit moved into the line to assume the position and weapons of his outfit, Cormier put his French skills to work. No one spoke French nearby, so Cormier said he "elected to show the French-speaking soldiers the GI way of knocking down enemy planes."

His heavy weapons unit had been on the line fighting for seventy days before being pulled back in favor of the French unit. Cormier stayed on for an additional week to assist the French in making the transition to the AAA heavy guns.[84] Cormier's citation read: "When an infantry division was relieved by a French Corps, difficulty was encountered due to the inability of the officers of both units to adequately express themselves in a language foreign to them. Sergeant Cormier volunteered to serve as interpreter for the changeover of the division field artillery forces. His ability to speak fluently both French and English, his knowledge of artillery methods, and his efficient liaison work were instrumental in effecting the relief with a minimum of disorder and misunderstanding. When his own unit had been relieved from the line for a rest, Cormier accepted the additional hazards and remained in the division sector under fire until his services were no longer needed." Major General Geoffrey Keyes, the commanding officer who gave Cormier the award, sent him a photograph of the event and short letter that read simply: "I desire to congratulate you upon your fine performance, and at the same time wish for you the best of luck in the future."[85]

Like so many Cajun veterans who spent considerable time overseas, Cormier returned home from the war and settled down in a small town and raised a family. He worked in the oil field most of his life. Although its likely he rarely talked about the war years, as was common for his generation, he kept newspaper clippings and photographs that documented his unique story as a French translator in Europe all these years. Cormier is one of perhaps a few thousand Cajuns who had the opportunity to utilize their French language to the benefit of military commanders in the field, in cities, and in rear echelon areas during the war. His story reveals the unique, if not ironic, circumstances in which many Cajuns found themselves during the war. Their native language, which had previously been so marginalized and discredited as substandard, had value.

Work As Interpreter In Changeover Of Infantry Unit On Italian Front Wins Bronze Star For French-Speaking Crowley Soldier, Citation Says

Louis Cormier's Bronze Star headline, The Crowley Post Signal, *1945*

When the Cajuns arrived in North Africa and Italy, they discovered a world that, from a language perspective, resembled their own. For many, the native French that they were instructed to forget in grammar school became a vital resource to military operations and to themselves. Their language kept many of them, particularly the well-trained Cajuns from the Louisiana National Guard, from the frontline fighting. These hardened infantrymen -turned-MPs were spared the grueling and violent combat engagements that other American ground troops faced. Wallace Thibodeaux of Company G once stated, "In the five years I was in the Guard, I never fired a shot in anger."[86] Warren Hebert, who spent more time in the boxing ring than in a foxhole, still questioned the army's decision to keep many of the French-speaking men from heavy fighting. "Perfect like we were and in good shape—I thought we would get into the battle with Rommel and Montgomery and Patton."[87] But they didn't. For the Cajuns of the Second Battalion, the war was seen from the behind the lines.

Nearly seventy years later, at a special gathering among fellow surviving members of the Second Battalion at the Acadian Memorial in St. Martinville, these aging veterans were asked to comment on their wartime experience. They agreed that it was their French language that dictated much of their journey during the war—and their safe return home after the war.

CHAPTER 2

FRENCHIE IN FRANCE

"Being of French descent and able to speak the language has been a great help to me."

—Harold Durio, France, 1944

The Allied invasion of Normandy, France, on June 6, 1944, is widely considered the most pivotal battle of the Second World War. For several weeks and months after the historic D-Day landings, tens of thousands of American troops came ashore in France. The French people welcomed their liberators with open arms and tears of joy, but the language gap prevented any meaningful communication among them. The French-speaking Cajuns GIs, spread out among the ranks, effectively bridged that language barrier. They were natural translators, not requiring any linguistic training to communicate directly with local authorities, civilians, and French Resistance groups. Their ability to obtain local knowledge of enemy whereabouts and navigate through the countryside all the way to Paris, across Belgium, and over the German border provided essential aid to Allied forces. Along the way, these Cajuns also met and befriended French families, developing relationships that, in some cases, continued long after the war. This experience in France made the Cajun soldiers feel as if they were back home in Louisiana; it gave them a level of comfort in an otherwise distant land far from Bayou Country. What is more, the Cajuns' regional dialect delighted the French people. As Allied forces raced across the French countryside, liberating town after town, word quickly spread that French-speaking Cajun soldiers from Louisiana were accessible and desperately needed as interpreters. "Frenchies," emerged as a valuable asset throughout the European theater.

Vive la France

Cajun soldiers put their language to use as soon as the Allies stormed the beaches of Normandy. Advancing over the bluffs and through the coastal hamlets, hundreds of small infantry units encountered scores of French locals who emerged from their shell-shocked cottages and farmhouses to greet the American liberators. But most GIs could only muster hand signals to communicate with the locals; someone needed to translate. Up and down the line, from Sainte-Marie-du-Mont at Utah Beach to Vierville-sur-Mer on Omaha Beach, platoon leaders and military commanders sent word through the ranks to rush French interpreters to the front. Cajun soldiers, who likely numbered in the hundreds early on in the campaign, answered the frantic call to extract information from the French locals. Some of these conversations produced valuable intelligence on enemy positions. Others led to the exchange of goods or the celebratory sharing of locally made cognac and wine. The gracious French people, who had waited four long years for this moment, embraced their French-speaking comrades from Louisiana. Numerous wartime letters, memoirs, and interviews with veterans tell firsthand accounts of how these two francophone cultures came together during the critical battle to retake continental Europe.

The invasion of Normandy was "without a doubt the greatest event the world has ever known," wrote Ellis Laborde of Avoyelles Parish in 1944 to his boss back home. "It was pretty rugged for a few days. We who had taken part in the Sicilian campaign knew what sort of problem we were confronted with, but still we were willing to take the chance, for we knew the only way home was via France. . . . I am using my knowledge of French here to some advantage."[1] Rodney Young from Church Point participated in the invasion as a naval officer aboard a landing ship. He wrote to SLI President Joel Fletcher shortly after arriving in Normandy. "Things are progressing very well over here. This morning while taking a walk over the beaches, I talked to several civilians who were on the beach at the time of the landing and are now working for the Allies. It certainly reminded me of 'good old Louisiana' to hear and speak French again."[2] Bunkie native Twyman Brouillette, a captain in an airborne division, jumped into Normandy with the first invasion wave. He wrote a letter home after D-Day that stated his knowledge of French was "a great aid to him, as he had no trouble in making the natives understand and thus got what he wanted—the only trouble being that when they learned that he understood their language they burdened him with their troubles and woes of the past four years under German domination."[3] Nelson Dubroc, an eighteen-year-old chief petty officer from Eunice, wrote his parents about the historic landing. "Our crew hit the beach at H-Hour on D-Day and we all came out okay. I didn't get a scratch. Thank the lord. Now it's over and I'm feeling fine. I met French people and felt almost at home. They were nice to me and I was glad I could speak French." Dubroc's reprinted letter in the newspaper captured the headline "Sailor's French Comes in Handy."[4] This line became an often-repeated phrase to describe the Cajuns' experience in France.

Jim Lanclos's Cajun French indeed came in handy the moment he landed on Utah Beach. "While we were down there near Normandy beach," he recalled in a 2003 interview, "this old French apple farmer called over my lieutenant and wanted to talk to somebody who knew French. My lieutenant called me over—they called me Frenchie, too—he said, 'Come here Frenchie, come talk to this farmer.'" Reared in a French-speaking community in Centerville along the Bayou Teche, Lanclos remembered his early days at a little country school in Loreauville where the teacher forced him to learn English. "They tried to scare the French out of me," he said. "We were taught not to speak French." But once in Normandy, his native patois and country-rearing kicked in. "I started talking to this old Frenchman. He had tears in his eyes. He called me 'soldier' and told me to follow him because he wanted to give me something. I thought, 'This poor old farmer. What the hell does he have to give me?' The Germans took everything from him; they took his property, occupied his barn. So this old farmer started digging in the ground like a damn dog. He came out with a little old keg of cognac. It had been buried there for five years. The Germans had their headquarters in his barn and they had been walking over it the whole time. He cleaned off the lil keg and told me to get my canteen. He poured us each a glass and we toasted. '*Vive la France. Vive la France*,' he said. I will never forget it."[5]

Charles Ducote Sr. from the Marksville area had a similar experience, one that no doubt saved the lives of his fellow American soldiers during the critical opening hours of the invasion. Ducote joined the army at nineteen years old and spent more than a year of infantry training in the states before sailing to England. He landed on Omaha Beach as part of the first wave of D-Day with the famed Twenty-Ninth Infantry Division. Once his unit made it across the beach and up the bluff, an officer called him up to interpret with a French farmer to identify the location of a hidden German bunker. Ducote retold the story in an interview many years later: "One officer came up to me and said, 'You're a French speaker. Our interpreter got killed. Would you wish to come up with me? We'll have to crawl up on shore to this first French house and see where the entrance of this pillbox is. We have to knock that out because they have some observers in there.' So we did." The assault team had to cross a deadly minefield to get off the beach and up to the Frenchman's home perched high up on the bluff. "And there I asked him, 'Where is the entrance to this tunnel, pillbox?' They were fortified in there. . . . They could see us [on the beach] easily. Point blank. Machine guns, shells. They had observers in there to direct other big guns in the rear." The Frenchman then said (in this instance Ducote says the French phrase first, followed by the English translation):

Monsieur, á propos quatre kilomètres.
A little less than three miles.

Tu vas voir deux grandes portes.
You going to see two big doors, with wooden slats.

Couvert de vignes.
Covered in vines.

Ouvrir cela et il ressemble à un palais.
Open that up and it looks like a palace.

"'And there you are,' he said. So, the officer radioed back to the tank destroyers, and they came over with three or four tanks and they bust up that place. And from then on, after they took the prisoners, and we captured them, troops were able to walk in. . . . And from there on I stayed with the Twenty-Ninth Infantry until V-E Day. . . . I was very lucky. The good Lord was with me."[6]

Another Louisiana-born D-Day veteran with the Twenty-Ninth Infantry Division, Clifford Borel, came ashore at Omaha Beach and found himself immersed in a tense battle. The local newspaper *Teche News* reported: "Because he spoke French, Pfc. Borel was selected to go from house to house as his men advanced through the village questioning the people regarding the retreating Germans. He was awarded the Purple Heart."[7] After thirteen days of continuous fighting in France, he was severely wounded by shrapnel near Saint-Lô and lost a leg. Born in Catahoula, not far from St. Martinville, Borel was the oldest son of nine kids and spoke only French until he attended school. Like so many others during the Great Depression, Borel dropped out of school to find work. He joined the Civilian Conservation Corps (CCC) and helped build Girard Park in Lafayette, earning a dollar a day to help feed his family. He was one of the 250,000 young men, ages fifteen to eighteen, who served in the CCC across the country in the 1930s. This group ultimately made up a core component of the American military in World War II.

In the days following the Normandy invasion, a local Louisiana newspaper ran this story: "Lafayette Man Saves Day by Talking French." It featured Alfred Benoit Jr., who's ability to communicate with the French people proved invaluable as the Allies landed on the French coast. Born in Carencro, Benoit joined the army in July 1942. He trained with a quartermaster battalion of the Eighty-Second Airborne Division and landed in Normandy on D-Day in a glider with a small infantry unit. The article listed Benoit's many contributions while in combat, including using his French language to speak to the locals. "During the operation, Pfc. Benoit became one of the most valuable men because of his ability to speak French." Through him the mayor of Cherbourg was contacted, and dozens of Frenchmen came to their aid for grave digging. With Benoit as interpreter, the quartermasters rounded up

LAFAYETTE MAN SAVES DAY BY TALKING FRENCH

Alfred Benoit headline, The Daily Advertiser, *1944*

Alfred Benoit with French people, 1944, courtesy of the Benoit family

parachutes that contained ammunition, rations, and medical supplies. With lines of communication open, he was able to obtain numerous fresh eggs and other scarce items for his comrades.[8]

Livonia native Lee Johnson landed in France at Utah Beach. His hometown newspaper carried a lengthy feature story on his brave action in combat. The headline read: "Livonia Sergeant Called One of the Best Soldiers on the Western Front." From Normandy, Johnson's unit made its way to the port city of Cherbourg on a reconnaissance patrol. Once there, the officers of his company recognized his unique skill set, "that of being able to speak French. Once when they were marching down the road near Cherbourg, a Frenchman came running out to them and started talking very rapidly. The other GIs, not understanding, just shrugged their shoulders and walked on, but not Johnson. He got the information which the Frenchman was trying to give them, and as a result the platoon went over to a neighboring barn and found 20 Germans who were hiding there, making them all prisoners."[9]

Of the 450 men in the US Army VII Corps headquarters that liberated the Cherbourg Peninsula, only one spoke French: Warrant Officer Ned Arceneaux from Lafayette. "I grew up speaking French and couldn't speak a word of English until I started school," he said. "I was drafted into the army on May 15, 1941, because Uncle Sam said, 'I need you! I want you!' I was twenty-two and working as a clerk at the post office." Arceneaux received infantry training in Louisiana, Florida, and Alabama and wound up in California as a supply officer in charge of getting all the food and equipment for the men in headquarters. He traveled across the country with the VII Corps and sailed to England to prepare for the invasion of France. "We left early that morning and landed at Utah Beach; it was about nine in the morning on June 6th. A lot of boys got sick going over. When we landed, you could see all the dead bodies floating all over. My first thought was, 'We're never coming back. We're never coming back.'" Arceneaux came ashore on a jeep, dodging light enemy fire on his way inland. After a few days of clearing the beach, his unit moved onto the town of Sainte-Mère-Église and set up a command post in a farmhouse. From there, he went to Carentan and then followed the coast north up to Cherbourg. On the outskirts of the major port city, the commander of VII Corps, General J. Lawton Collins, ordered Arceneaux and a chaplain to drive into the German-occupied area to find a French priest and deliver a

Ned Arceneaux and buddy with French girls, Cherbourg, France, June 1944, courtesy of the Arceneaux family

Ned Arceneaux, Oct. 1944, courtesy of the Arceneaux family

message: be advised that four army divisions would soon be arriving to capture this strategic location. The commander selected Arceneaux for this task—and for many others throughout France—because of his ability to speak French. For the next several months, whenever the general needed an interpreter, Arceneaux accompanied him.

Arceneaux grew up in a French-speaking community along the Vermilion River near Lafayette. His ancestor, Louis Arceneaux of Beaubassin in L'Acadie, came to Louisiana after the expulsion and received a large land grant from the Spanish government. He owned considerable parcels of land in the area known as the Attakapas District. In the early twentieth century, the family donated an acre of land to build a one-room schoolhouse in the country, where Ned Arceneaux got an early education. "We were not allowed to speak French on the campus," he recalled in a 2006 interview. "If you were caught, you were punished. You were put on your knees and then in the corner, oh, yeah."[10] At recess, the young rebellious Cajun often jumped the fence surrounding the schoolhouse to join his uncles and cousins working in the field. His parents, realizing that he would never learn anything in that environment, sent him to Lafayette for schooling, where he eventually learned English.

Everyone in VII Corps headquarters knew of Arceneaux's ability to speak French when they arrived in France. His comrades often called on him to find certain items of need throughout the French countryside. "My French and my Cajun helped a lot in the army," he said. "It helped a lot because I could go out in the country and supplement our food like getting eggs and stuff like that and vegetables for our kitchen to prepare for us. Yeah, getting all kinds of things. Helping out with the people—some of the fellows who didn't understand French—they wanted to go and purchase something for their wives back home or something, and then I'd always accompany them and interpret for them. . . . They called me 'Frenchie.' Yeah, oh yeah. Some of them called me 'Cajun.' I didn't mind at all. As long as they didn't call me 'coonass.'"[11]

As a quartermaster, Arceneaux had the organizational skills to run the logistics for General Collins's headquarters group. As a Frenchie, he had the unique ability to move about the French natives and acquire valuable items, supplies, and information. On one particularly rewarding venture, Arceneaux and an army chaplain named Father Gleason entered a fort in Cherbourg that the Germans had just vacated. Down the main hallway, the two Americans stumbled upon a warehouse stock full of liquor. They each grabbed a bottle of cognac and hurried out to radio their findings to VII Corps headquarters. When General Collins picked up the line, the two men exchanged information:

> "General, we captured this fort, and Father Gleason and myself discovered a warehouse full of liquor."
>
> "Go-head!"
>
> "Yep, we got all kinds: wine, scotch, whiskey, cognac, anything you want."
>
> "Ned, stay where you are. I'm sending six trucks your way. When they get there, start loading up as much as you can and send them back to headquarters."[12]

Later that day, when Arceneaux returned to the headquarters with the newly commandeered supplies, General Collins told him to deliver a truck full of liquor to each of the four divisional headquarters. "Tell them it's compliments of J. Lawton Collins," Arceneaux recalled his orders. After delivering the goods, there remained two trucks fully loaded with bottles of liquor. General Collins took one for himself; Arceneaux took the other. "So, we had those trucks with us from Cherbourg on," he said. Arceneaux's ability to dispatch vehicles and secure contraband for his unit served him well in the army. He later honed these skills as the postmaster general of Lafayette, a job he held for thirty years. He also coordinated all the VII Corps headquarters reunions after the war, including several held in Cajun Country.

Marion McGee, another Cajun who fought in the Battle of Cherbourg, wrote a letter to his father in Eunice about his experiences with the French people. "I was interpreter for the captain, taking information from the French so we had modern hotels to sleep in, even when everything seems to be popping open all around, it felt good to have a home-like bed. Dad, the French are nice. I stayed three or four days with a French family on a farm and had eggs, chickens, buttermilk, and also wine. I kind of hated to leave that good old country home. I often heard you say that the French language was quite different from our French. I don't see very much difference. I understand them very well. They look to me like pure Cajuns—some of them plenty dumb."[13]

The local French people expressed jubilation in meeting and talking to French-speaking American soldiers. In nearly every French village and country farm, the Cajuns encountered gracious French locals who raced out to share a drink of calvados—a locally made, potent, apple-flavored cognac—with their thirsty liberators. The GIs described calvados as "apple cider with a dynamite base."[14] The fiery calvados left a lasting impression with the Cajun troops. "I must say that our boys have had a few gulps of the powerful drink after I induced a Frenchman to exchange 20 lbs of sugar for the only two-quart bottles of cognac he had left to his name," wrote Abbeville native Harold Pastor. "The French people are more than glad to open their hearts to any Americans, in particular those who can understand their speech and can carry on conversations with them." In many cases, the French people used their hidden reserves of calvados and other fresh goods to barter for such items as soap, chocolate bars, and cigarettes, which the GIs had in abundance. "I made a deal with a nearby farmer to provide the boys from my unit with all the milk we can drink and I must say it's delicious," wrote Pastor.[15]

Curtis Myers, a native of Jeanerette, got a taste of calvados in Normandy and talked about it in his memoir. He was assigned to a heavy weapons company that manned antiaircraft guns on concrete block ships—codenamed "Phoenix"—towed and parked just off the coast. These giant structures, strung together across a few miles, formed a breakwater for the beachhead at Normandy. On the afternoon of June 8, a large seagoing tugboat attached tow lines to the concrete caisson and towed the artificial harbor, with Myers's unit aboard, across the English Channel to within sight of the Normandy beaches. "What a sight!" he wrote. "Hundreds of ships and landing craft in the beach area. Barrage balloons tethered to cables hung in the air like giant sausages." After spending several days on the concrete ship manning the guns, his unit went ashore to join the armada of men and machines moving en masse across the beach. One afternoon, he and a few GIs met a young French boy who led them to a nearby barn made of stone. "I was the only one in the group who knew a small amount of the French language," he wrote. "Inside, his grandfather greeted us and served each of us a glass of apple cider (the alcoholic kind). In the barn were several large barrels filled with cider. In this part of France, this liquid was distilled and turned into a 90-proof liquor called calvados. This product is named after the Calvados district of France and is marketed throughout the world for serious drinkers or connoisseurs of finer things in life."[16] Myers had the fortunate opportunity to return to Normandy for the fiftieth anniversary of D-Day, where he received a special award as a liberator from the French government.

Napoleonville native Robert Bourgeois tasting cognac, Cherbourg, 1944, courtesy of the Arceneaux family

The Office of Strategic Services (OSS) recruited several French-speaking Cajuns for the all-important battle of Normandy. Their job was to provide assistance to the French underground forces in tactical missions against German positions and movements all across France and Belgium. Robert LeBlanc, an Abbeville native, came ashore at Utah Beach ten days after the initial landings as the intelligence officer for OSS Special Forces Detachment 11. Within hours of arriving in Normandy, LeBlanc's commanding officer sent him out to find some calvados. He located a Frenchman who struck a hard bargain in exchange for the popular apple-flavored cognac:

> I went to a French farmer nearby and I started speaking in French to him and [he asked] are you French? I said no. I said, I'm American. But why do you speak French like you speak? (*Vous êtes français? Je dis non. Je dis je suis Américain. Mais pourquoi vous causez français*

> *comme vous causez ?*) The reason is very simple. I didn't know how to speak English until I was five years old. (*La raison c'est bien simple. Je ne connaissais pas comment parler en anglais jusqu'à j'avais cinq ans.*)[17]

Following the small talk, LeBlanc got down to business. He told the Frenchman that he wanted some calvados. When the Frenchman balked, LeBlanc had his driver bring over a carton of Lucky Strike cigarettes. He pulled out a pack to entice the Frenchman into a beneficial trade.

> I hand him a cigarette and I lit up a cigarette and I said now, you know where is some calvados? He says—*il dit, oui. Vous avez quelque chose le mettre dedans?* You have something to put it in? I said, yeah, I got a water can out there. He says, how much is it worth? (*Il dit, combien ça vaut?*) How much is it worth? Well, the can is five gallons. That's about six liters, you see. I said, I'll give you four packs of cigarettes. (*Le can est cinq gallons. Ça c'est à peu près six litre, you see. Je dis, je vous donne quatre paquets de cigarettes.*) The carton was four packs. He says, how many cigarettes are in a pack? I said, there's twenty. Well, he said, make it one hundred cigarettes. (*Quatre paquets. Il dit, combien de cigarettes il y a dans un paquet? Je dis, il y a vingt. Mais, il dit, fait-le cent cigarettes.*) So, he says alright. *Donne-moi le*, give me the container, and that bastard had it, excuse my English, he had it down in his cellar, you see. I got the five gallons of Calvados and I went back to the headquarters and the major said "Well, why don't you bring us a brie cheese?"[18]

Leo Thomas from St. Martinville had a front-row seat on a navy vessel for the Normandy invasion. "Our ship came here with the assault tide on 'D' day," he wrote. "We made our first beaching a couple hours after 'H' hour, and have been here since. A person had to witness what was going on to really believe anything about this invasion. The French were really swell to all the Yanks 'over here.' Knowing a little 'Cajun' French, I get along with the people fairly well. I also help my shipmates learn what they consider the toughest language out [there]. After they learn a few basic words, they find that it's fairly easy."[19]

Loreauville native Carroll Mestayer, who lost his best friend, Houston Duhon, while storming the shores on bloody Omaha Beach in the first wave, witnessed the historic battle from a Higgins boat all the way across the smoke-filled beach. After surviving the initial beach assault, Mestayer made his way into the interior and regrouped with the survivors from his unit. A machine gunner in an antiaircraft unit, Mestayer's men often called on him to speak to the locals, not only for information, but also to find certain items that were not readily available, such as eggs, fresh milk, and booze. "I was glad that I could speak a little French with those people," he said. "Now, it was two different kinds of French, you understand. They spoke that real French. And I bumped into some right quick there after the Normandy invasion. I went through them hills and I'd run into them, then they'd tell me stories about how the Germans had taken over in 1940 and the Germans would take all their butter. And the Germans would steal all their wine. The French was a wine growing people, you know. They'd store wine in their cellars and the Germans who come there take all that stuff away from them."[20]

Nicknamed Frenchie by his comrades in Europe, Mestayer possessed a skill set that many others did not. He showcased his native-born talents as a French speaker every chance he could. On the long road to Paris, his company commander asked him to talk to the mayor of a city about placing some antiaircraft artillery pieces nearby.

> We got to talk, finally got the mayor on, in the office and I asked him, I asked him what I wanted. We wanted to get some antiaircraft artillery guns on the edge of the cemetery—a good approach when the airplanes would come and bomb that rail yard, you understand. So, I spoke to that mayor. He said, "Where you from son?" He asked me in French. *Je dis,* well, well, *je deviens de la Loreauville, Louisiana* [I'm from Loreauville, Louisiana]. He said, "*mais, je peux pas croire. Il s'avait dit qu'il pouvait pas croire*" [But I can't believe. He told himself that he couldn't believe it]. So, we talked a little more. He was a busy man and he said, "*Tu peux mettre des*" [Yes, you can put some]—an artillery piece in French is *des armes contre avions,* a gun against airplanes. He said, "Yeah, you can put your guns there," but I don't remember his exact words, but he didn't want us to destroy the area. . . . So, I spoke to him for about fifteen or twenty minutes. He was glad to talk with me. But I said, "Listen, I can't talk your good French like you, but I can understand you a little bit."[21]

One afternoon, near the city of Versailles, Mestayer went into a barbershop for a haircut. The old, gray-haired French barber greeted him, to which Mestayer responded, "*Bonjour. Comment va le vie.*" The two struck up a conversation in French. When Mestayer told him his full name, the barber pulled back in shock. "He said, '*Mon nom est Raul Mestayer.*' I said, 'My daddy's name is *Raoul Mestayer.* R.A.O.U.L *Mestayer.* It's spelled the same way!' That was the most fantastic, amazing thing to meet up with that old man. Here I am about eighteen and a half years old, he was about seventy-five—same name. It's amazing. I'll never forget that."[22]

Aside from the horror of seeing his buddy killed on the bloody beaches of Normandy, Mestayer expressed how the experience overseas changed him. "I had never been anywhere, really," he said. "I'd been to New Iberia only, and I saw how greatly that changed me. You could say I went into another world. . . . The satisfaction of going through all of that and come back home, being able to work for a living, support your families and work for companies. And then thank God that we pulled through it."[23]

Mestayer and his fellow Cajun soldiers had participated in the greatest invasion of all time. They had breached Hitler's "Atlantic Wall" and secured a toehold in German-occupied France. As the Allies moved inland into the French countryside and cleared a pathway to Paris, French-speaking soldiers became evermore popular among the units and with the French communities. For the Louisiana Cajuns who fought in Europe from 1944–45, the language they had been told to forget became an equalizer on the battlefield.

Breaking Bread

With the Normandy beachhead secure, the Allied forces made their way into the maze of ubiquitous hedgerows that covered the interior. As American infantry units cleared out enemy positions, one hedgerow at a time, more French people came out of the woodwork. Every advancing infantry unit seemed to have a Frenchie Cajun in its ranks who could strike up a conversation with and gather information from the locals. Many natives were shocked to meet French-speaking Americans and expressed curiosity at the Cajun's familiar-sounding dialect, which resembled the "ancient French" of centuries old. "All over the western front our soldiers are having difficulty in finding directions, obtaining aid and solving hundreds of big and little problems—simply because they don't know the language," wrote a reporter for the

Times-Picayune in the early stages of the battle for France.[24] Clearly that was not the case for the hundreds, if not thousands, of French-speaking Cajuns spread out among the vast American army, all moving in unison, liberating one village at a time, to reach Paris. Through it all, the Cajun GIs established deep bonds with and respect for the French people. This experience changed their view of their own cultural heritage and their place within the francophone world.

"I'm enjoying the best of good health," wrote Lee Arceneaux from Normandy, "and getting along very well in all respects, including my French language. My first acquaintance with the French civilian was with the mayor of a small village whom I first met when our company was located on one of his farms. We had a long conversation and at the time of parting, he invited me to visit his family which I did shortly afterwards and still do from time to time and when my absence from the Post is possible."[25]

"The apple trees were in full bloom, and this part of France is one immense apple orchard," wrote A. J. Resweber of St. Martinville about a month after arriving in France. "This is great cider and calvados country. In England we shunned cider claiming that it was too mild, but here in France we have come to be great cider drinkers. . . . I have talked to quite a few Frenchmen, and I get along with them practically like a real Frenchman. French-speaking soldiers are quite popular now; to ask for cider, to get clothes washed, to ask for water and a variety of other things. While everybody was still eating rations, we were fortunate enough to get fresh meat and eggs."[26]

"I am now in France," said Breaux Bridge native Harold Durio in a letter to his parents. "The people have treated us exceptionally well since our arrival into their country. To the French, there is no one to be looked upon with greater esteem and respect than the American soldier. Nothing they can do is too good for us in France. The people are very friendly and do not hesitate one minute to show their gratitude which knows no bounds. Being of French descent and able to speak the language has been a great help to me. Rattling away in French reminds me of the good old days in Breaux Bridge. I never realized then that being a Frenchman could mean so much to me in so short a period of time."[27]

Letters like these written from France poured into Cajun Country in the fall of 1944 and found their way into local church bulletins and newspapers. These letters provide a vivid snapshot of the Cajun experience in France. The *Morgan City Review* paraphrased a letter sent home from Newton Mason, who

Pvt. H. Vidrine Is Interpreter

Son of Mr. and Mrs. Wilfred Vidrine Selected French Interpreter

According to information received by his parents, Mr. and Mrs. Wilfred Vidrine, Pvt. Howard Vidrine, has been selected to act as interpreter for his company in France.

Pvt. Vidrine was with the infantry on active duty, and his knowledge of French assisted in his transfer to a headquarters company to serve in a new capacity.

Pvt. Vidrine says that the French are very happy to meet French speaking Louisianians and are very interesting in relating their experiences.

Howard Vidrine Interpreter story, The Ville Platt Gazette, *1944*

participated in the Normandy invasion. "Says he wouldn't have missed this episode for anything in the world and that there is no need to worry about him 'cause everything is going along just as they would have it. His Cajun French is proving to be an asset too, he's managing real well talking with the native French. The only difficulty that he has encountered is that they talk too fast and when he can get them to slow down a bit, all goes well."[28] Percy Savoy wrote to his folks that he had been in France since June 6, and that he was taking good care of himself. He noted that he could speak to the French people without any hesitation, and "he is now very proud of the fact that he is able to speak the language."[29] Howard Vidrine from Ville Platte wrote to his parents shortly after the invasion that he had been selected to act as an interpreter for his company in France. His knowledge of French assisted in his transfer to a Headquarters Company to serve in a new capacity. He noted that the French were "very happy to meet French-speaking Louisianians and are very interesting in relating their experiences."[30] Al Villemarette from Bunkie landed at Normandy with the Ninth Infantry Division and fought in the Battle of Cherbourg. He was quartered in a beautiful section of France where his knowledge of French "is not only a great asset to himself, but to his entire company," his hometown paper reported.[31]

Writing from France, former students and alums of SLI described their experiences with local people and the benefits of having learned French

30 December 1944
France

Dear Mr. Fletcher,

Just a note to send you greetings from France and my new address. Haven't received the Vermilion and Alumni News in a long time because of my transfer. One of these days they will catch up with me and I will receive them regularly again.

I like France very much and feel perfectly at home. This particular spot where I am stationed reminds me so much of the French Quarters in New Orleans. My knowledge of French is helping me considerably, not only in my work, but also in meeting French civilians.

Zachery Sonnier (Capt.) from Scott is stationed here too. We certinaly had a 100 per cent S. L. I. conversation the other day. It is wonderful to meet someone from home when so far away from home.

Regards to Mrs. Peggy and Albertine.

Happy New Year!

Sincerely,

/s/ Merle Durand

Lt. Rita M. Durand, L. 804906
W A C Det., Hq. & Hq. Sqd'n.
A S C - U S S T A F
APO 633, c/o Postmaster
New York, New York

St. Martinville native Rita Durand letter to SLI President Fletcher, 1944, Joel Fletcher Papers, UL Lafayette Special Collections

back home. "My knowledge of the French language surely has stood me in good stead since I've been in France," said Homer Doucet. "Wouldn't give it for anything in the world, and spend half my time acting as [an] interpreter for the rest of the boys."[32] Thomas Clement wrote, "This is one place that my knowledge of Cajun French really comes in handy."[33] Thomas Doiron cleared the air of any preconceived notions about the Cajun's inferior dialect: "As

Ordnance Liaison Officer I have been able to see very much of France and my 'Cajun' French has been very handy; it fact, my French is more correct than most of the dialects I heard in Normandy and Brittany."[34] St. Martinville native Rita Merle Durand, a first lieutenant in the Women's Army Corps and one of the few women who wrote to SLI President Joel Fletcher, praised her ability to speak the native language. "I like France very much and feel perfectly at home. This particular spot where I am stationed reminds me so much of the French Quarters [*sic*] in New Orleans. My knowledge of French is helping me considerably, not only in work, but also in meeting French civilians."[35]

Another SLI alum, Sam Broussard, wrote several letters home during the fall of 1944. He traveled by jeep, often behind enemy lines, as a member of the OSS Special Forces. His responsibility was to communicate and coordinate with leaders of the French underground. In this critical role, he moved about freely, though covertly, among the French communities and French people, sometimes well ahead of the advancing Allied forces. "I travel a great deal and see much of the area already taken," Captain Broussard wrote in July 1944. "In fact, I know every town in the Cherbourg Peninsula. My work is still interesting. I like it so much. The war won't last much longer but I might ask to remain here after it is all over. So far, I like the people and they live a good life. Had a good dinner yesterday with good French people: 1st course crabs, bread butter and cider; 2nd rabbit fricassee with good rich gravy and good wine; 3rd fried steak with a second kind of wine; 4th peas and carrots bread butter wine; 5th lettuce salad, crackers and preserves; 6th coffee with calvados; 7th cognac; 8th champagne." Few Cajuns could attest to this level of French hospitality! "They discuss everything at meal time," he noted. "Incidentally, they say my French is very good and so is my accent. Have been practicing regularly and have learned much." A few days later, he wrote home again: "Had a good dinner Sunday with some good friends of Cherbourg. Have made myself a few homes since living here. I really get along with these people and they still say my French is very good and so is the accent. Of course, I improve as time goes on."[36]

Harold Pastor, who penned several eloquent letters to SLI President Joel Fletcher about his experience as a Cajun in France, described the French people, their habits, and their language in great detail:

> I definitely agree . . . that the Louisiana Cajun French can come in mighty handy, depending on where you're located. . . . I've been in

> France for over three months, having arrived shortly after D-day. At first, my French accent was a little different from that of the inhabitants, but after three months of practice, they can't tell the difference now—so much so that the French people I encounter nowadays find it hard to believe that I wasn't born and raised in France. It so happens that ever since I struck France, I've been on the look out [*sic*] to refrain from using Louisiana Cajun slang which definitely confuses these French inhabitants. As a result of my endeavors to avoid from using Cajun slang and attempting to find the proper grammatical French phrases in their stead, I can say that I've met with great success. Often times I catch myself using Cajun slang, then immediately back track and say it the proper way, which all adds up to give the Frenchman a big laugh. . . . My French tongue is working wonders these days. By merely speaking a little French in beer gardens or on city streets, somebody steps up, grabs me by the arm and before I know it, I'm being led into a home where good red wine and a hot meal is awaiting to be disposed of. . . . The exchange of conversations which follow these meals prove to be very interesting.[37]

As in North Africa, the military police (MP) units in France had almost daily contact with locals in the towns and cities and along the roadways. Captain William Winsberg of St. Landry Parish commanded an MP battalion with the Third Army in France. "My knowledge of French has been an open Sesame to knowing the French [people]," he wrote. "In addition, any south Louisianan would understand the people perfectly. They are clever, vivacious and have a charming sense of humor. First, the Norman peasant is a solid, rosy-checked, quiet, cider-drinking (also cognac and calvados) individual who is very frugal and hard working. His home is the traditional French farm—with farmyard, stables, etc. . . . In most towns they are blitzed out, but as we go down south, we are seeing more of the natural life of France. The people welcome us more and more with open arms. I have been pelted with thousands of flowers—been offered hundreds of drinks, and they wave and wave, salute and salute until our arms drop from waving and saluting in return."[38]

Corbett LeBlanc Jr. of Maurice met French people throughout Normandy who commented on his particular accent. "They seem surprised that I, an American, can speak French, and they are really nice to me," he wrote. "They seem to be much nicer to someone who can speak their language and they invited me into their homes, which you can hardly call a home." The locals shared wine and cider with him. He met an older French woman who told him, "You speak so good French." She offered to wash his dirty clothes for him as thanks. "P.S.," he concluded. "Give my regards to Gamie and the rest and tell her that my French speaking is really coming in handy. I'm just about the only American here that can speak French and I'm proud of it."[39] Little did he know that Cajun GIs stationed in France numbered in the hundreds, perhaps more, and, like him, they too trekked across the French countryside, meeting, greeting, and communicating with the French people and the French Resistance fighters using the language they had been taught from birth.

The regional dialect in the rural areas of France closely resembled the words and phrases spoken in Cajun Country. The Cajun vernacular—which had traveled from France to Acadie to Louisiana—had not change much in four hundred years. Lloyd Berard of Coteau Holmes found this out firsthand. As an army engineer, he was assigned to work on constructing the Mulberry harbour system used in the immediate aftermath of D-Day landings to offload men and equipment. As a plumbing and carpentry specialist in a construction outfit, his job was to find materials and tools to build temporary hospitals in Normandy; as a French interpreter, he was responsible for communicating the army's needs to a local hardware store owner. The two became good friends, and the Frenchman had Berard over for dinner on numerous occasions.

One afternoon, while sitting on the Frenchman's porch waiting for supper, Berard opened a letter that he had just received from home. In it were pictures of his two nieces. He showed the photos to his friend and commented in his French: "*Mes chiches* [my lil nieces]." Surprised by what he heard and how he heard it, the Frenchman called his wife to come outside and asked Bernard to repeat that phrase. He said to Berard, "*Dis come ta dis*" [say it like you said it]. "But then I tried to say it in real French. 'No, no,' he said, 'say it like you said it.' So, he tells his wife, 'They talk just like us. They speak the same patois.' I always tried to speak real French while I was there, but when I got excited, I spoke like we speak at home, which is the ancient French. This old man and his wife spoke the same way. Our French hadn't changed much."[40]

The French people in Normandy felt the same way about Sidney Vincent's accent. The St. Martinville native served in a field artillery battalion in charge of a 105 mm howitzer unit that supported the infantry in the breakout of Normandy at Saint-Lô. "My French did come in handy in France. I did a lot of interpretation," he said. "When we'd come to a little town, they'd often come and get me to talk to the people. They were a little confused why I spoke French, but then I'd tell them that I was from Louisiana. They'd say, 'Well, now we know why you could speak such good French.'"[41]

In Pat Mire's film *Mon Cher Camarade*, renowned Cajun folklorist Barry Ancelet explains how Cajuns easily integrated into the rural French communities. "They had to get to Paris. Paris is what they had to earn. The way they got there was in the provinces all around; they were in Brittany, Normandy, Poitou, Perry, and Bourgogne, and those were all the places where our ancestors came from. . . . They would have linguistically blended in perfectly. . . . Everything would have sounded familiar."[42]

David Meche, from Scott, was inducted into the US Army in September 1942. Two years later, he arrived in France equipped with an army-issued French-to-English translation book. He didn't need it. He did, however, find subtle differences between the two languages. "The French people could talk faster than [us]," he said. "Most of the time I could understand the French people. If they would talk slow, you see. But some of them, to me, they would talk like us. . . . And us, we gotta think a while before we say anything. Especially us Cajuns, you see. We don't speak exactly good French or English. It's a mixture, you call that. We always use part English and part French."[43] C. G. "Buddy" Simon Jr. agreed, "The French here is very similar to ours. However, along the coastal areas the dialect was a little tough to get on to. But the further into France we go the easier it is to understand."[44]

Like so many others, John Allen Brasseaux, a D-Day veteran with the Eighty-Second Airborne Division, found commonalities between the Cajuns of Louisiana and the country people in rural France, although some of the phrases spoken by the two groups were a bit different. "At first, I couldn't understand them too good 'cause they talk faster than we do," he said in a 1991 interview. "And it's not the same French. They pronounce it different than we do. You had to really pay attention to them, you know. But after about a couple of minutes then, I could get around pretty good. Like an airplane, we call it a plane, but they call it a *avion*." The French people called a car or truck a *camion*. These words were foreign to Cajuns, who had over time naturally incorporated some English words into their unique vocabulary. Nevertheless, the presence of French-speaking American troops thrilled the locals who wanted nothing more than to converse with their liberators. When they identified Brasseaux as a francophone, they yelled out: "*C'est un Américain! Il veut parler Français! Français! Français!*" Although the dialect was a bit different, the Cajuns adapted quickly to exchange the correct information with the locals. The safety—and comfort—of their fellow comrades and officers depended on it. "Most of them, nine out of ten, well 99 out of 100, they couldn't speak French. . . . And when the officers would go to town, they knew that I could speak French. So they'd call, 'Go get Brass,' and they'd get me to drive them to town or whatever to go to the stores and whatever they needed."[45]

Normandy was similar to the country lifestyle in Carencro, where Brasseaux grew up, with farmland, farm animals, and barns: "They was friendly people just like us," he said. "I mean, just common folks, you know, in the country. And we had a camp just outside of town there, and we'd go to town and just like it was anywhere else. Go to the store, bought a few stuff, and they were friendly." Brasseaux grew up with horses and spent his entire life around them. The French people in the Normandy countryside also had an affinity for horses, but oddly enough, Brasseaux observed that their animals lived in the front of the house, not in a barn in the back. "They took us in their homes. Funny thing about it over yonder, you don't have stables like mine. I've got my stables about a hundred feet from my house, but damn, [in France] it's all connected together. Everything was connected to the house. . . . You could see them in the morning, take their big horses out of there, close the door, go to the farm and work, you know. And I visited all those, I visited those people 'cause I was raised on a farm."[46]

Brasseaux's bilingualism and country upbringing indeed served him well overseas. As a member of an elite airborne unit, he participated in several glider missions in Europe and practically lived on the front lines. His French no doubt helped him and his comrades maneuver through the enemy-held territory in France, Belgium, and the Netherlands. It probably helped save his life a time or two. How ironic, then, that as a young boy growing up in a rural French-speaking community, he was denigrated for speaking his native language at school. "When I went, started school, I couldn't speak English at all. And at school, you couldn't speak French, but they'd spank you at school at that time because they wanted you to speak English."[47] A decade later, in a country halfway around the world from his home, that same French became a vital resource and a lifeline.

The "English-only" policy of the Louisiana public school system in the 1920s and 1930s is notorious in the annals of Acadian/Cajun cultural history. While not all Cajuns received the same harsh treatment at school, few escaped the prejudice. Norris Morvant who was raised in the country near Thibodaux and had a high-level security pass in France during the war, recalled that shameful period growing up, which had a generational impact on the culture:

> When I went to school, I didn't know a word of English. That was hard. At that time, the teachers wanted you to speak English, so if you spoke French, they would hit you or they would make sure that you didn't speak French, for sure. They wanted you to get away from that. They wanted the world to be all English and for us to forget what we were, and I think that was wrong, of course, because what you are is what you are. You can't change that. If you want to change that, you're going to have a problem, as far as I'm concerned. Like I had trouble in school. Oh, for the first two years in school, oh, man, I was lost. But, finally, I got with it.[48]

Morvant went into the service in early 1943. Following several months of radio and radar training in the Army Air Corps, he wound up in England, then in France, working as a courier and interpreter in General Eisenhower's headquarters. After the Normandy invasion, Morvant was issued a jeep to drive and tasked with passing along important information to leaders in the field. He had a special pass from the general's office to deliver messages and orders to field commanders. Few Cajuns had the level of autonomy to roam the French countryside as he did. In this unique capacity, he interacted with French people almost daily. His first assignment was to fly in a C-47 transport plane from England to Normandy to deliver a generator to Eisenhower's headquarters in Granville, about fifty miles to the southwest from Utah Beach. "Can you imagine the authority I had with being from the general?" he exclaimed. Much of the roadways in Normandy had been bombed out, and enemy units still lingered in the region. Once on the ground, he drove a jeep pulling a trailer with the equipment to the designated location, often veering off the damaged main highway onto backcountry roads. This would be his first of many interesting missions in France, some of which went deep into the interior, far beyond the Allied front line. "Most time, if they sent me somewhere, I could communicate with someone to find out where I'm

Norris Morvant and his jeep, France, 1944, courtesy of Norris Morvant

at or where to go and how," he said. "It was convenient."[49] His knowledge of French became an imperative to safely completing these important missions.

He remembered his first encounter with French people near the coast. When the friendlies attempted to greet him in broken English, Morvant responded that he could speak French: "I told them, '*Je parle français aussi. On peut se parler en français.*'" Shortly thereafter, a lieutenant from headquarters called him in for a special job. He said, "Frenchie, we got something for you to do. I want you to go in the country and find us some eggs. We want to eat some eggs, good eggs." When asked about a form of payment for the eggs, the officer replied: "You don't buy; you barter." With those instructions,

Morvant loaded up his jeep with "GI soap" and headed toward Brittany. He came upon a circle of homes and approached the residents with an offer. "I told them I could speak French and [said], 'I come from Louisiana. We speak French over there too.' Boy, we made friends all over."[50] He loaded up the jeep with eggs and headed back with his prized loot.

Morvant had the necessary skill set for this particular type of job; he spoke French naturally. Back in England, before the invasion, the men from headquarters picked up on his bilingual abilities. "It started one day when I was in headquarters," he recalled, "and they understood that I was French. 'So, you're Frenchie.' And it started. Everybody would call me Frenchie. Some of the soldiers I was with, they were from all over, you know, and they were kind of good with being someone different, and I was the only one that was named Frenchie, so whenever they would call for somebody Frenchie, that was me. It was all right."[51]

As the Allies advanced east toward Paris, Morvant went with the general's headquarters staff. He soon found out the subtle difference in the dialect. "When I got to Paris, they had some Parisian slang, and I learned it. Then one day I met somebody, and I was talking with the slang. They said, 'How

Norris Morvant (head of table) *at French wedding dinner, France, 1944, courtesy of Norris Morvant*

did you do to go to America and get to be in the service and come back?' This person had thought I was a French person. But when you get good at it with the slang, you know, threw the slang in, then that made the difference. It was fun. But the rest of it wasn't." On one particularly grueling mission, Morvant drove a supply truck for days on end, loaded with jerry cans of valuable gasoline. "When the last push was done to go into Germany across the Rhine," he said, "they were running out of gasoline for tanks, especially, and General Patton got in touch with headquarters, said, 'You need somebody to get some gas from Le Havre today to the front.' And I was one of them. Three days straight, that's all we did. I would bring a full one to the front, take an empty truck, go back again, for three days straight."[52] For completing these harrowing, long-distance treks across France, General Patton awarded Morvant a Bronze Star.

Throughout his many adventures in France, Morvant met countless francophone people, some of whom he remained friends with after the war. He actually returned to France a few times over the years to visit with them and

Norris Morvant with Bronze Star, France, 1944, courtesy of Norris Morvant

to cook Cajun cuisine for them. On one of these trips, Morvant attended a banquet held in his honor. "I was sitting at the head of the table. They honored me right there, and everybody thanked me for being in the *débarquement* [invasion]."[53]

These experiences created close connections among the Cajuns and the French. In correspondence and interviews, the Cajuns almost universally recount breaking bread with French people at their dinner tables.[54] "The French people surely have been nice to us," said Gustave Trosclair from Breaux Bridge. "I don't like to accept dinner invitations from them, because I know how little food they have, but they won't take no for an answer. Being able to speak French certainly proved to be a great asset."[55] Ed Broussard from New Iberia, who commanded an infantry platoon in France, became close friends with a French family and spent time in their home. "I had an invitation from a French family for their daughter, a teenager, who I had become friendly with," he said many years later. "She got married some years later after the war, and they sent me an invitation. I became friends with this family because I could speak to them. Our French down here is like the ancient Parisian French."[56]

Lucien Laborde, a descendant of Acadians and French immigrants, grew up in the French-speaking community of Marksville. He served as regimental adjunct officer—and interpreter—for the 115th Regiment of the famed Twenty-Ninth Infantry Division that landed on Omaha Beach on the morning of June 6. He had extensive training in intelligence and utilized his French during the Battle of Normandy. In the early weeks of combat, Captain Laborde was called upon to speak to a local Frenchman who had barricaded himself in the cellar of his home. He had stocked that hidden cellar with wine, cheese, and eggs in anticipation of a prolonged conflict. "His name was Pierre Lemoine," Laborde said in a 2013 interview. "And we got to be good friends. I spent a lot of time in that hole with him. We drank wine and ate cheese and bread. I learned a lot from him about what they were doing in that country because I was interested in agriculture."[57] Thirty-five years later, with an invitation from this brother, C. E. Laborde, the two brothers and their wives traveled to France to tour the Normandy battlefields. Laborde guided the group to the small village where his old friend Pierre Lemoine had lived in 1944. There, in a nearby home, he found the old Frenchman, who was completely deaf and suffering from a heart condition, sitting peacefully at the end of a long dining room table. The lady of the house passed a note to

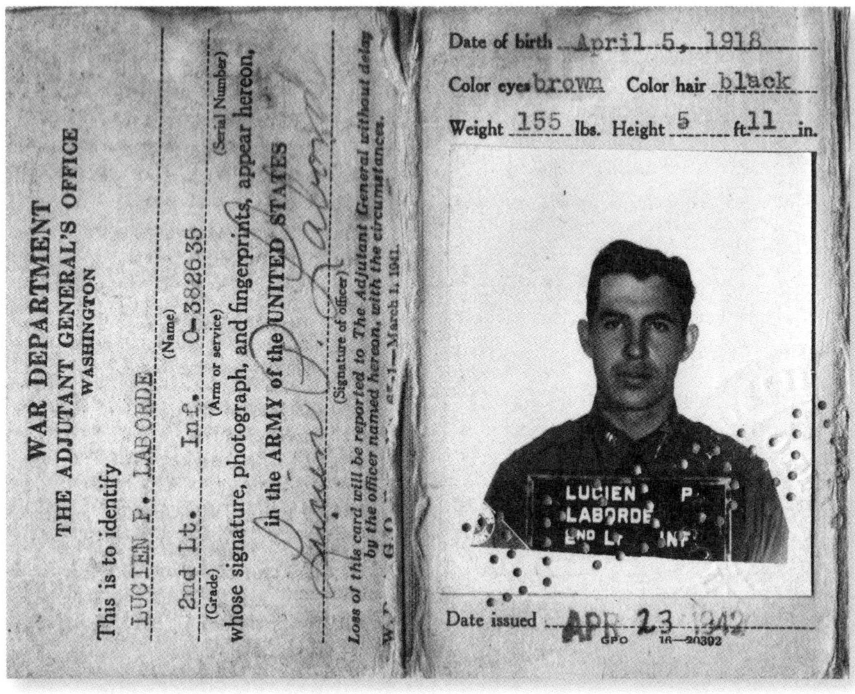

WAR DEPARTMENT
THE ADJUTANT GENERAL'S OFFICE
WASHINGTON

This is to identify LUCIEN P. LABORDE
(Name)
2nd Lt. Inf. O-382635
(Grade) (Arm or service) (Serial Number)
whose signature, photograph, and fingerprints, appear hereon,
in the ARMY of the UNITED STATES
(Signature of officer)

Loss of this card will be reported to The Adjutant General without delay by the officer named hereon, with the circumstances.

—March 1, 1941.

Date of birth April 5, 1918
Color eyes brown Color hair black
Weight 155 lbs. Height 5 ft. 11 in.

Date issued APR 23 1942
GPO 16—20392

Lucien Laborde military ID, courtesy of the Laborde family

Lemoine, informing him of the American visitor. "She invited me in, and she wrote a note to him," Laborde recalled with emotion. "He read it, and he read it again, and he stood up and he grabbed me, and he said 'Mon Capitaine!'"[58] Laborde and his family returned to France again for the fiftieth and sixtieth anniversaries of the Normandy invasion.

As it did for Cajun GIs in North Africa and Italy, the *L'Echo du Teche* bulletin carried numerous excerpts of letters from Cajuns about their exploits in France. Nearly every letter from Europe mentioned encounters with French-speaking people. Vincent Blanchard wrote that he was in safe company and no longer on the front line. "Although I am far from home, the house in which I am staying reminds me of home, because I can talk French with the people."[59] Valerie Huval noted: "I have not yet seen much of the country, but I have enjoyed talking French with the people."[60] Dempsey Thibodeaux, Milton Wiltz, and Maurice Perez wrote a group letter that described their surroundings: "France so far is a wonderful place; we certainly feel at home, being able to speak their language. Some think that we are really French, so we have to give them practically our whole life history."[61] James Begnaud said that he liked France better than England because "I feel more at home among the French-speaking people. They are so surprised to hear an American speaking French so fluently. I was an interpreter for the C.O. I will have to go out with him or other officers when they need someone to speak for them." Percy Goulas noted, "I get all the stories because I speak French. Everyone calls me the interpreter. I had a chance to trade a pair of shoes, 2 coveralls and a loaf of bread for a calf. Boy, we had a good steak."[62]

After a few months in France, Ames Rees wrote to his mother in Breaux Bridge about the new francophone friends he made overseas: "My French is really coming in handy. You should hear me talk to those Frenchmen. The fellows keep me on the run getting their laundry done for them. I don't mind it; as it helps me to learn French words that we do not use back home. I have been going around with a Colonel to do his talking for him; it not only gives me a chance to go out, but I find it lots of fun. I made friends with an old farmer; he took me over to his farm to see his livestock. He has some beautiful horses. Tell Mrs. Neuville Thibodeaux that I have found a family here with the same name as hers."[63] Weston Trahan of Abbeville added this perspective: "I'm writing this in a foxhole. Keep on praying for me mother. These French people over here were in a pretty bad fix. They tell me they are very glad to see us. I'm sure they are. I have no trouble at all in understanding and talking to them; in fact, don't be surprised if I talk much better French when I come back."[64]

Ambroise "A. J." Champagne from St. Martinville was a section leader on a halftrack vehicle with the Sixth Armored Division that stalled on the drive to Metz in the fall of 1944. "When I'd come to the little towns, I could speak French, so I'd say to the people, '*Bonjour*,'" he said in a 2004 interview. He spent six weeks near the city of Nancy, France, awaiting new orders. "When I was there, these three or four families had taken a liking for me. When it wasn't our week to stay on the line, watching to make sure the Germans wouldn't come back, they'd cook and we'd drink wine all afternoon. That's how they are. This one family was Jobert. They kept on writing me after the war. I'd go and visit with these families during the day. I got along well with them. We drank some good wine in France. Our reconnaissance officer always wanted me to go with him because I could speak French. I went with him a lot of times, sticking our nose around behind the German line. We got into some tight places sometimes."[65]

The Cajun soldiers not only wrote letters but they also kept letters received from their French friends. Mansel Mayeux, from the French-speaking community of Marksville, wrote about his European adventures in his memoir. When the United States entered the war, he, like everyone else his age, shipped out to military training far from home. "World War II scattered Cajuns all over the US," he wrote. Following Officer Candidate School at Harvard, he was assigned to an engineer combat battalion and landed in Normandy about a month after the invasion. From Saint-Lô to Paris his unit repaired and built bridges and cleared minefields. Because of his upbringing, he carried some additional responsibility for his unit. "Since I spoke French while we were in France I was often on the point or advanced party when we were moving forward. That was at times fun, but at others it was a dangerous position." He was shot in the shoulder during an ambush in Holland by German troops. During a long recovery in Paris, he befriended a French couple, Marcel and Claudine Colas, and stayed with them as a guest on many occasions. "Their home was my home whenever I was in Paris," he wrote.[66] Shortly after the war, he received a letter, written in French, from his newfound friends:

> Paris, December 11, 1945
>
> My Dear Mansel,
>
> Claudine and I were very happy to receive your letter, but we were very surprised to see that you are not in the United States, but rather in Germany. What a disappointment it must have been when you left Twenty Grand camp for the East instead of the West. These are the mysteries of the army, which you should not try to unravel. I hope this change will allow us to see you soon. If only you could get a 7-day leave for Christmas or New Year's Day, we could have a good time together. You must tell your Colonel that you have a good friend in Paris, who loves Americans very much and who repatriated several hundred of them during the German Occupation, who is absolutely counting on you for the festive season. I am sure that he will give you a "Seven Day Leave" to please me.
>
> My dear friend, I have already chatted too much, and I would like to finish my letter here. Claudine joins me in sending you all our regards, and on the threshold of the year that is about to begin, we

wish you all the best for a Merry Christmas and happy New Year. We hope that you will be able to return home soon and resume your civilian occupations.

Best wishes to you, Marcel
Claudine sends you a big hug.[67]

Joseph Delcambre, from the Lake Arthur area, served with the Fourth Infantry Division and landed in Normandy around D-Day. He befriended a family in France as well and corresponded with them after the war. His family discovered this letter among his most cherished possessions from the war:

My Dear Comrade,

It's with pleasure that I received news from you that I welcomed with joy. The little ones and the gown-ups recognized you in the picture accompanying the letter. We hope you are in perfect health and I echo everyone's sentiment in sending you our sincerest wishes of joy, happiness and health for the New Year. After your departure from Ciral, my husband tried to see you again in Paris, and then write to you in Paris, then we wrote another letter as well. . . . Since then, we were wondering what could have become of you. When your letter arrived, there was a shout of joy throughout the house. . . . What are you doing? I see that you are married. Do you have children? Is life in the USA pleasant, in France, it leaves a bit to be desired, the lack of money paralyses commerce a lot. I am sending you a few pictures of our large family that you may have difficulty recognizing, in order to guide you, the names and ages are inscribed. Hoping to have news from you, on behalf of everyone, I send you our fondest memories. Are you thinking about a trip to France?[68]

Letters like these highlight the special bonds that the Cajun GIs established with French locals while serving in France and later Belgium. Meeting these families and maintaining contact with them after the war certainly left a lasting impression with the boys from south Louisiana. They held onto these letters for decades, stashed away in a special box or drawer, along with their medals and photos with army buddies.

Letter to Joseph Delcambre from France, 1948, courtesy of the Delcambre family

Romance in France

In France, Frenchie was indeed a popular GI. He could get things. He could translate for army commanders. He could help locate and root out the enemy. With this linguistic advantage, meeting French girls came much easier for the Cajuns. "It's easy to make friends, especially if you *Parlez Francais*," wrote Alton Latiolais, who, according to his letter, attended dances nearly every night while in southern France.[69] Leo Thomas wrote to his friend "Blackie" Bienvenu at the *Teche News* about meeting French girls. "The French are still pretty nice to us. Wish you were here to get an eyeful of the girls around here. They are really good looking and very nice. I have talked to quite a few. Believe me, Blackie, that old 'Cajun' French is really coming in handy."[70]

Some romantic encounters lasted a week; a few lasted a lifetime. Dennis Neal from Terrebonne Parish brought a French war bride home to his community in Point-au-Chene. Like most Cajuns from down the bayou, Dennis Neal grew up speaking only French and later learned English in school. During World War II, he served in a special military intelligence unit assigned to Supreme Headquarters, Allied Expeditionary Force. He worked as an interpreter and jeep driver for both an American and a British colonel. These two officers collaborated with the French underground forces to identify, locate, and bring back downed Allied airmen who had evaded capture by the Germans deep behind enemy lines in France and Belgium. Working on the edge of the front lines was touch-and-go for his small unit until they reached Paris, where a grand liberation celebration took place for days on end. It was in Paris where he met his future wife.

"We took off, just me and the two colonels, we went and joined a group of the French Resistance, the FFI, they had a group that was waiting to go into Paris," Neal recalled.[71] "And we went toward Paris. We went all the way to the Champs-Élysées, where they had the big parade the day after the liberation of Paris." Once in Paris, Neal drove his commanding officer to the home of the FFI leader for consecutive nights. There, he met a French girl, Ginette Cardinal—and the romance began. Neal stayed in Paris for eleven months, during which time he courted his soon-to-be-wife. "I kept seeing her every little chance that I had, I go see her. And then it really got serious, and that's when we got married."[72]

Dennis and Ginette Neal, cir. 1945, courtesy of the Neal family

When the war in Europe ended on May 8, 1945, Neal was in Épinal, France, near the German border. With considerable effort, and with contacts from his bosses, he was able to get his wife and newborn son safe transportation to the United States. From New York, she and her baby boy arrived in her new home near Houma. Although she could not speak any English, she felt right at home in the French-speaking Cajun community. Their arrival in south Louisiana generated so much fanfare that the local newspaper covered the story. The *Houma Times* ran this article, "Paris to Point au Chien is Hard Road, Says War Wife," about her

Paris to Point au Chein Is Hard Road, Says War Wife

The Houma Times *announcing the arrival of Ginette Neal and her baby boy to Terrebonne Parish, 1946*

travels. The paper featured a photograph of Ginette Cardinal Neal and the couple's baby boy—Mitchell—on the front page. "The road . . . was long and hard, but the people were so nice," she told the reporter. The language in western France is quite similar in sound that is spoken here, explained the young war wife, who said that she had no trouble in understanding French in south Louisiana.[73]

Dennis Neal's wife was one of dozens of French war brides who moved to south Louisiana with their American husbands after the war. Eighteen-year-old Monique Charrier met her husband Henry Stutes from Rayne while she served as an interpreter in the American army at the Seine base section in Paris.[74] In early 1946, she traveled by ship from Europe to the United States along with a few hundred other French war brides, then by train to meet her new husband in Terrebonne Parish. Micheline Mathieu Picheloup, wife of Gus Picheloup of New Iberia, was another war bride. She met her husband, an original member of the local National Guard, Company G, in her hometown of Dijon, France. Upon arriving at her new home along the Teche, she told reporters: "*J'aime beaucoup la Louisiane. C'est un très joli pays.*"[75]

Reaux Meaux married a French girl, Lucie Truphemus from Chambly, France, and brought her home to St. Landry Parish after the war. Meaux landed at Normandy on June 6. He was immediately assigned to interpret for his commanding officers. "After D-Day, I have to translate from French to English," he told an interviewer in 1991. "All those officers didn't know nothing about French. A lot of times, I couldn't understand the French and it was hard for me to translate English too. I didn't know much English." He was the only one in his outfit who spoke French. "Cajun French they call it here. I understand most everything they say, but I have to think. Just like them."[76] While in Normandy, he met his future wife, who had been brought to the coast and forced to cook for the German soldiers building the concrete bunkers on the beach.

Back in Louisiana, the newly arrived French war brides had the benefit of moving into French-speaking communities. In Cajun Country, they had amenities and advantages not found in rural France. United Natural Gas, a company headquartered in Louisiana, depicted a French war bride in a

Natural gas advertisement in Louisiana featuring a "French war bride," The Weekly News (Marksville), *1947*

newspaper ad to promote the benefits of its clean-burning, affordable energy supply for home cooking and heating. "*C'est Merveilleux*," exclaimed a "Mrs. Micheline Hager," a fictitious French war bride, who's likeness appeared in the ad that ran in nearly every local newspaper in southern Louisiana in 1947. "This natural gas service YOU people take for granted," said the ad. "But to me it is still amazing! *C'EST TRÈS SUPERBE!*" The ad featured an image of Mrs. Micheline Hager holding her newborn child.[77] The French war bride spoke directly to the veteran GIs, who no doubt sympathized with and related to those who married French girls during the war and brought them home to enjoy the comforts of post-war prosperity in the United States.

Three Cajuns in a Tank

Not all Cajun GIs had the opportunity to stick around for long duration in French towns and cities to get to know people. Those in the armored units stayed on the move. Erath native Lee Bernard clipped along at lightning speed in a Sherman tank, stopping occasionally—and often abruptly—in French towns as they sprinted to the German border. Bernard had an interesting experience as a tank driver and interpreter in the race across France. He served with the 739th Tank Battalion of the Eleventh Armored Division with a few other French-speaking Cajuns. These young soldiers faced ridicule and discrimination from officers and other trainees from Texas and Oklahoma. "They called us 'coonass,'" Bernard said.[78] All that changed, however, when the Cajuns arrived in France in late 1944 and encountered French people during months of intensive fighting and advancement through cities, towns, and rural countryside all the way to Germany. Having French-speaking Cajuns among the ranks proved invaluable in the field.

The discrimination that Bernard faced in training camps was nothing new to him. Raised in a predominantly French-speaking community, he struggled in the English-only school system of Vermilion Parish. At ninety-six years old, Bernard vividly recounted the harsh punishment he received in school for speaking his native language as a kid. "One time I had to write five hundred times, 'I will not speak French on the school ground.' I had to write that. In English." Bernard put one over on the teacher, however, by joining together a pair of pencils and reducing his punishment by half. But he could not escape the physical abuse that young Cajuns were subjected to during that unfortunate period in Louisiana history. Teachers notoriously hit the kids' hands with paddles when caught speaking French at school. "Slapped!" he demonstrated with his wrinkled hands. "That would burn. Lord! Burn you up to the elbow."[79]

That same prejudice followed him into military service. Bernard joined the service in 1943 and trained in Camp Bouse, Arizona, in a tank unit with enlistees from the US Southwest. When he was assigned as a driver for a four-man Sherman tank equipped with anti-mine detonation capabilities, he found himself in the company of two other Cajuns: Donald Blanchard from Houma and Dunis Faulk from Kaplan. Throughout months of training, the commanders, like the teachers back at school, scolded the Cajun soldiers because of their accent and persistent use of the French language among themselves. "I had some of my buddies in the service that would speak French, and if any one of the bosses would hear us, they'd raise hell or they'd punish you for speaking French on the campground. I used to speak French lots. That was, like I say, my main language was French." As punishment, the commanders made them clean latrines or run around the block. "Excuse the expression, but they called us 'coonass,'" he snickered. "If they knew you was from around Louisiana, that's what they'd call you, 'coonass' . . . because a lot of young people my age, they didn't know how to speak a word of English when they went to school. Me, well, I knew, but I wasn't all that smart in English."[80]

Notwithstanding their broken English, many Cajuns proved to be mechanically inclined and adept at running and maintaining an armored tank. Growing up, Bernard took care of his father's car; he often washed it and drove it into the garage, even though he could barely see over the dashboard. "The thing is, we who was in the service, the Cajun people knew how to work, work with their hands. You get them—we called them 'city slickers,' they didn't know—they could walk on the sidewalk and that was about it," he said sarcastically. "But do physical work? They didn't know how to work. If they had any problem with their tanks, they didn't know where to start."[81]

Bernard and his Louisiana-led tank crew landed in Le Havre, France, in November 1944. They made a mad dash toward the city of Reims, about a hundred miles northeast of Paris. When they stopped in small towns along the way, the officers asked Bernard to translate conversations with the French people. "When they found out I could speak French, well, they used me as an interpreter a lot of time, talked to them in French. . . . I went and talked to them in French, *et quand on se parler, justement parle en français, parle pas en anglaise* [and when we talked to each other, we speak in French, not English]. And every time I'd go talk to them, they'd give me some champagne. I left there, and I had I don't know how many cases, bottles of champagne I had."[82]

His unit spent a week in the small town of Mailly-Champagne, where Bernard mingled among the locals. He made friends with an older Frenchman and would drink wine with him every afternoon. "When I left, I had five cases of wine in my tank," he laughed. While there, he met a French girl named Solange Fuselier and wrote letters home about her. She, in turn, wrote a letter to Bernard's mother back in Erath. Several weeks later, as his unit neared the German border, he received a letter from his mother asking questions about his new admirer. "I get a letter, and when I saw the return address, it was [from] my mother. 'Please, don't get married over there. Come home before you get married.' I wrote back to her: 'Mom, I'm about thirty-five miles from where that woman lives, and I'll never see her again, so don't worry.'"[83]

Bernard's tank unit was involved in several battles from winter 1944 to spring of 1945, including the Battle of the Bulge. "We almost lost that," he said. "They was getting the best of us till finally we had the best of them."[84]

All throughout the campaign, as the armored columns rolled across France, the officers of his unit often called on Bernard and his fellow Cajuns to speak to the locals and gather information. "It's the American people that wanted to find out something from the French people in their community," he said. "A lot of time they'd call me to go, and we'd go like in a new area to go talk to somebody in the community. One of the main things they asked for was freshwater to drink." In his Erath French, Bernard would ask them: "*Est-ce que vous avez de l'eau à boire, bon pour boire*? [Do you have water to drink, good to drink?]" Of course, the officers also wanted French wine. "A lot of time they'd call me to go talk for some officer, called me to go talk to some of them people in the farm, if they want something. Oh, Lord. And go talk to them French people. They always made their own wine. Always had a bunch of wine in my tank."[85]

The French dialect in lower Vermilion Parish had not changed much since the Acadians first arrived there in the late 1700s. In Europe, Bernard discovered that some of the words spoken in the rural French countryside had not advanced in modern times. "It was pretty much you didn't have trouble finding out what they were saying. . . . Oh, yeah, they could tell I was from Louisiana."[86]

Although often picked on by his Anglo comrades at training camp, the name-calling never seemed to bother Bernard. In fact, he had a tendency to push back a bit when it came to returning the jest to those who poked fun of his peculiar cultural traits. Bernard was the type to openly taunt his oppressors with consistent use of French slang. It pushed their buttons and earned him the nickname "sarcase coonass," among his comrades. "See, when you went in the army, you went in there as a private, then got up to be a sergeant, a first-class private, a sergeant, and it was like that, and every time I'd get a promotion, they'd get on my butt about being a coonass." The taunting and teasing fell by the wayside once the soldiers landed in France, however. Their commanders and comrades immediately saw the benefit of having French-speaking Cajuns within the ranks. "We got to France, instead of calling me a coonass, they called me Frenchie," he said with pride.[87]

To Cajuns serving in Europe, the nickname Frenchie became a badge of honor. "They changed their tune," Bernard noted. "Like I say, they called us 'coonass,' but then after we got in France—'Frenchie.'" Bernard spent his entire life in Erath and became a pillar of the community. He lived to be ninety-eight years old and spoke French every day. "I'm proud of my French," he said. In 2009, he traveled back to France and received the French Legion of Honor Award from the President Nicolas Sarkozy for his service during World War II. As one of the few Cajun war veterans to receive that prestigious award, Bernard's personal contribution to the Allied war effort represents the broader impact of the Louisiana francophones in liberating Europe. Their ability to speak French distinguished them from the tens of thousands of American troops who could not.

RACE TO THE RHINE

By fall 1944, the Allies had liberated much of France and the Low Countries. They brought the "Arsenal of Democracy" ashore in Europe and dismantled the vaunted German army. However, the Allied drive to the German border bogged down at the Siegfried Line. Following Hitler's winter counteroffensive in the Ardennes Forest, known as the Battle of the Bulge, the Allies regained the momentum and pushed forward to the Rhine River. All through the rapid advance across France, Belgium, and into Germany, US Army commanders relied on Frenchies for swift intelligence. Conversations and personal visits with French-speaking people were often brief, some lasting only a few days. Those in the forward echelons tended to have more run-ins with enemy forces fighting a defensive retreat to Berlin. Land mines, snipers, blown-up bridges, and German holdouts hiding among buildings, barns, and churches posed considerable danger. The level of intensity and anxiety grew as American GIs neared the German heartland. Some Cajuns wound up in hospitals with injuries from fighting; others became prisoners of war. In the midst of this relentless sprint across war-torn Europe, the need for rapid, effective, and trustworthy liaisons with the local people became all the more critical.

Broussard native Alton "Ton" Girouard drove a jeep throughout Europe with a reconnaissance company attached to the Sixth Armored Division. He served as a messenger from company headquarters to the command post. His citation for receiving a Bronze Star stated: "For heroic service in connection with military operations in France, Belgium, Luxemburg and Germany during the period 28 July 1944 to 1 May 1945. As liaison agent, he constantly traveled enemy infested roads, through mortar and artillery fire, to deliver urgent messages for his troop to high headquarters."[88] Another citation lauded him for driving his jeep, often during bad weather and darkness, to keep his unit in close contact with higher headquarters—where his French no doubt served him well during these missions. Decades after the war, he received a letter from a former commanding officer who related many stories of their exploits driving the backcountry roads and meeting French people. "With your French we talked a bakery into making us the hard crusted French bread to supplement our K and C rations," the letter read. "Also, one trip we stopped at a small villa near St. Nazaire and you talked the restaurant owner into making us French fries and chicken for our return trip (we gave them GI lard and flour plus $). Another patrol we stopped at a bar to get Capt Dan Moore a bottle of wine and I stumbled upon VIN ROUGE or something and bought a cheap vintage. You with your 'French' went in an talked the owner into giving us a great vintage bottle from his special supply in the basement. I am not saying which bottle we gave to Capt Moore and which one the two of us took care of."[89] Girouard certainly knew his way around the kitchen. After the war, he founded a very popular local diner, "Ton's Drive-In," which has remained a mainstay of the town of Broussard for more than fifty years.

Isadore Labbe used his French skills to roam freely about the French countryside in search of mechanical and automotive parts to repair army vehicles and equipment. He was reared in the French-speaking communities of Duson and Scott and learned about tractors and implements on the family farm. During the war, he served with the Eighty-Third Infantry Division in an automotive unit and landed in Normandy a week after D-Day. His main job was to drive across France, and later Belgium, in search of spare parts to fix army jeeps, trucks, and related equipment. Labbe's French language was invaluable to his daily task, running the back roads and talking with French people to obtain what he needed. In addition to mechanic parts, he also gathered food, wine, and other items to share with his unit. He carried around a camera and took many pictures of the French countryside and of the people who he befriended. While in France, he located the family of his maternal grandfather (Louis Francois Pellissier). He discovered that some of his cousins had moved from southeast France to Paris, where he found them and shared food with them. When he came back from the war, he started a service station where his French remained necessary to communicate with the local Cajun customers.[90]

Cajuns played a role in air-to-ground support in the final push to the German border. Kaplan native Lionel Abshire drove a colonel around in a jeep delivering important information for air-to-ground missions. In his

Isadore Labbe with French people, 1944, courtesy of Joan Boudreaux

Isadore Labbe working on army truck, 1944, courtesy of Joan Boudreaux

memoir, he noted: "My upbringing, in a small country town, with French- and English-speaking ancestors, served me well as I was able to converse with the farmers, who came out to work in the fields [in France]. I could bargain for fresh milk and butter to supplement our daily hard rations, and I could negotiate with the women to have my clothes washed and ironed in exchange for cigarettes and soap." While in France, he was reassigned to army headquarters near Fontainebleau, south of Paris. There he met Lt. Colonel Irvin Patrick "Pat" Murray and became his clerk and his personal driver, as a member of the G-3 Air (Air-Ground Liaison), Third US Army. One day, he met a young lady walking with her two children. "We became friendly very quickly," he wrote, "when she learned that I spoke French. She then invited me to dine with her family in Fontainebleau that night and she gave me her address with instructions for reaching the house." He obtained a pass and went to her house. They were enjoying a meal of rabbit, vegetables, bread, wine and "good conversation" when they heard someone kick in the door. He grabbed his helmet and carbine rifle and walked to the balcony that overlooked the patio. There below he saw American soldiers who were "looking for women." His prompt action dispatched the GIs from the French home.[91]

Abshire provided transportation support and translation for Colonel Murray, whose job it was to call in close air support to assist with units pinned down by heavy enemy fire. Nearby squadrons of P-47s would be directed to strafe enemy positions at a moment's notice. When not driving the colonel around, Abshire often took reconnaissance flights in an artillery spotter plane or drove vehicles back to headquarters. His unit was stationed at Nancy, France, near the German border, when Hitler launched the Ardennes campaign. Abshire flew several missions in a B-26 bomber toward the end of the Battle of the Bulge. As a French-speaking G-3 clerk for Headquarters Detachment, Third Army, he had a unique experience in the European theater. According to his military discharge papers, he drove a jeep to transport commissioned personnel to various frontline units. He assisted in maintaining accurate data on tactical maps in connection with air liaison. And he prepared map overlays and routed map overlays to units concerned.[92]

Familiarity with place names, road conditions, and safe routes through the many villages and towns in France became vital for the rapid Allied advance toward Berlin. Reconnaissance units, attached to armored columns, raced ahead to gather intelligence. Addy Melancon, who initially joined the local National Guard, Company F (Breaux Bridge) in 1940, commanded a small "recon" team. He arrived in Le Havre, France, in July 1944 as a replacement officer with the Eighty-Third Reconnaissance Battalion in support of the Third Armored Division's sustained drive across Europe. He rode in a jeep, ahead of the tank units, all the way to Germany. His job was to communicate with the local people and relay information back to the commanders directing the advance. "We had to contact the mayors in those towns and have some people sponsor us," he said, "and when they found out we could speak part of their French, they used to get their younger ones to get us together and make us translate our Cajun French to the real French. It didn't take long [but] we had to tell them to slow down, speak slow, and we got along that way."[93]

As soon as Lieutenant Melancon arrived in France, he tested out his Breaux Bridge French on the locals. He quickly learned that he had to make adjustments to communicate properly with the French people:

> I got off a ship at Le Havre, France, and they find out I could so-so speak French, and the train was supposed to come pick up some troops. When they got there, I started talking Cajun French. An old

> Frenchman on the train says, "*Quoi vous dites?*" [What did you say?] I talked to him in Cajun French [and the Frenchman responded], "*Je ne comprends pas ce que dis-tu.*" [I don't understand what you are saying.] I said, "Well, why not?" He said, "That's not French." So, I realized I had to change my language, so I said, "You talk to me." And didn't take long for me to adapt myself to their French, but they could not adapt their selves to Cajun French because most of the Cajun names and words sound pretty close to what they used to do, so it didn't take long for me to learn to speak the real French because of what I knew of the Cajun French. But that guy laughed. He wondered what in the world I said.[94]

Some of the phrases were different, but close enough for Melancon to get his point across. For example, when he asked around for some food or something to drink, he would tell the people of the town: "*Comment ça serait du manger?*" The people understood the word *manger*—to eat, so they would bring out some food—"*On a dû manger pour vous-autres* [We have food for you all]," said Melancon, "That's how we started to get along with them."[95]

His recon unit consisted of six jeeps, three light tanks, two half-tracks, one artillery piece—and one French-speaking Cajun. "We could find out from the French people where the Germans were," Melancon said. "I was asked to talk to the French people to find out what was ahead. Not all the time, but most of the time they were helpful, and it helped a lot. It protected me because I wasn't in the front; I was in the back listening to French people, and we relayed the information to the Air Corps, or if they told us the Germans were in a certain place, then we had some airplanes circling to protect us, we could get them to destroy them before we'd get there." The commanders certainly knew of his French-speaking abilities. He recalled hearing of requests for bilingual officers back at Fort Riley, Kansas, where he received his training. Once on the battlefield, his French proved invaluable to his unit's success and survival. "Everybody in my company called me 'Cajun'—*Le Cadien*—that was me."[96]

Melancon credited his French with saving his life: "It's part of me being alive today. A lot of times the unit was in the front fighting. I was in the back getting information in French, and I may have saved a life. Some of them got killed. I might have, if I'd been in front, I might have gotten killed. Thank God I was not. But I think that French helped me."[97]

Even in Belgium and Germany, the Cajun GIs found their French to be useful. Lester Armand wrote from Belgium in late 1944: "We went through France and Belgium . . . and we certainly enjoyed the short stay there. That Cajun French of mine certainly came in handy throughout. Belgian people are practically all French-speaking."[98] Damas Romero wrote to his mother in Lafayette in January 1945 from Belgium: "Dear Folks: Glad to receive cigarettes and fruit cake from home. We are living at some old French people's home, taking it very easy. My French really comes in handy. Now I really get a kick. I am the only [one] that can speak it here, so anything they want they come and get me."[99] Doris Johnson from Crowley fought with the 104th Infantry Division in several battles in Germany. At the famous Remagen Bridge on the German border, where hordes of American infantry and armored units swarmed to cross the Rhine River, Johnson put his French to good use. According to his hometown newspaper, "While there he acted as a French interpreter on the bridge to question all who crossed and made certain that no Germans used the bridge as it was forbidden to Germans."[100]

Prigeon Fontenot left the family rice farm in Rayne to join the army in World War II. He arrived in France in February 1945 as a replacement in an armored halftrack unit with the Ninth Armored Division. As a

Breaux Bridge native David Guidry (left), *original member of the Louisiana National Guard, Company F, France, cir. 1945, courtesy of Fred Guidry*

French-speaking Cajun from the prairie, he quickly grasped the French dialect spoken overseas. “If you could speak French, you pick up on the French right away,” he said. “The other guys would try to talk to them, but [the French] wouldn’t associate with them too much; they couldn’t understand them. I’d walk up to a few people and try to visit with them and I’d start speaking French. Well, of course they want to speak with a Frenchman. That’s how they were. They wanted to speak with somebody they could understand and could understand them.”[101]

That spring, his unit sped through Belgium and eventually crossed the Rhine River into Germany. His use of French became particularly valuable in communicating with Germans and German prisoners—all of whom could speak some French. “If you could speak French, you could understand the Germans better than the other guys who couldn’t speak French,” he said. But sometimes, it was touch-and-go, with little time to identify friend from foe. With so many German soldiers retreating, surrendering, or attempting to avoid capture by pretending to be civilians, it was critical to have GIs like Fontenot who could speak to the local population. “It was always dangerous; we knew we didn’t have any friends around us. You couldn’t turn your back to nobody. You didn’t know who was who. Every day was a different day; we didn’t know what we would face up with tomorrow.”[102]

The Cajuns who made it deep into German-occupied territory skirted the line of danger at every turn. Sidney Hardy, who served as an interpreter for General Patton’s Third Army, was captured behind the lines and sent to a prisoner-of-war camp. Prior to his capture, he rode in a jeep, gathering information from local people, as the armored units raced across the territory. “I had some skills that the rest of them didn’t have,” he said. “They couldn’t speak French, and didn’t know what was said in French, so I’d re-speak it again in English and interpret for what they needed to know.” Like Prigeon Fontenot, Hardy had to be extra vigilant when speaking with the native people as the Americans got closer to Germany. “I enjoyed being an interpreter. I was liking that because it was things that I knew when to say something and when not to say something at all. It makes a difference. Because you don’t know who you are talking to, to start with. You don’t know them and they don’t know you. Period. So, you had to be very, very careful when you interpreting.”[103]

In one hair-raising incident, as his unit passed through a small town, a Frenchman ran out and warned Hardy about German soldiers hiding out in a nearby church. Hardy quickly interpreted that information for his commanding officer, who then ordered the Americans to encircle the church. Using his French, Hardy called out for Germans to come out with their hands up. When one German made a run for it with his rifle, he was immediately cut down, forcing the remaining enemy troops to surrender. It was one of many occasions where Hardy's Cajun French saved the day. "It was very, very valuable because my commanding officers didn't know how to speak French," he said, "and all the things they were telling him in French, he didn't know what they were saying. But I knew, so I interpreted back to him. And he says, 'Boy, we sure glad we got you Frenchmen over here to interpret.' And it helped a whole lot."[104]

Hardy later spent seven months in a German prisoner-of-war camp. He was surprised by the similarities between the French and German vernacular. "They could speak it just as I spoke. Same thing," he recalled. "When I was a prisoner, I learned to speak German. . . . That helped me out a whole lot the whole time I was over there being a prisoner of war. They were always talking about the Americans were getting close to us."[105] The German guards kept moving Hardy farther back behind the line. By the time he was freed, he had been moved to a location about 150 miles from Berlin. He credited his knowledge of French for giving him the ability to learn a bit of German while a POW.

After the war, Hardy's French remained important to his line of work as a detective for the local sheriff's department. On occasion, when a judge needed someone to help with translating French to English for a court hearing, the sheriff called for Hardy to serve as an interpreter. On his ninety-ninth birthday, the city of Breaux Bridge honored this hometown hero by proclaiming "Sid Hardy Day."

Another Frenchie, Meus "Pie" Hebert, served with the 104th Infantry Division and was wounded and later captured outside of Aachen, Germany. During a tense battle near the Belgian-German border, his unit was pinned down by the heavy enemy fire. Hebert recalled his commanding officer requesting: "Frenchie, we gonna need 1,500 crosses and 1,500 [body] bags." Hebert thought, "Wow, now we playing for keeps." He was severely injured, paralyzed from the waist down, and sent to a field hospital in Germany as prisoner of war. There, he met and talked with French-speaking medical personnel. A nurse helped him out with a little extra serving of the only food they had, mashed potatoes. "Hey, that French came in handy," he said.[106]

As the war in Europe came to a dramatic ending in the late spring of 1945, Shirley Guidry found himself on the banks of the Elbe River, near the German city of Magdeburg, not far from Berlin. He was part of a combat engineering battalion group tasked with building pontoon bridges across waterways for the fast-moving Allied forces. As his unit raced through the towns, he was called upon to talk to the locals. They talked fast and used different phraseology than his Cajun French, but he managed to get the message through. Even the greetings were slightly different, he explained. "It's just opposite, you know. Cajun is '*Comment ça va*?' The French says, '*Comment vous sont, monsieur*?' It's a difference, you know. I didn't have no problem. They were so happy to hear somebody, an American, talk French, you know, broken French, but I got along with them."[107]

Like most rural Cajun children reared in the 1920s, Guidry did not speak a word of English until he started school at six years old. "When I was growing up, it was all Cajun. All the people in the country was Cajun." His first-grade teacher taught him how to speak English before he learned to write it. He grew up on a farm in Rayne where few adults spoke English, but everybody, including the kids, worked. "At the age of six years old, on the day of my birthday, 1931, I started picking cotton," he recalled. "Later on, at twelve years old, I was on a wagon in the rice field, feeding the rice to the old tractor. I was twelve years old. I was on a wagon, so I know what work is."[108] At sixteen years old, he worked at the Civilian Conservation Corps. Then, when the war began, he took a welding job at the Consolidated Shipyard in Orange, Texas, making seventy-five cents an hour, before joining the army a year later.

Shirley Guidry, France, 1944, courtesy of Joe Guidry

Guidry landed in France on Christmas Day 1944. It didn't take him long to put his French to use. "When we got in France, I was the only one that could speak Cajun

French, so naturally they called me over." His buddies would say, "Hey, Guy-dree, Guy-dree, come here!" They wanted him to interpret with the French people who were elated to meet the American liberators. "They were happy to see the Americans," he said. "Because I talked to them, see. That's what got them all excited. 'Oh, an American talking in French!' Of course, the GIs, friends of mine, called me over, talking to them, didn't know what they were saying, so I had to come and interpret. They were so happy to be able to talk to somebody in French, you know. They treated us like we were kings. . . . So it came in handy, it really did, you know. My Cajun ancestry really came in handy."[109]

When the war in Europe ended in May 1945, the Cajuns eagerly awaited their return trip home. But a few stayed behind, primarily because of their language abilities. Lester Guillory from Mamou was one of them. He flew thirty-two combat missions over Europe as a bomber pilot. As the son of French Cajun parents, his first language was French. His fluency with the language led to his assignment as a liaison officer between the US Army Air Corps and French workers at Orly Field in Paris during the last months of the war. "With an excellent knowledge of French, he was like a 'Gift from Heaven' when he arrived at Orly last June," a US military newspaper noted. "Lieut. Guillory learned to speak French back home in Louisiana before he learned to speak English, so it is not unusual to walk into his office and find him discussing technical problems with one or more of the French mechanics whom he supervises." In this capacity, he was assigned to Project Patriotism, an Allied effort to identify, recognize, and, in some cases, reward courageous French citizens who helped downed airmen to evade the German occupiers and return to safe haven. In 1948, the French government awarded Guillory with the Croix de Guerre.[110]

Glady Trahan who served with the Crowley National Guard, Company I, in Europe, ended up working as a printer for the military's printing service in France. "His training as a printer and his ability to speak French fluently took him away from his buddies in Company I, with whom he had entered the service in November 1940 and crossed the ocean in 1943," the local Crowley newspaper reported.[111] Trahan went to work at a printing plant in Reims, distributing material to dozens of French printing firms. "Among his tasks was that of acting as interpreter for the commanding officer there. This was one time he enjoyed his mastery of the language of Louisiana's founders. After learning to speak French at home, Trahan had two years of French grammar at

Catholic school." He was involved in making photostatic copies of the German surrender terms, signed by General Alfred Jodl, chief of staff of the German army, on May 7, 1945, which brought an end to the war in Europe.[112]

As American troops began a mass exodus from Europe in the summer of 1945, Addy Melancon volunteered to stay in France for another six months to assist with the sale and distribution of surplus army equipment to the local governments and town mayors. "I got assigned to the Army Surplus Command selling vehicles, trucks, and stuff to these town mayors, and, naturally, they wanted to take care of me with everything they had," he said. "Everybody wanted to treat me fine so I could give them some vehicles, half-tracks, deuce-and-a-halves, jeeps. . . . So, I led the life of Riley for six months." He stayed in hotels, ate good food, and drank French wine with the town elders, eager to please a young American army officer who spoke their language. "If I didn't speak French, I wouldn't have a job," he said. "They didn't want a guy that couldn't speak French, because the people they talked to couldn't speak English. Half of the mayors and stuff in these towns had very little English. . . . When I shook hands, that was the deal for whatever was bought."[113]

When he finally returned home from the war—an experience like few others—Melancon reunited with his comrades in the National Guard and reestablished the old Company F as new guard unit. He was sent to Fort Polk and taught young enlistees about military operations and maneuvers that he learned firsthand in combat. "When we'd go to Fort Polk in the summertime, a lot of us were chosen as the interpreters in the classrooms to teach part of the class in French if we could. And I did part of that when I went to Fort Polk, and I liked that, because when I was teaching, I was teaching something that happened during the war, something I knew about, not what the book says. Most of them, they would teach by the book. I would teach by experience."[114]

Melancon commanded the famed Company F National Guard unit for the next two decades, retiring as a major. When he was interviewed in 2021, at ninety-nine years old, he was the last living World War II-era Louisiana National Guardsman. During the entire span of his life, which took him halfway around the world and back, his French followed him and he never lost sight of its value. Even though teachers tried to beat the French out of him at school, and he was ridiculed during army training, it was his native Cajun French that proved so important and impactful throughout his military career and long life. "The French language helped me a lot in life, before the war, during, and after," he said.[115]

Addy Melancon receiving honors, 2021, photo by author

As one of the last surviving French-speaking Cajuns of World War II, Addy Melancon finally received long-overdue recognition by the local media and civic leaders for his service. At a small gathering at the Melancon home in 2021, State Representative Mike Huval presented the esteemed veteran with a special certificate from the Louisiana legislature honoring his service. "Thank you for everything you have done for us," Huval said. "A lot of people don't realize it, but your French language helped y'all in the service and helped the Americans to speak to the local people to where you could translate it for the officers." Melancon responded, "I did more translating than I did fighting, because I could speak French."[116]

At the same event, Melancon received as special honor as an inductee into the Acadian Museum's Order of Living Legends to preserve his legacy and the legacy of the Louisiana National Guard. Warren Perrin, chairman of the museum, said: "You stood up proudly, didn't try to hide your Frenchness, but used it as a badge of honor and a way to serve your country. Stories like that inspired the Louisiana legislature to create the twenty-two-parish area called Acadiana in 1971, and in 1974 our [Acadian] flag. . . . You have served your country by honoring your culture as an interpreter throughout Europe. And because of your special skills, you were allowed to see the world, not because you were a Melancon, but because you were a Cajun, and you spoke the language positively for a good reason and a good cause."[117]

Addy Melancon's story is representative of the thousands of Cajuns who left home for the war not realizing that their language and upbringing held much value beyond the confines of their small communities. Yet they found a new purpose for their language in France and Belgium and with it established deep connections with other French-speaking people. This new purpose revealed the importance of their Cajun French inheritance, passed down from many generations, all the way back to the original French settlers of *Acadie*—the Acadians. The Cajuns' native language, once reviled as backward and taboo, became revered and valued by the military in the march across Europe.

CHAPTER 3

THE CAJUNS OF OSS

"All of us had the same training, the same skills, same weapons, same specialty, and we all spoke French,"

—Roy Armentor, Operation Group Peg

In October 1943, the commander of Camp Wolters, Texas, received a dispatch from Washington, DC, requesting the services of two French-speaking soldiers for special operations with a new intelligence gathering outfit, the Office of Strategic Services (OSS). One of the men, Sam Broussard, a Cajun from Breaux Bridge, answered the call. By the end of the year, the secret agency had recruited a dozen or more French-speaking Cajun GIs for Special Forces operations in Europe. For six months, these high-caliber recruits underwent extensive and unusual training, all in preparation for the invasion of France. As the campaign unfolded, they were deployed, in small groups, into various sectors of the battlefield, usually ahead of the regular army, to coordinate activities with the French Resistance. Those American agents who joined the OSS had to be proficient in a foreign language. For the select group of Cajuns who volunteered, their linguistic expertise came naturally. Once imbedded with leaders of the French underground, it became clear that the distinct, age-old dialect of the Cajuns melded almost perfectly with the local leaders of the Resistance. Their survival and the success of their collaborative missions depended on effective communication in French. In no other aspect of the Second World War did such a small group of Cajun soldiers contribute so much to the war's outcome. They worked undercover and behind enemy lines to help defeat the German army in France. Their accolades are legendary, their contributions to the liberation of France, immeasurable.

Ike's Spies

The Office of Strategic Services played a critical, though less known, role in the Allied victory in Europe. In 1940, William "Wild Bill" Donovan, himself a hero of World War I, created the OSS, which was a forerunner to the US Central Intelligence Agency. By 1944, the OSS had grown into a powerful intelligence gathering arm of the American military. The organization specialized in unorthodox warfare such as sabotage, counterintelligence, and guerrilla activities behind enemy lines. Donovan's agency combed the army ranks in search of qualified individuals with unique talents required for Special Forces operations in combat. Those selected for OSS training had to agree to volunteer for hazardous duty, which included parachuting out of airplanes. They had to be physically fit and possess sound communication skills. Above all, these soldiers had to be fluent in a foreign language. The rich American melting pot of cultural and ethnic backgrounds provided Donovan's agency with specially trained bilingual agents capable of handling the most dangerous missions in enemy-occupied countries.[1] When it came time to select French-speaking agents for the invasion of France, OSS recruited several Cajun soldiers who were born and raised in the heart of the bayou country in south Louisiana.

Before becoming an agent, however, volunteers had to prove themselves during training at the OSS Assessment School in Washington, DC. There, agents-to-be were tested for memory skills, inquisitiveness, and aptitudes. They were subjected to "Gestapo-style" interrogations to test their ability to handle stress and make quick decisions. Aspiring agents learned to be proficient in Morse code, radio operations, weapons, demolitions, sabotage, and hand-to-hand combat, among other necessary skills needed to survive and complete a mission behind enemy lines. They also took French classes, instructed by French officers, who taught the men how to master the local customs, mannerisms, and dialect of the areas in which they might be operating.

In December 1943, the new members of OSS traveled to England to prepare for the invasion of France. Once there, the training for espionage activities continued rigorously under the tutelage of the British Special Operations Executive (SOE), including locksmithing, "breaking-and-entering" techniques, and urban warfare. For the final phase of training, the soldiers dressed in civilian clothes and went about the city. They boarded a bus and rode out to a designated street corner while being "tailed" by British secret agents.

After successfully eluding their followers, the undercover operatives were to break into an office building, steal documents from a desk, and escape without getting caught. The purpose of this unusual spy-like training was to simulate clandestine activities in enemy-held territory.

As the date for the invasion approached, the top brass split the agents into three categories: Jedburghs, Operational Groups, and Special Forces detachments—all specially trained military teams of various sizes. Each had their own special mission, which entailed coordinating activities with French Resistance groups, known as the *Maquis*.

The OSS and the SOE had direct lines of communication with the leaders and secret agents of the French underground. As night fell across France on June 5, coded radio messages from the BBC in London reached Resistance groups spread out in villages, farmhouses, and cellars in various districts of France: "The dice are on the rug" and "It is hot at Suez." The flood of coded messages like these signaled to the thousands of Maquis that the invasion had started. Throughout that night, and even days before, bands of vengeful French guerrillas sprang into action; some raced to sabotage railroads and German communication centers while others gathered intelligence and organized raiding parties. Throughout the night, and for weeks following the invasion, half a million men and women in the Resistance conducted hundreds of raids on German columns, lines of communications, and troops movements, which effectively crippled enemy transportation all through Normandy, Brittany, and the Cherbourg Peninsula. Resistance forces sabotaged a thousand railroad targets in France; they knocked out bridges and fuel dumps.[2] Not a single enemy tank made it to the beaches during the crucial first forty-eight hours of the battle.

In *Ike's Spies*, author Stephen Ambrose quoted General Eisenhower's 1945 remarks about the contributions of the Free French: "I consider that the disruption of enemy rail communications, the harassing of German road moves and the continual and increasing strain placed on the German war economy and internal security services throughout occupied Europe by the organized forces of resistance, played a very considerable part in our complete and final victory."[3] Supplying, communicating with, and sometimes leading these small bands of Maquis were a handful of specially trained, French-speaking agents from Cajun Country. Their stories would become the stuff of legend.

Sam Broussard—Special Forces Detachment Ten

With D-Day fast approaching, General Eisenhower decided that Allied operations in France would be better served if a handful of OSS officers were assigned to army units in the field. He therefore established Special Forces Headquarters and assigned thirty-five liaisons and staff officers to individual army groups. The mission for these Special Forces detachments would be to collect intelligence from battlefield OSS agents and Maquis; coordinate activities and operations with the French Resistance; and provide tactical intelligence to London and the various corps headquarters as to the location of enemy forces. This was the final phase of the invasion and liberation plan that married the Allied forces to the army of French underground fighters. The level of collaboration with clandestine activities among agents from several countries was unprecedented in the history of warfare.

Breaux Bridge native Sam Broussard led Special Forces Detachment Ten. He came ashore on Omaha Beach on D-Day and served as the intelligence officer for the First Infantry Division. Once the Allies secured a beachhead, Broussard made off into the Normandy countryside to locate and organize Resistance fighters. With his mastery of the French language and knowledge of the country's prior guerrilla activities, he recruited several underground fighters to lead American infantry units through the heated hedgerow battles of the Cotentin Peninsula, into the port of Cherbourg, and eventually to capture all of Brittany. "My job was to interrogate the French people behind enemy lines to find out about the German forces," he wrote to Stephen Ambrose many years after the war. "We supplied the underground with weapons and explosives. I organized bands

Major Sam Broussard, cir. 1944, courtesy of the Broussard family

of Maquis and attached them to various American infantry units as our forces moved into occupied areas, where the French were experts at infiltration."[4]

Broussard had a deep connection to his Acadian ancestry. He was a descendent of Joseph Broussard dit Beausoleil, the legendary leader of the Acadian resistance who fought against the British during the period of the Acadian exile from Canada in the mid-eighteenth century. After years of fighting a guerrilla war in Nova Scotia, Beausoleil and his brother were exiled from their homeland and established a flourishing farming community in southern Louisiana. "Apparently, the Broussard brothers came down to the Bayou Teche," he said in an interview, "and they must have been good lovers, because they really populated the area with Broussards." Growing up in the 1920s—almost two hundred years after the arrival of the Acadians in Louisiana—the people of Breaux Bridge and surrounding areas still spoke fluent French. English became a secondary language for most Cajuns, if they learned it at all. "Everybody spoke French back then," Broussard recalled. "My daddy spoke French, my mamma spoke French and English; we spoke French at church and always spoke French at home."[5]

He came from a long line of Cajuns reared to be hard-working, agricultural people. With fifteen acres of cotton, a dairy, and farm animals to tend, life on a bayou farm left little time for leisure, except for hunting and going to school. "Hard living," he said, "everybody [in the family] worked. There was no way around that."[6] He'd wake up before dawn to stoke the wood-burning stoves; the Broussards had no running water and no electricity. After morning chores, he'd deliver milk to the neighbors on his way to school. Every afternoon, he raced home and picked cotton until well after dark.

Following high school, Broussard joined the local National Guard and paid his way through college with savings from his milk-delivery business. He graduated from SLI in 1934 and went to work for the Soil Conservation Service. He was called to active duty in 1942 and was sent to a special army engineering school—one of the first of its kind—at Fort Wolters, Texas. This school specialized in engineering-related skills: bridge building, rigging, field fortifications, cutting down trees with TNT, laying mines, demolitions, camouflage, and setting booby traps. This experience would prove vitally important for his future OSS operations in the backcountry of France.

During his stint at Camp Wolters, his commanding officer received a dispatch asking for junior officers with bilingual skills to volunteer for a special assignment. The message gave no indication as to the type of work the officers would be doing; however, Broussard speculated that it might have something to do with working with the French underground. It sounded intriguing and adventurous, so he signed up. The next day, he received a telegraph to report for temporary duty in the nation's capital.

> CAPT SAMUEL S BROUSSARD 0439763 INF WILL PROCEED FR CPWOLTERS TEX TO WASHINGTON DC REPORTING UPON ARRIVAL TO TAG ROOM 1048 MUNITIONS BLDG FOR TEMP DY APPROXIMATELY 14 DAYS CONNECTION OSS ACTIVITIES STOP TRAVEL BY COMMERCIAL AIRCRAFT IS DIRECTED AND NECESSARY FOR ACCOMPLISHMENT OF EMERGENCY WAR MISSION STOP OFFICERS FOUND SUITABLE WILL BE ASGD TO STA OUTSIDE CONTINENTAL LIMITS US PRIOR TO COMPLETION OF TEMP DY END[7]

For ten days, government officials questioned and interviewed him for this special assignment. Investigators contacted his family and associates back home to double-check his background. They even contacted the SLI President Joel Fletcher and asked him questions. In a letter of recommendation on Broussard's behalf, President Fletcher wrote:

> I am sure that he does not have any relatives in a foreign country for these people have been in Louisiana for over two hundred years; coming here from Canada about 1765. I am sure that Sam has never been out of this country. His morals are unquestionable, his intelligence of the highest, and if he ever takes a drink, he is perfectly capable of handling himself as a gentleman.[8]

After probing into the recruit's personal life and rushing him through an intense interview process, the OSS accepted Broussard into its ranks. The department sent him home to Breaux Bridge to take care of his personal business before beginning his new job. Within a few weeks, he would be bound for England in preparation of the invasion. "I can hardly wait for that time to come," he wrote to his parents just before departing for overseas. "We're going over by air plane which makes it much better. There are a bunch of officers here on the same thing. They all speak French and we're all going together."[9]

Once in England, he, along with hundreds of other agents, trained for special operations and the standard beach assault from a landing craft. While in the office, he kept track on a map of the location and details of the various Maquis groups and the individual French agents awaiting the big offensive. With anticipation of the invasion building, he wrote a letter to his sister outlining the intense preparation: "We leave the house at 7 am and don't get back until way after dark. There is always plenty of work to do and you know that you are really working towards an end. Things are looking good and it can't happen too soon. I feel about the invasion as the June bride did about getting married. I know it is going to happen but I don't know how it is going to feel."[10]

As D-Day approached, Broussard participated in a meeting with General Eisenhower's staff to discuss the beach obstacles, enemy defenses, and resistance activities. Because of his background, headquarters assigned Broussard as the intelligence officer with the US First Army. For the invasion, he and a dozen officers from his detachment landed on Omaha beach with the First Infantry Division. As the lead intelligence officer, he led the advanced party in a jeep with two other men. His ability to communicate effectively with the French underground would be imperative to his mission.

When he came ashore, bodies were strewn across the sand, smoke billowed from the cliffs, and the shoreline resembled a massive military junkyard—remnants of the costly battle that had taken place hours before across the open beach. He immediately dug a foxhole to protect himself from incoming enemy artillery attacks. Although the Allies had advanced a few miles inland, the German defenders were still heavily entrenched and firing from fortified positions. In his records, Broussard described the magnificent fortifications along Hitler's Atlantic Wall: "The Germans had actually built homes in the embankments and the camouflage work was perfect. They had their guns so inlaid in the embankments that it was impossible to see their positions from the air or from the sea. Most of the guns were still intact and the only way to clean those Jerries out was to get in their trenches and dig and burn them out."[11]

German snipers were masters of the Normandy hedgerow country. In one of Broussard's first missions in France, he led a platoon of Black soldiers on an enemy sniper hunt. Three days after D-Day, members of the news media had arrived in Normandy looking for stories. One crew photographed

Captain Broussard climbing down a ladder leading to the second floor of a barn where snipers had been spotted. The photograph made headlines back in the states. The caption read: "A platoon of American Negro soldiers, the first mentioned as participating in the assault upon French Normandy, and led by Captain Samuel S. Broussard, Breaux Bridge, Louisiana, surround a farm house as they search for a German sniper during mopping up operations by the allies in the liberated section of northern France. These boys mean serious business."[12]

As soon as American forces secured the beachhead, they pushed up on the right flank to liberate the Cotentin Peninsula and capture the vital port of Cherbourg. It was during this operation that Broussard's French-speaking abilities, his skills at sabotage, and his born leadership qualities helped to make a difference on the battlefield. He and his jeep squad rode way ahead of the advancing forces to locate Resistance fighters and assign these individuals to support American infantry units in advancing through enemy-occupied territory, "where the French underground were experts at infiltration," he noted in a report.[13]

Map of Brittany with locations of French Resistance groups, post-invasion, courtesy of the Broussard family

Broussard rendezvoused with a French Maquis leader named Lieutenant Emile Boin, who had contact with several heads of the local guerrilla groups located in the northern and southern regions of the Cotentin Peninsula. The Maquis, Broussard described, "were poorly clothed and poorly armed, but they wanted to fight."[14] These local Frenchmen penetrated through German strongholds and reported back to Broussard on exact enemy locations. He then called in airdrops of weapons, ammunition, and explosives to arm these men, along with French francs to pay them.

The Frenchmen knew the locations of enemy machine gun and artillery emplacements. They knew the terrain and the locations of mine fields and obstacles. In his report to headquarters, the newly promoted Major Broussard stated, "From the tactical point of view, the attaching of organized French resistance workers to military units is the way in which resistance could do the most good." This group in the northern Manche sector had been "extremely well-managed and operated by very able leaders," he remarked. Some of their surnames reminded him of Cajun families back home: Robin, Laroux, Guerrand, and Olivier.[15]

Unidentified French Resistance fighters, Normandy, cir. 1944, courtesy of the Broussard family

On June 17, on his ride back to headquarters, he spotted a German soldier retreating from the front lines. Broussard took him prisoner only to find out that his captive was indeed a German general. He confiscated the general's sword as a souvenir and gave it to his comrade, Lieutenant Emile Boin, for safekeeping. When Broussard returned to Paris many years after the war, his old Maquis friend Boin had the sword waiting for him. This precious souvenir, a symbol of Broussard's contributions to the liberation of France, held a place of honor above the mantle in the family home in New Iberia for many years. The two men visited for the last time in 1994 when the Broussard family went to France for the fiftieth anniversary of D-Day.

From June 17 to June 24, American forces advanced through the Cotentin Peninsula, aided by the local militia and their OSS counterparts. This one week of fighting proved the effectiveness of joint OSS-Maquis activities. Through coordination with the leaders of different sectors, Resistance fighters set up roadblocks and ambushed German columns. They cut all the communications in the area and provided crucial intelligence on enemy strength and positions. One of Broussard's field reports from that week listed the actual coordinates of enemy gun batteries and tanks provided by intelligence from the Maquis:

> One AA Battery at 224075
> Enemy installations around Part 223076, radius of 300 yards
> Two disguised tanks at Castle at 228071[16]

In 1982, Broussard gave an interview in French on the Louisiana Public Broadcasting program *En Français*, in which he explained his involvement with the Maquis during that all-important breakout of Normandy:

> My goal was to take care of them [Maquis] and then question the French to be sure that they were people involved in the Resistance because there was a lot of resistance in France. The Maquis, what we call the Maquis, their work was very, very, very interesting. We got the information to send to the American army. That way you could know where the ammunition was, where the oil was, where the general staff was, where the guns were, where their forces were.[17]

In late June 1944, Broussard reported that officers from the Ninth Division reacted positively to the assistance from the local Resistance workers who he had recruited. One American officer stated, "We didn't know what to expect from these Frenchmen when they reported to us, but we handed them rifles and they started to bring back dead Germans and destroying machine gun nests." One officer described them as "a brave bunch of Frenchmen."[18] Bill Donovan's vision for coordinated intelligence using bilingual agents on the battlefield had indeed been tried, tested, and proven to work when it mattered most.

From there, Broussard and his mobile team, which included a radio man and jeep driver, moved farther south in search of additional Resistance fighters to lead the American forces deep into the heart of the Normandy bocage. On July 8, they located a few and attached them to the Fourth and Eighty-Third divisions to guide the frontline troops through the region. In a memo, he wrote, "After sufficient interrogating and checking with the resistance groups in the vicinity of Carentan, four men were found suitable and volunteered for this work. It was agreed that those resistance workers would be given GI uniforms, rations, and when necessary, arms, to carry on their respective duties. Their jobs were to lead reconnaissance patrols, contact civilians for enemy information, and select positions and routes of approach toward enemy territory. . . . It is felt that there will be no time lost when information is passed through such members of resistance." Broussard learned quickly that rapid and reliable communication with the French on the battlefield could make a difference in real time, especially in the weeks after D-Day with American forces pushing to breakout of Normandy against well-entrenched German panzer units.

From Normandy, his detachment advanced into the center of enemy-occupied Brittany, an area from where many of the pioneering Acadian families originated. He wrote his brother, "There are a number of Broussard[s] in Brittany I've been told, so will have to look them up as we approach in the direction." In late July and early August, Brittany became the epicenter for OSS Special Forces operations. Mission ALOES involved a coordinated parachute dropping of several OSS Jedburgh teams and equipment to supply the French underground with weapons. Racing to the center of the region ahead of the drop, Broussard and his team made contact with the leader of the Resistance forces there, a Colonel Eon, at his headquarters in the town of Kerien. From there, Broussard and his French counterpart led coordinated attacks against

Major Sam Broussard and his OSS Special Forces Detachment, Normandy, cir. 1944, courtesy of the Broussard family

enemy columns and secured the opening of a major highway for General Patton's fast-moving Third Army. Some years later, the French colonel wrote to Broussard about this important mission: "I will always remember you during that night of combat firing away at my side with your small US team in the middle of my French Resistance fighters in their wooden shoes."

Years later, Broussard spoke in French about his convert operations with the Maquis in Brittany, the deadly encounters with German units, and how he hid out in a barn to evade enemy capture.

> I worked in the village of Kerien with a group of Maquis. We even dropped ammunition and then rations, a bit of clothes and all the things they needed. I was the one who led the group. In the afternoon we attacked a group of Germans. We killed several. I was the one who gave direction to fire. We killed several in the evening. We got the information that they were strengthening their positions and they would surround the village. So, I was the only American who was there. The French told me that. They took me to a neighbor and I slept in the hay barn at night to be sure [the Germans] couldn't find me there. The next morning, they woke me up with a cup of café au lait, saying that the [Germans] had backed off rather than coming. And then finally, we organized again, and the Americans finally joined us there.[19]

A French newspaper article, published some years after the war, memorialized this mission in which Broussard played such an important role: "The guerrilla warfare explosion unleashed by the French Forces of the Interior enabled the PATTON Army, rushing in from Normandy, to penetrate almost without firing a shot to the very depths of Brittany."[20] According to the story, the Maquis were positioned in ditches and undergrowth alongside the road where the enemy would pass. As the unsuspecting German column advanced down the road with horse-drawn artillery carts and supply wagons, Broussard gave the order to fire. Caught in an ambush, the 125 Germans dispersed in confusion and fled the scene, leaving behind much of their equipment and five dead comrades.[21] With a small band of lightly armed guerrillas, a cunning American intelligence officer from south Louisiana had orchestrated the surrender of an entire German company and helped secure the town of Kerien. That evening, guards were posted throughout the town. The Maquis escorted Broussard to a secluded barn out in the country for a safe night of sleep, knowing that enemy patrols would be out searching for the lone American spy.

Over the course of the ensuing weeks, Broussard continued to work as an OSS freelancer, using his French language and his knowledge of Resistance groups to affect the battlefield and clear a path for the armored columns to penetrate deep into the French interior. He befriended several Frenchmen along the way and no doubt picked up on the particular patois and phraseology of the different areas. In July he wrote home: "Was at Cherbourg when it fell and when they had celebrations which were very interesting. The French people feel good to see such places liberated. . . . Had a good dinner Sunday with some good friends of Cherbourg. Have made myself a few homes since living here. I really get along with these people and they still say my French is very good and so is the accent. Of course, I improve as time goes on."[22]

At thirty-two years old, Sam was much older than the average American GI in combat. But regardless of his maturity level, his background, or his training, he had to rely almost completely on his ability to communicate with foreign allies and to trust their judgment and experiences—and vice versa. Every little nuance in his French vernacular had to be understood and interpreted—his survival depended on how well he spoke to the French people and how well he understood them.

Broussard's adventures with Resistance forces did not end with the Allied victory in France. After spending several weeks working out of an office in Paris, Special Forces command sent him behind the lines into Belgium to coordinate activities with underground forces there. His primary point man was an underground leader out of Bastogne named Lieutenant Joseph Michel. The two French-speakers became lifelong friends. They first met at Michel's home in late 1944 to coordinate Resistance activities in and around the Bastogne area (prior to the Battle of the Bulge). They arranged for supplies of rifles, ammunition, and rations to be sent to various guerrilla groups. The Cajun officer helped to organize these forces to occupy a sector along the Belgian-German border in the Ardennes. As the Battle of the Bulge raged on for five weeks, Broussard assigned Belgian Resistance forces to secure roads and bridges leading to the besieged city of Bastogne. These efforts helped General Patton's forces reach the city in time to save it, and its defenders, from certain destruction.

In his letters home that winter, Broussard made sure not to give away any valuable information on his exact whereabouts or his top secret missions.

Instead, he told them about "life in the office" for a French-speaking officer with high-level credentials who apparently wore many hats:

> The people are nice and the girls are *tres jolie*. If one can mix up a little French with it all, it isn't bad. . . . I act as everything at camp, from officer in charge of the Belgium-French-Luxembourg and German Liaison Section, to interpreter for cooks and generals. All civilian problems and difficulties with Belgium and Luxembourg troops are thrown in my lap. Most of the time it goes smoothly, but at times I hit bumps as on all paved roads. All in all, I'd say it's working pretty good.[23]

On June 5, 1945, almost one year to the date of his arrival in France, Broussard's tour in Europe ended. It would be thirty-five years before he met up with the Belgian officer Joseph Michel again. After a ceremony in 1980 that paired the town of Woluwe-Saint-Pierre, near Brussels, Belgium, and his hometown of New Iberia, Broussard made contact with Michel and the two reunited with personal visits in Belgium and Louisiana.

In 2005, ten years after Broussard's passing, Michel wrote a letter to Dot Broussard, Sam's widow: "Sam Broussard was a courageous officer and served his army and our country the best he could in those horrific moments. Thank you Sam and your 'boys' for having given back to us our most precious possession: LIBERTY."[24]

For his contributions, the Belgian government awarded Broussard the Croix de Guerre with a palm engraving and made him an honorary citizen of Bastogne. Likewise, the French government awarded him their own Croix de Guerre with palm for his role in liberating France.

Sam Broussard, the poor, Cajun farm boy from south Louisiana, spent most of his young adult life serving his country; first with the National Guard, then with the US Army, then the OSS, then again with the National Guard, where he retired from military service in 1947. After the war, he started his own trucking business, served in politics as a state senator, and became deeply involved with the Council for the Development of French in Louisiana (CODOFIL) to help preserve the French language and Cajun culture in Acadiana. His obituary in 1995 listed his life accomplishments: war hero, battalion commander of the National Guard, businessman, rancher, crawfish farmer, horseman, and state senator, "but his role in helping to form CODOFIL may be his most important legacy."[25]

Jedburghs

Prior to the invasion, multinational Jedburgh teams, known as "Jeds," paired up to form three-man commando squads.[26] Beginning on and after D-Day, these individual units dropped into occupied France to coordinate activities with the French Resistance.[27] In the pre-dawn hours of August 4, 1944, team "Ronald," led by Lieutenant Shirly Ray Trumps, a Cajun from Breaux Bridge, rolled out of a customized B-24 Liberator and parachuted into an area near Quimper in the heart of Brittany. For the next several weeks, he and his team remained embedded with the French underground, conducting numerous hit-and-run forays against enemy forces using the strategy of "*surprise, mitraillage, énvanouissement*," as the Maquis called it; surprise, kill, vanish.[28]

Like Sam Broussard, Trumps grew up speaking French along the Bayou Teche in St. Martin Parish. He too served in F Company, Second Battalion of 156th Regiment of the Louisiana National Guard. In late 1943, Trumps found out about the need for French-speaking soldiers to train for special missions. He volunteered for the OSS, a decision that forever changed his life. "It was a very different community at OSS headquarters," he stated. "We were trained separately; they kept small groups apart, so you didn't know too much about the people who you were training with." Of the eighty-six officers trained for Jedburgh operations, Trumps was the youngest—at nineteen years old—and least experienced of the bunch. But he had a slight edge in one important category. "They were all really educated people, like William Colby, Aaron Bank, and John Singlaub," he said. "The only thing that I had over them was that I spoke French better than most. I think that's why they kept me in and encouraged me along."[29]

American soldiers, even those in the elite units, had not experienced the level of unorthodox warfare training required for the OSS. "We had no Special Forces that were combat capable," Trumps said. "We had the Rangers, but they were not trained to get into people's minds like we were." In the beginning, no one knew how to train these young officers. British spies operating in obscure regions around the world were called in to lecture and instruct the American OSS volunteers. "The British were hard taskmasters; you knew you were trained by the best," he stated.[30] In England, following intensive training in Morse code and silent killing, the international Jed teams came together. Trumps teamed up with a Frenchman named Lieutenant J. Dartigues, who had been a sportswriter in his civilian life and spoke German. Sergeant E. B. Esch from Michigan joined the team as the radio operator.

When Trumps jumped into France on his first mission, he carried a carbine rifle, a pistol, two grenades, a dagger, a canteen, rations, a silk map of the region, a compass, a money belt, and a flask of rum. The team's initial mission was to locate the headquarters of a Maquis leader in the area and deliver to him 250,000 francs for procuring men and arms. From there, team Ronald provided liaisons between French Resistance headquarters in Brittany and the leaders of the French underground in the region. The dozen or more Jed teams that dropped into Brittany organized and led a dynamic attack plan with French Resistance fighters that effectively eliminated the German threat and secured the region for the Allies. When Patton's Third Army sealed off the peninsula, the German forces imbedded in the region were trapped. Some units surrendered; others fought to the bitter end. But with bridges destroyed, roads damaged, and communication severed—thanks to the Maquis—the German forces in Brittany lost the ability to maneuver quickly into battle or to conduct an effective defensive retreat. Working in teams, the OSS agents and Maquis fighters ambushed the enemy at every turn, killing hundreds and capturing thousands. This unique collaboration amongst multinational francophones proved to be a game changer in the battle to take Brittany.

Shortly after arriving in the region, team Ronald was informed that the underground had surrounded a four-hundred-man enemy garrison of the elite German Second Parachute Division in the town of Quimper. The enemy commander was willing to surrender to American forces only. Trumps wrote a letter to the commander saying that he was in charge of an advanced armored unit and gave the Germans two hours to surrender. During that time, German patrols discovered that there was no "advanced armored unit" in the area, and thus called Trumps's bluff. A firefight erupted between the two factions. In Trumps's after-action report, he noted the outcome of the siege of Quimper: "We joined up with the Maquis troops and were fighting in the streets of Quimper. After three days of street fighting, the Germans attempted to leave the city and reach Brest. They were ambushed all along the road and very few reached their destination."[31]

The ensuing firefight resulted in several Germans killed and more than 180 taken prisoner. A few days later, Trumps and his team—operating on no sleep since their arrival in France—made their way south and ran into an enemy patrol in the town of Rosporden. The streets suddenly became a battle zone. Trumps and a member from another Jed team climbed up to the top floor of an abandoned building to seek cover. Three trucks of enemy troops appeared out of nowhere and began firing on them. "At this time all hell broke loose," he reported. "We began throwing grenades and firing like hell. The Maquis troops were all in positions in houses and I don't think one German escaped."[32]

A few days later, team Ronald participated in the battle of Concarneau, where the Maquis had bottled up three hundred German troops. During a firefight, Trumps was wounded in the head by flying shrapnel and his radioman had to administer immediate first aid. The Jeds were able to slip away from the fight and brought their wounded lieutenant to a nearby French hospital for treatment. He returned to action later that day. Team Ronald continued to harass enemy troops all the way to Paris. In September, with the work of the special forces winding down in France, Trumps flew back to England to prepare for an OSS assignment in China.

After the war, he returned home to Breaux Bridge, but only for a short stint. He ultimately decided to make a career in the military. He served thirty-four years of active duty in military intelligence, living most of his life on the East Coast. He retired as a colonel in 1975. The Cajun paratrooper who got his start in the Breaux Bridge National Guard would go on to become one of the town's most highly decorated soldiers of World War II. He died in 2006 and is buried in Arlington Cemetery.

Robert LeBlanc—Special Forces Detachment Eleven

In July 1944, Lieutenant Robert J. LeBlanc came ashore at Utah Beach as the lead officer for Special Forces Detachment Eleven, attached to Third Army headquarters. LeBlanc and his team rode in a jeep ahead of the armored units and worked closely with the French underground forces from Normandy all the way across France to the city of Metz. His harrowing experiences running with the Maquis behind enemy lines for several months left no doubt in the value of his upbringing and bilingual abilities.

Growing up in Abbeville with a father who was in politics, Robert LeBlanc learned French and English at a very young age. "My father happened to be able to talk very good English, but the neighbors spoke mostly French," he recalled. "We were taught to speak French to the neighbors, not to speak in English, because my father was in politics and he wanted to keep the people interested. And the kids had to learn to talk French, and that's what we did. . . . I went to the convent and I went to school and learned how to speak English, but the minute we start going to Grandpa's and Grandma's, they wanted us to learn how to speak French and speak French to them, so we did that. We utilized that knowledge to do different things afterwards, and those different things were primarily involved in the military because we needed that knowledge in military to be able to do it."[33]

Like many young men from the region, LeBlanc joined the Civilian Conservation Corps, where he earned a dollar a day. At age sixteen, he joined the Citizens Military Training Corps and learned the basics of military training, discipline, and teamwork. In 1941, he enrolled at Louisiana State University as a cadet in the ROTC. When war broke out, he received a commission and took infantry training at Fort Benning, Georgia. In the fall of 1943, he was sent to Fort McClellan, Alabama, for additional training as an officer. There, he found himself in a unique situation, with a unique opportunity.

Early that fall, he attended a special meeting for officers who could speak, read, and write a foreign language. Recruiters from a "special department" in Washington, DC, gave a short presentation. They were looking for volunteers to join up for a strenuous mission and parachute out of an airplane. That was all they said, and that was all it took for the adventure-seeking Cajun from Abbeville. LeBlanc thought about it for a moment. "Well, I'm at the mercy of Uncle Sam," he said, "so whatever I can do to help, I'll do it."[34]

Growing up a French-speaking Cajun, LeBlanc, like so many others, had a special talent listed on his personal military file that followed him throughout training. His ability not only to speak a foreign language, but also to read and write it, gave him several notches on his army qualifications known as Form '66. Prior to the age of computers, the military used this punch card system to keep track of soldiers' specialty skills. With LeBlanc's language qualifications, he was a prime candidate for the new secret organization, the OSS.

At OSS training in DC, he and a few hundred other volunteers went through a rigorous program. "There were a lot from the Ivy League colleges in the United States who were in OSS, from California and from the New England states, whose English was impeccable. However, their knowledge of French and ability to speak the French language was not all that it was thought to be, and guys like [Ray] Trumps, myself, Roy Armentor, and

[Claude] Galley were able to prove that we were better equipped to deal with the French than a lot of these other individuals were."[35] The OSS training regimen, largely influenced by British commando tactics, ran the gamut. "They taught you demolitions. They taught you how to make nitroglycerine and different things to make plastic [explosives]. They taught you how to dig to diffuse booby traps and they taught you all of the blasting caps, how to put blasting caps on dynamite or on plastic C3. They taught you the techniques of cutting a railroad so that the train would flip over. . . . They taught you how to put sand in the gear box of trains, of boxcars so that one hundred miles down the road, the brakes would lock off. They taught you all these types of ambushing techniques."[36]

Once in England, the training intensified as the D-Day invasion approached. Because of his previous training at the Army Censorship School in New Orleans, LeBlanc participated in disseminating false radio traffic and troop movements to deceive the Germans in what became known as Operation Fortitude. "We were sending information back and forth to fool the enemy into thinking we were going to land at the Pas-de-Calais or Norway," he said.[37] Inflatable tanks, dummy landing craft, troopless exercises, double-cross agents, and false radio broadcasts made the fake "invasion of Calais" seem a likely landing spot to the Germans. To further perpetuate the deception, the Third Army was issued cold-weather equipment and clothing, such as long jackets, to fool the Germans into believing that an Allied thrust or a possible diversion would come through the snow-capped mountains of Norway farther north. American and British secret intelligence were major players in this deceptive operation and were hence major contributors to the success of D-Day and the subsequent build-up in France.

In May, the military commanders created a battalion-sized headquarters for Special Forces operations and assigned LeBlanc, along with a jeep driver and two radio operators, to a separate armored unit to go ashore at Normandy and coordinate the activities with the French underground. "I was fortunate enough to be chosen for Patton's headquarters," he said. "My team and my detachment, Special Forces Detachment Number Eleven, was assigned to Patton's headquarters in England before the invasion. Well, then when we did this, they didn't send us to jump school because there was no need and they needed us immediately to do this sort of a function. So, we did this, and we trained for the post-invasion for when we were employed."[38]

Lt. Robert LeBlanc (left) *and OSS officers, cir. 1944, courtesy of the LeBlanc family*

LeBlanc and his team came ashore at Utah Beach on July 17 to begin their operations to track down agents of the French underground. The beach was still a nightmare. "What we witnessed as we were unloaded . . . was as appalling a sight as you [would] care to witness," he wrote in his memoirs. "The ships and vessels that were lying on the beaches and submerged in the water indicated to us the savage fighting that must have been necessary to secure this tiny amount of real estate." He elaborated, "We knew that from now on it was a matter of life or death."[39]

The terrain inland from Utah Beach was flooded marshland and passable only through the narrow causeways that led to the interior. "It was much like landing at Avery Island [with] causeways coming out of the marsh," LeBlanc described. Passing through Sainte-Mère-Église, his team arrived at Third Army headquarters, which was located in an apple orchard in the small town of Bricquebec. His unit stayed nearby until the Allies broke out of Normandy. Operation Cobra, launched on July 24 and 25, began with a massive bombing attack designed to blast a hole through the

Saint-Lô corridor. More than three thousand bombers laid waste to the area, "like they were plowing the earth with a great big bulldozer," he recalled. "That was a sight that I'll never forget."[40]

Four days later, the Allied forces were on the move. On August 1, General Patton's Third Army became operational. LeBlanc was then assigned to the Fourth Armored Division, which spearheaded the drive to cut off the Brittany Peninsula. From Périers to Avranches, LeBlanc's team drove ahead of the armored columns and witnessed the powerful destructive force of war.

Along the way, he met countless local French citizens who delighted in meeting a French-speaking American soldier. When approaching a French local, he would say: "*Bonjour, mon ami! Comment ça va aujourd'hui*?" They wanted to know how an American learned to speak French. He often responded: "My grandma and my grandpa *ont parlé français. Ça fait il fallait moi, je l'apprends comment parler français*." LeBlanc found out quickly that the dialect in Vermilion Parish and in the rural areas of France were similar. "You could speak to them, and you'd swear you were speaking to a Frenchman from Louisiana, because they would speak that type of French and we'd speak the same French."[41]

When he left headquarters at Périers, LeBlanc had the code names and locations of every French agent in the area. One of the first agents with whom he came in contact was a French priest known as *le curé Berel*, "Father Berel." Following a phony confessional in a small church with LeBlanc, the priest revealed himself as an agent. He then confessed that he had killed a German soldier who came looking for water. As the story goes, the priest pumped the water while holding the enemy soldier's helmet. As the Nazi bent down to get a drink from the well, the priest whacked him over the head with the steel helmet, killing him. To encourage the troubled priest, who "had done some good underground work for us," LeBlanc assured him, "Don't worry about that, Father, the Pope will forgive you."[42]

Once out in the French countryside, having the ability to speak a similar French dialect as his local counterparts—who were always disguised as normal French citizens—certainly made a difference in communicating information and building trust. Code-named "Underfoot," LeBlanc's team raced behind the lines, ahead of General Patton's tanks, and coordinated with Resistance agents to secure strategic bridges, railroads, and transportation routes. The OSS teams, using "suitcase" radios, made contact with OSS headquarters in London twice a day. "We all had a schedule," LeBlanc explained. "They would feed us information and we would feed that back to the Fourth Armored, down to Corps, and so on. Every few weeks, I would go back to headquarters to get the names and information on the new [French] agents in the area."[43]

LeBlanc's travels took him through Brittany, an area from where he had retraced his ancestral roots. After making his presence known to the locals, the guerrillas would emerge wearing arm bands, carrying bottles of wine, and offering their support to the French-speaking American soldier. The French patriots were eager to assist, and LeBlanc quickly put them to work. For the next several days, he coordinated with the local underground units to secure and defend vital bridges, which allowed the rapidly advancing Fourth Armored Division to drive south almost unimpeded. LeBlanc's team protected the lines of communication for the advancing units all the way back to Third Army Headquarters, while French forces attacked and reduced pockets of enemy soldiers ahead of the advancing Americans. As General Patton's tanks smashed through the German defenders, liberating town after town, the underground and the French Forces of the Interior (FFI) subsequently took on the role of guarding vast numbers of captured enemy prisoners. The Special Forces Detachments' efforts paid off in spades.

By August 6 and 7, the Third Army had reached the outskirts of Nantes—a major city on the southern periphery of Brittany—effectively cutting off a German escape from the peninsula. In addition, American units had reached the coastal fortresses of Brest and Lorient, pinning down the enemy forces in the area. Within a week, the Allies had liberated most of the region.

In his memoir, LeBlanc's analysis of the outcome in Brittany points to a lesser-known, but rather poignant, aspect of liberating a people from tyranny:

Lt. Robert LeBlanc, cir. 1944, courtesy of the LeBlanc family

> We were now in the breadbasket of France and [the] harvest season would soon be here. [We] have saved the crop from the German army [and] the French were delighted, now they would not have it taken from them to feed the German army and the German people. They could now enjoy the fruits of their labors and they gave thanks to the American boys who had made it possible, with fruits and wine.[44]

With lines and flanks secure, LeBlanc ventured back to the Third Army Headquarters to report on the situation and to receive new orders and a new list of French agents. From headquarters in Fougères, his team headed back to the Fourth Armored Division, which had, by the middle of August, begun an unstoppable drive from Nantes to the Seine River in the heart of German-occupied France. From Saint-Calais to Orléans to Sens and to Troyes, LeBlanc's mobile squad drove ahead of the advancing troops. He conducted vital missions contacting key Maquis leaders and coordinating guerrilla activities with the growing Resistance forces.

One of the hazards of OSS operations was crossing over into enemy territory to find French agents. After receiving orders for a new mission, LeBlanc's team took off in their jeep and traveled into unsecured territory. When the four men reached the front line, LeBlanc sometimes continued alone on foot. He would rendezvous with a French underground guide, who would lead him to the commanders of various militia units. Following a cordial greeting—and the exchange of the appropriate secret call sign—LeBlanc and his French counterparts shared information, assessed the battlefield terrain, and discussed the plans for the ensuing mission.

Through portable radio systems, LeBlanc and fellow OSS agents had direct contact with London. The mini radio that fit in a briefcase could be quickly strung up, then taken down, with a concise coded message sent to the command center before enemy directional finders could pinpoint their location. They would then immediately move on to a new location, set up the receiver, and wait for a response. The information flowed from LeBlanc to London then back down to the Fourth Armored Division Headquarters, which had a direct link to the tank commanders steam-rolling ahead on roads and bridges guarded by the French. The coordination among the Allies worked brilliantly.

It was not always easy going, however. The danger only intensified when LeBlanc entered a town unannounced and unescorted. He described a typical scenario when looking for a French agent in an otherwise precarious location:

> When you walk into a bar, you look around, and the unusual [is] safe; the usual are not safe. In other words, if you were an agent, and I was to go looking for you at a certain bar or hotel, and I walked in, and all of these guys had their shirt collars flipped up, you didn't ask questions. But if the situation looked normal that meant that there was somebody in there who didn't want to talk at that time. There might have been a German agent sitting in the corner or something. You always observe the area you are in. If the area is normal, it's not safe to talk.[45]

Concerning run-ins with enemy troops, LeBlanc, who carried a Marlin sub-machine gun, commented, "We had a few problems, but we took care of the problems." In retrospect, he added, "We coordinated the missions then slipped back through the lines to rejoin our units. This got ticklish at times, but the Lord was with us. Many times, my radio operators and driver would wonder if I was coming back. My ability to speak French was crucial."[46]

> The Cajun Frenchies didn't have any trouble in OSS because they always had a location they could send them in and do that business, and it worked perfectly. . . . They used [Cajuns] all over France, and when we went to France, it was no problem for us. As long as we weren't speaking Parisian French and we were dealing with people that was local, it was okay, but when you got close to Paris, then you were speaking Parisian French, and Parisian French is an entirely different ball game. I knew it, but I didn't know it as well as I knew regular French. . . . I was fortunate I got in the area of France where the French were very eager to talk to Americans and very eager to help the Americans. So I was able to do a lot of things with them, and I never had any incident where they refused. It was something that you never forget when you got your life on the line, and that's what it is. You're a Frenchman stuck in a foreign country, you don't know whether those Frenchmen are going to kill you or whether they're going to help you, and it depends how you talk to them, what they're going to do, because the French, when we first went ashore, there were different areas of France, and if they would like you, they supported you 100 percent. If they didn't like you, they didn't try to hurt you, but they didn't support you like they supported us, because when we needed help, we knew who to talk to and they would help us.[47]

Throughout the Third Army's infamous pursuit across France in August 1944, the Fourth Armored Division—"Patton's Best"—spearheaded the drive. The Americans' audacious advance was accelerated through the efforts of Special Forces Detachment Number Eleven, led by LeBlanc, and the groups of French underground fighters that he helped organize. By the end of August, Allied forces took Troyes and crossed the Seine River. In September, they pushed through to Nancy, then Metz, before Third Army's forces ran out of fuel. After a 700-mile run, the drive ended. When the French discovered an abandoned German liquor warehouse in the area, LeBlanc arranged for twenty deuce-and-a-half army trucks to load up the cases of cognac to aid the rest and recovery process for General Patton's exhausted army. "I was fortunate to be assigned to the Third US Army commanded by the US Army's greatest fighting General George S. Patton," LeBlanc wrote. "He was a genius of warfare, a no-nonsense commander who believed offense was the greatest weapon of war. I believe his total understanding of the French enabled him to utilize the ability of the French underground and the Special Operations Staff as no other commander did."[48]

(Ret.) Brig. Gen. Robert LeBlanc receiving the Congressional Gold Medal and the Presidential Medal of Freedom, 2018, courtesy of the LeBlanc family

In November 1944, OSS reassigned LeBlanc to the China-Burma theater where he served as a special operations officer with a detachment in Kunming, China. He was released from active duty in December 1945 and returned to Abbeville following a month-long boat ride back to the states. After the war, he settled down, got married, and started a family, yet his military service continued. He started up the local National Guard unit and climbed the ranks to eventually became commander of the entire 256th Infantry of the Louisiana National Guard. He retired from the military as a brigadier general. In 2018, he received the Congressional Gold Medal and the Presidential Medal of Freedom as one of the last living members of the OSS from World War II. LeBlanc, one of Louisiana's most decorated veterans, died in October 2023, one week shy of his 102nd birthday.

Operational Group Peg

In addition to the Jedburghs and Special Forces Detachments, the OSS deployed fifteen-man commando units known as Operational Groups into sections of France. The "OGs" specialized in demolition and ambush tactics. They trained as a unit to parachute into occupied territories and rendezvous with French underground groups. They dropped in with caches of weapons and explosives to target enemy forces in strategic areas and to cripple German transportation. Once on the ground, the American paratroopers—all of whom spoke French—had to rely almost completely on the local knowledge and intelligence of their French counterparts. Language and effective communication were key elements in the success of these dangerous missions behind enemy lines. Roy Armentor from Abbeville and Claude Galley from Montegut both served in the same Operational Group, codenamed "Peg."

"Our job was different from a regular GI," said Roy Armentor in a 2004 interview. "We lived in danger; there was danger around you all the time. I was so sure that I wasn't coming back."[49]

Andrew Roy Armentor grew up in a French-speaking community. "We didn't speak any English at home at all," he said. "Everyone around us spoke French; our friends, our neighbors, everybody spoke French." Like most Cajuns raised in the 1920s and 1930s, he had a hard time adjusting to the new school-board standards, where English was required and French was ridiculed. The teacher sent him home three times for speaking French on school grounds. "They were trying to do away with the French-speaking language," he said. "But once you know French, it stays with you all the time."[50]

He was drafted in February 1943 and sent to Camp Butner in Durham, North Carolina. While there, Armentor met a small group of French-speaking boys. Some were from the New Orleans area; one lived in Maine. Another, Claude Galley, was from lower Terrebonne Parish, and the two Louisiana Cajuns became fast friends.

That summer the group noticed an item posted on the bulletin board at the camp, announcing: "We are looking for volunteer officers . . . Secret and extremely dangerous overseas missions . . . Close quarter combat . . . Job similar to that of operational commandos . . . If interested please fill out the enclosed application form."[51] Soon thereafter, representatives from Washington, DC, held a meeting at the camp to solicit volunteers. The criteria to join was simple: a candidate had to be willing to volunteer for hazardous duty and jump out of an airplane. And he had to be bilingual. Both Armentor and Galley decided to join. Within days of signing on, the FBI conducted a thorough background check on each of them. Once approved and accepted into the program, however, the recruits learned very little information about this special assignment; the new members of OSS were kept in the dark about the operations for which they were training. "None of us had any idea what we were getting into," Armentor stated.[52] "We joined this outfit we didn't know what we was doing in it," said Galley, "all we knew was that we might be jumping out of airplanes and we'd be going overseas soon, they told us that."[53]

Claude Galley grew up along Bayou Terrebonne in a coastal community just south of Houma. His father trapped, fished, and worked in the oil field. Back then, few people spoke English in the bayou communities of lower Terrebonne Parish. "The teachers, they spoke English. But at home it was all French," he said. "All the regular people they all spoke French."[54] With very little formal education and few jobs available, Galley decided to join the army in 1943. He wound up at the same training camp as Roy Armentor and joined the OSS, primarily because of the additional $50 a month in "jump pay."

In November 1943, the volunteers traveled to DC for OSS training. The instructors emphasized map reading, night reconnaissance, and demolitions. The new agents soon became proficient in the use of explosives, weapons (foreign and domestic), knife-fighting, hand-to-hand combat, and first aid. They even learned martial arts. Galley excelled in compass and map interpretation, which earned him a promotion to sergeant. "They trained us to drop us in the mountains, find your way back to the camp," he recalled.

> They'd tell you what azimuth it was, well with your compass you could do that. I was pretty good at it. Matter of fact, after a while the company commander, he was a captain, he called me in his office, he said, "Sit down Galley." So, I sat down and I said, "What can I do for you captain?" He said, "I want to give you a raise." I said, "Whatchu

> mean a raise?" He said, "I want to make you a sergeant." A tech sergeant they call it; it was a staff sergeant with a "T" in it. So, I said, "Captain, I don't know if I can handle that." "Why?" I said, "Because I don't have that much education." He said, "I've been watching you." He said, "I want you to take it and if you get any problem at all, any kind of problem at all, come to me with it." And I took it. That was an honor for me. And I went overseas with that, and we went to Africa.[55]

In early 1944, they sailed across the Atlantic to North Africa and landed in Casablanca, French Morocco. From there they boarded boxcars and rode the slow-moving train to Algiers. There were no bathroom facilities onboard, but the train moved so slowly that the soldiers could jump off, relieve themselves along the tracks, and jump back on. "The toilet was outside," Armentor remembered. "You held on if you had to go do a number two and you did the best that you could." As the trainload of American GIs rode through the French towns, the locals would shout, "*C'est la guerre*!" he recalled.[56]

Roy Armentor (top left) *and Claude Galley* (standing next to Armentor), *OSS training in Washington, DC, cir. 1944, courtesy of Roy Armentor*

Operational Group Peg, cir. 1944, courtesy of Roy Armentor

Operational Group Peg was attached to the 2671st Special Recon Battalion. "All of us had the same training, the same skills, same weapons, same specialty, and we all spoke French," Armentor said. The Algiers base became the epicenter of American, French, and British Special Forces training operations in the Mediterranean. The maneuvers in the Atlas Mountain taught these commandos how to live off the land. Once deployed to the battlefield, it could be several weeks before the OGs met up with other American infantry units, so they had to learn to fend for themselves. Having been reared in the swamps, marshes, and bayous back home, Cajun soldiers had an advantage in this regard. "A 'coonie' is hard to beat when he gets on the outskirts," Armentor said.[57] "He knows what to steal; he knows what to kill. He knows what he likes and what he doesn't like, and he knows how to prepare it."[58] During survival training in the mountains, the men sent out hunting parties during the night and returned with wild (and domesticated) animals from the area, including goats and javalinas. They skinned the animals and cooked the meat with vegetables taken from local gardens. Armentor remembered that he especially enjoyed training alongside the Moroccan soldiers, who all spoke French.

During one foraging episode in the mountains, Galley—a trained demolitions expert—found a small, clear watering hole that contained fresh fish. He lit a stick of TNT, dropped it in the pond, and recovered several dozen fish that floated to the top. At camp, he instructed the others on how to gut, scale, and wash their fish. "Then I got me a little stick with a fork, and I made me a fire and I barbequed 'em. And we all done the same thing. . . . Of course, we didn't have no salt on it. But we didn't go to bed hungry."[59]

In training, these paratroopers learned to work as a team and to rely on each other. In combat, they were masters at sabotage and demolitions. "We were trained to cut rails for trains, blow up bridges, and attack an enemy column," Armentor said. "It was a hit-and-run deal—we'd hit then run, but we stayed in [the combat zone]. And we did all this in conjunction with the French underground. They would gather the information for us, and then we prepared the attacks and went to work."[60]

Members of OG Peg (Roy Armentor on right) *and French girls, France, cir. 1944, courtesy of Roy Armentor*

On August 12, 1944, Operational Group Peg parachuted into the mountainous region of Aude, in southern France near the border with Spain. A few days later, the Allies launched Operation Dragoon (initially called Anvil)—the invasion of southern France. The mission for Peg was to cover the German escape route into Spain while destroying enemy communications and supply lines along the way. The team jumped from a British bomber in the dark of night. Each man carried a rifle, a .45-caliber pistol, a trench knife, a machete, a canteen, ammunition, grenades, and rations. Their explosives were dropped in separate containers. Upon landing on the rocky terrain, three men were injured on the jump, including Armentor, who injured his back. However, after receiving medical attention, they were able to continue with the mission. The Maquis had secured the area and were waiting when the Americans landed. The Frenchmen then guided the Americans up through a secret path in the mountains that led to their hideout.

Throughout the next two weeks in combat, Armentor's back pain grew worse. He spent time resting in the homes of the local French people, who would soothe him with medication and wine. He managed to sneak into a hospital in Toulouse, but not without detection by his enemy counterparts. He recalled how the French locals saved his life from Nazi spies. "The first night I was there, the French had shot some German agents who were trying to get to me," he said. "They were on our tail all the time because we were with the French underground and they knew where I was. If those Germans had gotten into that hospital, that would have been it for me. I would not have come back; they would have done it right there in the room."[61]

The tactical objective for team Peg was to cut the bridges and causeways of route nationale 117, one of the main highways leading from the south of France into Spain. Beginning on August 13, the commandos put the plan into motion. By the following day, four bridges and one bypass had been destroyed, effectively cutting off the main road and a German escape. On August 15, Allied forces began making beach landings in southern France.

Two days after the invasion began, team Peg and its raiding party of Frenchmen set out to capture an enemy food warehouse in a nearby village and destroy a bridge. A firefight erupted as the group came upon superior enemy forces. The unit's commander (Lieutenant Swank) and Galley laid suppressing fire with machine guns, as the bulk of the outnumbered Allied force retreated. Swank was killed during the attack and Galley was severely wounded. More than sixty years later, Galley retold the harrowing story:

> When we went to blow up a bridge, the Maquis told us that the Germans were going to pass by there at night and our job was to stop them anyway that we could. And when we got to the railroad bridge across the highway, we stopped and we all got out—there was about six or seven of us—to go check where we would place our [explosives]. . . . Our job was to blow up the bridge to stop the Germans . . . that night. And well when we got to the bridge we started looking at it and here comes the Germans. They seen us before we seen them. So we ran back to our little truck and the lieutenant told them other boys to get out of sight, and he told me to stay with him to stop the Germans so that them boys could get away. So they got away. Well, he got killed. He was laying behind the right front wheel of that little truck, and I was laying on the pavement behind the left rear wheel of the truck, and I was shooting from that side, and he was shooting from the other side. And all of a sudden he said, "They got me." That's the word he used. And then I crawled a little bit to go help him and they got me . . . in the hand and in the heel.[62]

Just then, the few soldiers who got away returned fire, which allowed Galley a brief moment to escape. With bullets flying in his direction, he managed to reach a hill where two Maquis grabbed him and escorted him down a safe path. Bleeding profusely from the hand and foot, he managed to walk, several hours, to a roadside where other Frenchmen picked him up in a truck and brought him to nearby house. A local woman took care of him and dressed his wounds. "I'll never forget," he said, "she was dressed in black, and I was sitting at that table and she brought me a big glass of wine—about a twelve-ounce glass of wine—and she told me to drink that; it was gonna help me. So, I drank a couple of sips of that and I passed out. See, I had lost a lot of blood. And when I woke up sometime during the night, I was in a clean bed, they had put clean clothes on me and the next day they brought me to a French hospital. Didn't know nobody, nobody knew me, all they knew was that I was an American soldier." Galley spent the next several days in a hospital, which had long ago been ransacked by the Germans. The French doctor did the best he could with the medical supplies to sew up and treat his severe wounds. The French fighters came to check on him regularly and moved him around from one hospital to the next so as to evade any run-ins with German units in retreat. "Those two

Maquis, they saved my life from when I got wounded to when I got to the hospital, they took care of me," he said.[63] Eventually, with aid from the Maquis, Galley reunited with his unit.

Once their mission was complete and France liberated, Galley and Armentor boarded a ship and headed home. They made it back to their respective bayou communities after the war and went about their separate ways. They did not see each other again until sixty years later, when they began receiving letters (and emails) from a veterans' group in France, members of the former resistance fighters of the *Maquis Jean Robert et Faïta* who fought alongside Operational Group Peg in August 1944. The letters revealed that every year on August 17, the remaining veterans from that Maquis association and their families visited the grave site of Lieutenant Swank to honor his sacrifice. "Our association has often met at the place known as Salvezines where the *Maquis Jean Robert et Faïta* met up with your group in August 1944," a letter to Armentor noted. "We have visited many times the Drop Zone (Le Clat), where you placed your feet on French soil for the first time, and in the Gorges of Alet [Alet-les-Bains], where Lt. Swank lays according to his wishes."[64] That chain of correspondence

Veterans of the Maquis Jean Robert et Faïta *Resistance group that fought with Operational Group Peg, 2003, courtesy of Roy Armentor*

(Left to right) *Author Jason Theriot with "Cajuns of OSS" Claude Galley, Robert LeBlanc, Roy Armentor, Houma WWII Roundtable, 2005*

ultimately brought the two Cajun commandos back together for a memorable meeting as participants in a World War II "roundtable" program in Houma in 2005.[65]

Operation Adrian

Bill Donovan, the founder of OSS, created the Operational Group concept based on the idea that America's diverse ethnic background could produce a specialized unit of bilingual soldiers, trained in commando tactics and organized into small groups, to parachute behind enemy lines, work with local militia groups, and immediately impact the battlefield. In its nationwide search for participants, the OSS recruited a French teacher and coach from Golden Meadow High School in Lafourche Parish named Orleans Pitre. Born in Cut Off, Louisiana, in 1917, Pitre had already received a degree in education from LSU and had started his teaching career when he entered military service with a commission in 1942. Two years later, he wound up in England in charge of the OSS training school. As the Allies raced across France in

September 1994, Major Pitre led an Operational Group, codenamed Adrian, into the Côte-d'Or region of France, southeast of Paris.

"When I went to school at the age of six, I did not know a word of English," Pitre recalled in a 1992 interview. "I had to learn English for eleven years throughout the years of school. I came back and spoke French all the time. . . . As far as in the community, it was French people and strictly French."[66] At Pitre's school, young Cajuns were taught in English, but they could speak French on the school grounds without repercussions, a rarity for the time.

Growing up, he never heard of the term "Acadian," but knew that his family had its French origins in Nova Scotia. "We consider ourselves French, but we always consider ourselves Cajun," he said. "Even in those days, because in those days they spoke the Cajun, and we were the Cajuns. . . . Everyone spoke *le cadien* as people coming from Nova Scotia. In those days everyone was *le cadien* because it was the French that we spoke, and I would assume that it came down from Nova Scotia and come through the Acadians that settled all along Bayou Lafourche from Lafayette all the way to Golden Meadow and past to Leeville."[67]

Pitre graduated from high school at age sixteen and received a scholarship to attend LSU from 1934 to 1938. Like many college students at the time, he joined the ROTC. By then, his English had improved, and although few people spoke French on campus at LSU, he did run across a few Cajuns. "I met a lot of Cajuns from Marksville," he said. "There were a few from the Lafayette area. I'm not talking about Lafayette proper; it was the little communities like Scott, and probably New Roads, New Iberia, St. Martinville. They all spoke French and they spoke French at home. When we were together, we might speak a couple words of French together."[68]

In 1942, he entered military service and received officer training. A year later, he was promoted to captain and sent to Fort Sill, Oklahoma, to train with the 166th Infantry Regiment with troops from the Ohio National Guard. He was older, talked differently, and didn't quite fit in. "I was a Cajun boy from Louisiana," he said. "I was not mistreated, but I was not one of the boys. You had to kind of bow to their ways."[69] But he did outshoot them on the pistol and rifle range. Because he scored high in marksmanship, the army sent him and a few dozen other officers to Maryland for more intense training. Little did he know at the time that was training with the OSS. Six months later, he was in England, assigned as an assistant instructor for the

OSS training school there. Just prior to the Normandy invasion, Major Pitre became the chief of the training section.

Around midnight on September 9, 1944, a group of thirty-one agents jumped from converted British Liberators into an area just north of Dijon, France. The mission was to support additional OSS groups already on the ground working with French Maquis units to ambush retreating German units. Among the team members were four French women commandos. When the commanding officer of the group was killed on the drop, Major Pitre took charge. Once on the ground, a party of French Resistance met them and escorted the group to their mountainous hideout in a nearby town. "We went hunting for Germans," he said about his mission in eastern France. "Everyone around me spoke French. . . . They understood what you were talking about. Most of them speak the same way. There was not much difference in the French, especially not around Paris, but around the surrounding areas of Paris. It's like when you go to Canada; one part of Canada is just like you're over here in Cut Off and Golden Meadow and Galliano. Yet, in another part of Canada its strictly another French."[70]

After making contact with other detachments in the region, Operation Group Adrian set out to attack a German column in full retreat out of France. The team set up an ambush, fired a bazooka round into an enemy armored car, and killed or wounded two hundred German troops in the ensuing firefight. For the next few days, team Adrian conducted similar ambush operations against the retreating Germans with similar results. Five days later, the group arrived in Paris and, with the mission complete, flew back to London.

At war's end, Pitre made it back to the United States and continued his military service with the special forces, serving as an instructor for the organization that ultimately evolved into the Central Intelligence Agency. When his service to his country came to an end, he returned to civilian life back home on Bayou Lafourche and continued his education career as a teacher, coach, and administrator.

The overall accomplishments of Bill Donavan's special forces teams cannot easily be calculated, nor can they be overlooked; only recently with the opening of OSS records at the National Archives have scholars begun to uncover the depth of the OSS missions and their importance to the overall Allied battle plan to defeat the Germans in France. Using Jedburghs, Operational Groups, Special Forces Detachments—and the French underground—the Office of Strategic Services was able to provide the Allied forces in Europe with a network of intelligence and resistance support unprecedented in warfare. "Many lives were saved because of them," said Robert LeBlanc.[71] The Cajuns of OSS had a unique opportunity to use their language talents to aid in missions behind enemy lines where it counted most. For the all-important battle for France, where the outcome would be decisive, these Cajuns soldiers and their teams played a crucial role. The harrowing and life-changing experiences on the battlefield with other French-speaking comrades gave them a renewed appreciation for their language and heritage. As LeBlanc summed up:

> The low esteem that we had when we were young with other people—people of other cultures felt we belonged to a culture beneath them. But as I grew through this stage and visited all over the world, I became knowledgeable in what goes on in all the different cultures all over the world and realized that the fact that we were not the best speakers of English, [but] we had value both to ourselves and to the country, and this we could demonstrate with our ability, so that it was recognized that these people here in south Louisiana were a valuable resource to the United States. . . . Here was a ready-made, prefabricated, no-cost individual who could provide this service, and that, to me, is what "Wild Bill" Donovan demonstrated to the active army, that there were second- and third-generation individuals throughout the army and throughout the community, throughout the United States, who had a valuable foreign language ability, and he was able to mobilize this talent, this skill, and get it in operation within a short period of time in World War II.[72]

CHAPTER 4

FRENCHIE IN THE PACIFIC

"That Louisiana French is something worth knowing around here as the native Caledonians are all French. Many northern Yanks would give anything to know as much French as I do. That is what I like about good old Louisiana; you can get along all over the world."

—Ford Gremillion, New Caledonia, 1944

As in European countries, Cajun soldiers stationed around the world found their French language to be useful, even in the Pacific. Cajun soldiers, sailors, marines, and pilots participated in the island-hopping campaigns of the vast Pacific theater, where numerous locales contained thick jungles, busy ports, and, in some cases, French-speaking residents. These Cajuns felt right at home in the subtropical, swamp-like environs. Moreover, their knowledge of the French language made them valuable interpreters in strategic areas, in particular the French island of New Caledonia—a key Allied supply base in the South Pacific. Wartime letters and testimonials demonstrate how the Cajuns in the Pacific yearned for a connection to their culture, whether it be geography, cuisine, or simple conversation with fellow Cajuns in their native language. Whenever two or more Cajuns met up randomly on a ship, at port, or at a dank cantina, their French "lingo" and talk of Cajun Country always dominated the conversations. These occasions served to reinforce the connection to their group identity, and their bilingual advantage and use as interpreters helped to perpetuate the Cajuns' distinct ethos.

A Jungle Paradise

Cajun soldiers quickly recognized the commonalities between the Pacific Islands and the landscapes in south Louisiana. There were oddities, to be sure, like coconut trees and coral reefs, but there were also sugarcane fields, farms, and lush jungle that resembled Louisiana swamps. The letters written by these young service members, many of whom had never been outside of their bayou communities before, reveal a deep curiosity with the environments of the islands. The thick vegetation, rich soil, and wet weather reminded them of conditions back home. Having grown up in swamps and speaking multiple languages, the Cajuns felt well prepared for the adventures on these far-off islands.

"The vast pineapple fields of Hawaii are a beautiful sight," James Cormier wrote. "But even if it is nice to see the world, I am anxious to get back to the fields of the Teche Country."[1] Roy Pontiff, writing from somewhere in the Pacific, said "I like this island; it grows a lot of sugar cane, which reminds me of home."[2] Conrad DeRouen, a marine from Erath, loved the smell of burning cane: "The cane sits in the field much longer than ours and is planted much thicker. When it is ready to be cut, they set fire to the fields. Evidently, the fire doesn't harm it. Finally, it is cut and sent to the mills via water ducts. I assure you as a Louisianian I have been chewing my share. The smell of burnt cane fields can really bring back memories of good old Southwest Louisiana."[3] Ray Broussard, stationed on the Admiralty Islands, noted, "This island isn't bad, as islands go. It is beautiful, clean, sandy, and covered with luscious tropical vegetation, which we call 'jungle.' The chow is excellent, but oh, what I wouldn't give for a heaping big plate of steak, rice and gravy. . . . Oh, how I long for a cup of good strong, black 'Cajun' coffee!"[4]

Ellis St. Germain, a young doctor from Breaux Bridge, served on a hospital ship at New Guinea, an island which he described as "a land of tropical beauty lavishly endowed with luscious fruit, flowers of exotic beauty, beautiful birds, towering mountains, thick jungles, gorgeous sunsets over the water." His letter also underscored the unusual creatures on the island. "In the bargain, we also have insects, bats with 4-ft. wing span [*sic*], crocodiles and pythons. Days are warm, nights are cool," he said.[5] Jerome Domengeaux, writing from New Guinea in 1944, agreed: "The heat, mosquitoes, the swamps . . . are truly an incentive to get this war over with in a hurry, and get back to that good old 'Cajun' country."[6]

Another Breaux Bridge native, James Burton Angelle, who later in life had a career as a public servant and served as a state representative and secretary of the Louisiana Department of Wildlife and Fisheries, wrote many letters home about his travels throughout the Pacific. He too noted the interesting geography of the islands and how it compared to the bayou life back home. "It's been raining for the past thirty minutes, and it looks like that good old rain in Louisiana, pouring down like nobody's business," he wrote. "I merely mentioned that to some of the boys, most of who have never seen so much rain, as most of them is from Texas and other dry states. It started another argument about the value of the different states. Of course, you know me; I stick up for Louisiana and always have some remark to make about their states. As a result, they call me 'Frog' and 'Frenchy,' etc. By the way, do they get a kick out of my reading the French articles in *L'Echo* to them. They just can't get over it. I've met quite a few boys from home since I am here. It's always good to see somebody like them as it brings home so much closer to us."[7]

Vernon Sonnier from Crowley felt at home in the Pacific jungles. Prior to joining the military, he worked for the US Army Corps of Engineers as a survey man on the Atchafalaya Spillway, so he had plenty of experience in the swamps. He served in an anti-tank battalion and went to several islands in the South Pacific: "Some people refer to it as a hell hole," he wrote, "because of the heat, rain, flies, malaria-carrying mosquitos, and the rest of the drawbacks, but anyone who can remain in the swamps of the Atchafalaya for nine weeks, working all the week, then hunting and fishing on Sunday (and enjoying it) should not find life too unbearable." Sonnier concluded his letter by saying that he could remain in the Pacific "indefinitely," but wanted to return to his "Southwest Louisiana jungle" after the war.[8]

The US Marine Corps, experts at amphibious warfare and trained in jungle fighting, became the cornerstone for military operations to retake the Japanese-controlled Pacific islands. Otis Courville, raised as a swamper in the Atchafalaya Basin, did not meet the minimal physical qualifications to join the highly competitive Marines. "Nine out of ten, if I wouldn't ha' been a Cajun, I wouldn't na been in the Marines," he stated in a 2006 interview.[9] Courville, native of Catahoula, a small enclave on the basin periphery, grew up on the edge of the swamp and learned from his father how to fish, trap, and pick moss in order to earn a living. His father never did hold a "real" job—he harvested resources from the basin and passed those skills on to his children. When Courville turned eighteen years old, he hitched a ride to Lafayette to join the Marines and fight for his country. He soon discovered that his weight, 137 pounds, disqualified him from the elite unit, which required that new recruits weigh at least 145 pounds. After dismissing offers to join the navy and the army, Courville met face-to-face with a hard-noised marine sergeant. Determined to become a marine, the pint-sized Cajun questioned the reasoning behind the designated weight requirement. The sergeant explained that due to the Marines' prolonged missions in often inhospitable places, a marine needed to be physically capable of carrying a "double-pack," which weighed eighty-six pounds. The recruiter brought out the heavy pack and informed Courville that at 137 pounds, he wasn't strong enough to carry it. The determined Cajun laughed and set out to prove him wrong. He strapped the heavy load to his back and took off running down the hall. He said, "I can run with that for a week. . . . Me, ever since I was a little bitty boy, I used go in the woods, I had a little sack, not all that big, I'd pick up black moss in the woods. Now, when I go in the woods, I got a big sack, and I pick moss until I got about a hundred pounds . . . and I put that on my back and sometimes I have to carry that two miles to get out."[10] Astonished, the recruiter signed him up on the spot. Courville excelled at marine boot camp and later fought at Tinian, Saipan, and Okinawa with the First Marine Division. When the war ended, he volunteered to go to China, where his knowledge of French came in handy with the local French concession. Once the US military discovered his bilingual abilities, they assigned him as an interpreter for an American colonel, who interviewed people about Japanese atrocities.

The educational reforms of the early twentieth century that threatened to subdue the Cajun French dialect caused some bitterness among some of the younger people in Cajun society. Jefferson DeBlanc, a marine pilot from St. Martinville, resented the state bureaucracy for forcing English exclusively in the schools. He spoke French, English, and even broken Spanish growing up along the Bayou Teche. Like other Cajuns who attended college before the war, he recognized the benefits of knowing more than one language. In the competitive realm of higher education and especially in military training, every added advantage helped. The knowledge of French—even a little Spanish, as in the case of DeBlanc—and the experience growing up in the swamps gave these Cajuns an edge in training and overseas in the jungles of the Pacific.

"If you can pick up a language or if you know it, more than one language, you have an advantage, in my estimation," DeBlanc stated in a 2006 interview. "When you start in the uniform and you're American and you show them and they have been listening to you in English all the time and all of a sudden you come out there and you want to talk to this guy, 'Hey, Boog, *vient ici. Comment-tu vas? Allons boire maintenant.*' Then that's something and the natives will spot it like that and they'll come out there . . . this way you have a sort of an insight to communications with the islanders rather than just by brute force. So, I think it's a sport to it. The Cajun has a way of, you know, he recognizes the situation . . . especially the idea of the jungle and the idea of the swamp."[11]

DeBlanc, who piloted an F4F Wildcat off Guadalcanal for the famed "Cactus Air Force" ("Cactus" being the codename for the island), spent much of his childhood around the Atchafalaya swamp—an experience he attributed to saving his life. Once DeBlanc got acclimated to his surroundings on Guadalcanal and studied the maps and topographical features of the many islands within the Solomon Islands chain, he quickly realized that the jungles looked like familiar territory. "[I] felt as if I were home in the Atchafalaya Basin," he wrote. "The names of most of these islands in the Solomon chain were French and Spanish. Both languages were common in Louisiana, and I could speak each fairly fluently. This was a good omen for me, and I felt that the world was young and I would never die here. I could survive in the jungles of this island chain if I were forced down. That this was a home away from home gave me an added edge of confidence in the air combat battles which followed."[12] He would ultimately come to rely on that experience for survival.

During an escort mission in January 1943 flown deep into enemy territory, the external fuel tanks on DeBlanc's Hellcat fighter malfunctioned. Having just enough fuel remaining to support a squadron of bombers to their targets, but not enough fuel to make the 290-mile trip back, the Cajun ace made a fateful decision. He decided to stay with the bombers, knowing that he would have to ditch his plane somewhere in the Pacific once he ran out of fuel. "I took the option," he said. "I figured that I was born and reared here in the swamp country, and I could survive this type of territory, [compared] to someone from New York City or Los Angeles who is not familiar with the ways of the jungle."[13] After shooting down six enemy aircraft (credited with five) near the island of Vella Lavella, enemy bullets from a Japanese A6M "Zero" brought DeBlanc's plane down. He parachuted out of the burning Wildcat and swam for hours using celestial navigation to find his way ashore on a nearby island. His experience in the Atchafalaya Basin swamp gave him the skills needed to find food and refuge in the jungle for a few days. A group of Indigenous people later captured him, but another, friendly Indigenous "coastwatcher" secured his release by trading his life for a ten-pound sack of rice.[14]

His epic story of heroism and survival in the South Pacific reached all the way up the chain of command. On December 6, 1946, President Harry

Capt. Jefferson DeBlanc (with his wife, Louise), receiving the Congressional Medal of Honor from President Harry Truman, 1946, courtesy of Jefferson DeBlanc

Truman presented the Medal of Honor to DeBlanc for conspicuous gallantry and intrepidity at the risk of his life above and beyond the call of duty. For this Cajun ace, it all boiled down to his upbringing. "Being a Cajun, we had it all over the others," he said. "We had the advantage, there's no doubt about it."[15]

Jefferson DeBlanc, post-capture, dressed in Japanese uniform with spear, Solomon Islands, 1943, courtesy of Jefferson DeBlanc

Frenchie in New Caledonia

The French island of New Caledonia became a hotbed for French-speaking Cajuns. The island was the second-largest producer of nickel in the world. American forces arrived there in early 1942, shortly after the attack on Pearl Harbor, to support the Free French government and colonists and to protect the island's rich mining resources. Less than a thousand miles east of Brisbane, Australia, the airbase on the island's main city and chief port, Nouméa, served as a strategic location for Allied operations in the South Pacific. The mountainous island, larger than the state of Massachusetts, had more than fifty thousand inhabitants working the mines, plantations, and ports. A third of the people spoke French, which delighted the Cajun service members and made them feel like they were back home. It didn't take long for the military to make use of the Cajuns' bilingual skills on the island.[16]

The *Abbeville Meridional* featured a story on one of their own, Numo Benoit, a dental technician in the Army Air Corps who served in New Caledonia. "He proved himself very popular with members of all American units he came in contact with," the article noted. "In fact, he was a main source of communication between these units and the French populace of New Caledonia."[17] Purvis Theall missed his gumbo from home but not his French. The Abbeville newspaper printed a letter that he wrote to his aunt, in which he spoke fondly of his experience on the island. "It's all French people there," he wrote. "After we were there for a few days, they put me working with the French Police, and after they did, well

Benoit, in South Pacific Finds French Invaluable

Headquarters, 13th AAF, South Pacific—Corporal Numo Benoit, son of Mr. and Mrs. Gilbert Benoit of Theall, has found his knowledge of the French language invaluable during his travels in the South Pacific. He proved himself very popular with members of all American units he came in contact with. In fact, he was a main source of communication between these units and the French populace of New Caledonia.

Corporal Benoit is a skilled dental technician in the medical department of the 13th AAF famed "Sun-Setters" P-38 Lightning fighter squadron. He holds the Army's Good Conduct Medal, the American Defense Ribbon, and one Battle Star to his Asiatic-Pacific Theatre Ribbon. In civil life he was a farmer.

Numo Benoit article, Abbeville Meridional, *1944*

everything was all set, I'd go around the Island with him, and soon made lots of friends. Had a little trouble at first in understanding their French, like it's a little different than ours is, but soon caught on."[18] Eno Bares sent a short note to SLI President Joel Fletcher about his tour there with the Seabees (naval construction battalions): "I like it here in New Caledonia cause the climate is very much like home and the natives speak French. I get by much better than the Yankees out here, but I would prefer being in good old Louisiana."[19]

Many lady Cajuns received recognition for their efforts on the French-dominated island. Alice Rita Bourgeois of Raceland spent thirteen months on New Caledonia as a nurse in the US Navy. Because she was the only one who knew French, for two months she trained French-speaking housekeepers. "I would love to have stayed, and I want to go back," she told a newspaper reporter.[20] Living and working conditions gradually improved for the medical staff on the island. When they first arrived, they bunked in grass huts with thatched roofs. They washed all linens by hand until they received their first washing machines. Bourgeois had received her training at Charity Hospital in New Orleans and worked at Baton Rouge General Hospital before joining the service.

Upon arriving in New Caledonia in April 1942, Grosse Tete native Joseph Pourciau was surprised to find so many French-speaking people around him. He wrote in his wartime journal: "Had the advantage over some of the boys, knowing how to speak French freely. These French people thought I was Canadian, treated me nice. I was chief interpreter for the officers in my battery."[21] Valex Doucet found his language useful, though not as well polished as the locals. He wrote, "The language of the colony is definitely French, and very good French. In fact, they speak possibly a little better than I do."[22] Even Jefferson DeBlanc, the future "Cajun ace," got in on the action. When a ship transporting DeBlanc's marine fighter-pilot unit, bound for Guadalcanal, landed in New Caledonia in late 1942, the commander of the ship called on the French-speaking Cajun to translate. "Since I was from Louisiana and could speak French, I was selected to be among the first ashore as an interpreter," he wrote in his autobiography. "The expression on the faces of my Ivy League colleagues made my day as I walked with an aristocratic gait down the gangplank. I really rubbed it in!"[23]

Another marine from St. Martinville, Rex Chauvin, reported to the *Teche News* in late 1943 about his experiences on the French island. He arrived just after his friend Jefferson DeBlanc had come through and left with the Cactus Air Force. Chauvin missed him, but he did get to witness some aerial dogfights over the island involving marine aviators. "I've had the opportunity of seeing some of Jefferson's buddies do their stuff, and can they do it!" he wrote. "One time they rolled the score from 94 to 6." Chauvin worked in a service supply outfit that provided fuel for the military, and he apparently sidelined as an entertainer during USO events. He noted that two impressive acts, Ray Bolger and Little Jack Little, toured the island to entertain the troops on stage. When Chauvin met the performers after the show, he was introduced as 'Frenchy.' "Of course, Ray took his cue from that and he started his monkeyshines in French and I helped him along," he noted. In his closing remarks to the local newspaper, Chauvin described the mix of ethnic groups within his bunk house. "P.S. This is truly an all-American Army. In my tent, the roster reads this way: Larkin, from Boston; Hennessy, from Chicago; Thune a big Swede from Seattle; Bardell from South Dakota; and this Cajun from home."[24]

Harris Callahan of Bayou Dularge found his French useful in New Caledonia as well. He enlisted in the navy in 1942 and advanced to carpenter's mate, second class. He later served aboard the aircraft carrier USS *Shangri-La*. Although he only had a sixth-grade education, he could speak two languages. While stationed at New Caledonia, Callahan became an interpreter. Like so many other Cajuns stationed on the French-speaking island, he made friends with the locals. In late 1944, his mother received a letter, written in French, from one of the islanders who had befriended her son during his time in Nouméa. Callahan kept this letter—one of his few precious items of wartime memorabilia that he held onto throughout his life. Translated, the letter reads, "Dear Madam: You may certainly wonder who is writing to you as you receive this letter? Well, it's a lady from New Caledonia who has gotten to know your son, Harris, and is delighted to write a few words to you. Your son, who left us two days ago, was hosted at our home. We appreciated him for the few months we've known him. Needless to say, Madam, how happy he was to be designated to go back home to you."[25]

Agricultural specialist John Bacqué, from Lafayette, had a unique experience in New Caledonia. In 1943, the US Army sent him to the island to develop a large-scale farming operation to provide food for the troops. Prior to taking the job, Bacqué held the distinguished position as District Farm Security Administration supervisor in Lafayette. "Bacqué was asked to head the New Caledonia project," the newspaper reported, "not only because of

John Bacqué (center front), *New Caledonia, cir. 1945, courtesy of the Bacqué family*

his valuable agriculture background, but because French rolled easily off his tongue." He started from scratch on a 150-acre plot of land and, with help from the Indigenous people and French colonists, developed a highly productive farming operation. Within a growing season, they shipped about fifty tons a week of tomatoes, lettuce, radishes, sweet corn, and cucumbers, along with a hundred tons of watermelon.[26]

With such fertile fields and French-speaking people on every corner, New Caledonia must have seemed to the Cajun GIs more like New Iberia than an island on the other side of the globe. Ford Gremillion from New Roads fished, hunted, and spoke French to the locals while stationed there—all traits that made up the way of life for Cajuns in south Louisiana. He served with a supply depot for automotive parts and wrote a series of letters to SLI President Joel Fletcher about his experiences. New Caledonia, he said, was a "choice spot in the South Pacific. . . . That Louisiana French is something worth knowing around here as the native Caledonians [all speak] French. Many northern Yanks would give anything to know as much French as I do. That is what I like about good old Louisiana; you can get along all over the world."[27] The military put him in charge of a mechanic shop, where he met

1 November 1944
In the Mariannas

Dear Mr. Fletcher,

I've been threatening to drop you a few lines for a long time. You see, I've been receiving the "Vermilion" for some time now and have often wondered how you got my address as I did not attend S.L.I. I'd like for you to know, sir, that I've really enjoyed reading your wonderful paper. It always gives me the straight dope on guys that I've lost track of since this damned war started. Thanks a million for favoring me with a copy of each edition.

I first started receiving the "Vermilion" when I was in the States. When I shipped out, it followed me soon after and also to every place I went to. When the first one reached me out here I was still in an old, stinking foxhole.

Mr. Fletcher, I'm not a stranger around Lafayette. You see, I lived in Southwest La. all my life, so far. I lived in Opelousas, Abbeville, New Orleans and finally Lafayette. I worked for Mike Donlon, the Real Estate Agent, for a year and a half. Incidentally, I'm another "cajun" as you can tell by my name. Proud of it too. Haven't run across very many French-speaking "gyrenes" out here.

In order to receive the "Vermilion" more pronto, I'm sending you my new address:

Sgt. Jim Brignac, U.S.M.C.
General Supply Company
7th Field Depot,
c/o Fleet Post Office
San Francisco, California

Bye now, and write me sometime when you have a chance.

Sincerely,

Sgt. Jim Brignac

Letter from Jim Brignac to SLI President Joel Fletcher, 1944, Joel Fletcher Papers, UL Lafayette Special Collections

an interesting local business owner. "On my way to the shop last night to see how my night shift was getting along, I picked up an old Frenchman who was walking down the road. He could not speak English, so we spoke French and got along very well," he wrote. "In our conversation I became aware that he was a very intelligent man. During the course of our conversation, I learned that he had studied to be a machinist during the early part of the century and has since been engaged in that line of work for the past thirty-four years. He owns the largest machine shop on the Island which is located in Noumea [*sic*]. Today, I visited his shop and to say the least I was amazed when I walked in. . . . We are now old friends and I have already accepted an invitation for dinner at his home next week. He has a very nice home and not a bad looking daughter I hear. He has also invited me to go deer hunting with him."[28] Sure enough that fall, Gremillion made several deer hunts with his new friend, who happened to be a police commissioner in the capital city. "I have been hunting with him on my occasions," he added. "Deer hunting out here is by far the best I have ever seen. It is common to see forty to fifty deer on one hunt."[29] The Cajun mechanic went so far as to purchase a thirty-foot boat for deep sea fishing off the island. With experiences like this, it's no wonder the Cajuns recalled such fond memories of their time on the island.

When Gremillion's unit left for the Philippines in 1945, he stayed behind to manage two million pounds of cargo at the harbor. Because of his French, he was assigned to division headquarters for special duty—to assist with cargo movement and to work with the local landowners. He received a commendation from the commanding general for this special assignment. "In all tasks assigned him, Lt. Gremillion rendered fine service," the citation included. "Largely because of his fluent command of French and his tact in all contacts, the Division's relations with the local people have been friendly and satisfactory. I commend him for his attention to duty and manner of performance."[30]

On the way to the Battle of Leyte Gulf near the Philippines in the fall of 1944, Mike Trahan's ship stopped in New Caledonia to receive orders. His captain knew that he spoke French, so he called on him to interpret with the locals once then got ashore. Trahan related this story many decades later to his grandson in an interview at a family gathering: "The captain said, 'Frenchie, I need for you to come with me to New Caledonia to get our orders to go to Leyte. You must understand that you will have to do all the talking.'" The ensign and his captain went ashore and obtained the information by translation from the locals. Then the island spokesman invited them, in French, to partake in some ice cream, made with goat milk. "It was good" Trahan recalled. "It was the first time and the last time I ever ate that. The captain said, 'That was good goat ice cream,' and we started laughing. But when we got to Leyte, we wasn't laughing any more. That was one of the worst invasions that we had went through."[31]

That Cajun Lingo

With so many service members moving about freely at ports and islands throughout the Pacific, Cajun soldiers inevitably ran into other boys from home. When these chance meetings occurred, the Cajuns instinctively jumped right into their native French language to speak to each other. Sometimes they learned of the whereabouts of their friends from letter chains or church bulletins from back home. Most of the time, these run-ins with old friends or classmates were random. What is more, whether someone was a native of south Louisiana didn't matter to the Cajun GIs; if they heard people talking in French, they flocked to them. The sound of a French dialect was like music to their ears. "Seldom a week passes that my ear doesn't pick up a few phrases (welcome ones, too) of that 'Bayou French,'" wrote a Cajun serviceman stationed on New Guinea.[32] Whether sailing at sea or enjoying some rest and relaxation at a safe port of call, Cajuns found every opportunity to express their cultural identity, uniting an entire generation, and to share it with others.

Vernon Sonnier wrote a series of letters to his family that appeared in a collection of wartime stories titled *Letters Home*, published in 1944. On a ship headed across the Pacific to New Zealand, Sonnier overheard a strange-sounding French dialect. "They were Frenchmen alright," he wrote, "but of Canadian parentage and their homes were around about Maine. . . . While I was speaking to the above mentioned 'Canucks' as they're called, someone next to me asked what I was speaking, and being it was asked in English, I listened and heard one of the Canucks say, 'He's from Louisiana, that's real French he's speaking.' Well I was flattered but I do remember your saying on a number of occasions that our French at home was nearer to correct French than were any of the dialects spoken in any other locality around part of the state. You further stated that when spoken fluently it was a more beautiful language than Parisian French, to which I agree."[33]

In October 1943, Sonnier reported in *L'Echo du Teche* that he was stationed near three Breaux Bridge boys—Joe Huval, Percy Hebert, and Kerney Broussard—who were cooks at the Regimental Command Post, likely on New Caledonia or New Georgia. "We spoke nothing but French," he said, "but strangely enough, no one commented; they had become accustomed to hearing us talk French among ourselves. From all I can see and hear, our Cajun boys from south Louisiana have a nice record as soldiers."[34] Sonnier clearly understood and appreciated his rich French heritage. His father wrote a short foreword in *Letters Home* that suggests an appreciation for and knowledge of the family's Acadian roots: "Vernon, on the paternal side, is a descendant of those brave Acadians who suffered exile and persecution rather than give up their faith. . . . I was about 18 years of age before I could speak a word of English," wrote his father, "speaking only French. All of my children, seven sons, speak good French and are extremely proud of it."[35]

Jonas Perrin, from a small community south of Erath, was a gunner on the USS *Reno*. He, too, spoke only French as a youngster. Perrin recalled his first day of school under the newly implemented English-only educational system in Louisiana of the early 1920s: "The first day I peed in my pants because I didn't know how to ask the teacher to go to the bathroom because I couldn't speak English." When his older brother died of a ruptured appendix, the younger Perrin was forced to take on more responsibilities. He realized quickly that learning to speak good English was important to his family. Even though nearly everyone in his rural community spoke French as their first language, the age of progress and industrialization in the 1930s (primarily due to oil and gas development) rapidly Americanized the Cajun people of lower Vermilion Parish. Perrin's mother was a Broussard, and a direct descendant of Joseph Broussard dit Beausoleil, the legendary Acadian patriot. Perrin acknowledged that his parents knew of their Acadian roots and shared that history with their children. "We knew where we came from, that's about all. We came from Canada. The queen of England had expropriated us all."[36] When he came of age to join the military during World War II, he signed up with the navy. In Hawaii, he ran into a number of local boys. He said the impulse to speak French with other Cajuns was automatic, especially being so far away from home for so long. While cruising the Pacific, he discovered two other francophone shipmates from Maine who spoke a similar French dialect to his. The trio became friends and spoke French whenever they could.

"I was glad to see the boys," wrote Lester Trosclair about meeting up with old friends at port. "When we Cajuns get together, we just forget that we can speak English."[37] From New Guinea, J. A. "Blackie" Arceneaux wrote that he had met up with another SLI alum, L. D. Bernard, from the town of Broussard. "We certainly were surprised to see each other," he said. "As usual, when two Cajuns meet, they have to speak French over a cup of coffee. We celebrated our meeting by having a drink; at least a bottle or two of [Japanese] beer. Not so hot, but it was beer."[38] Clayton Badeaux from Breaux

Bridge wrote from the South Pacific that he met up with Joe Theriot on the street. "We went out and had a very good time together, talking in the good old French lingo upon the good times we used to have back home," he said.[39]

Ervin LeBlanc had a similar run-in with hometown friend Burton Angelle somewhere in the Pacific. "I have met quite a few of the boys from back home," he said. "Wherever we meet, you hear the Creole French all over the place and everybody staring at us and wondering what's going on."[40] Raymond Zeringue who served on the USS *Idaho* ran into Burton Angelle as well, along with Buddy LeBlanc and Mitchell Trahan—all from St. Martin Parish: "I met a couple of French soldiers the other day and I never saw anybody more cheerful, especially when I addressed them in their own native tongue."[41] Harry Bonin teamed up with J. S. "Puts" Angelle in Australia. They sailed across the Pacific together and discovered they were both from south Louisiana. "And then from there on the good old Cajun French just flew," Bonin wrote.[42] When Anthony Roberts met up with six local boys somewhere in the Pacific, he said that local French language "really flew fast and furious for a while."[43] Charles Perilloux wrote a letter to his wife about a large gathering of boys from Lafayette Parish somewhere in the Philippines. They had lunch together and drank cold beer. "It was nice to be with a good bunch of good ole 'cajuns' from home and to hear the racket of French speaking once more. . . . Truly this was one of the most wonderful picnics that any of us had had in quite some time."[44]

Ovide Lancon, another French-speaking Cajun in the navy who was raised on a plantation in Iberia Parish near the town of Lydia, had a similar experience onboard his ship, the USS *Ranger*. One of his shipmates was from Rayne and the two often talked in their native Cajun French language: "You just had that urge, all your life you spoke French, then first thing you know, you go where nobody speaks French, so you kind of missed it, and whenever you heard somebody speak French, you wanted to speak French." Lancon came from a family of twelve children, and he did not know a word of English until he went to school in the first grade. "To start school, you had to speak English; you could not speak French," he recalled. He said his older siblings, who were the first to learn English, helped teach it to the younger ones. But it wasn't the proper English spoken today; it was a mixture of whatever words they could pull together from both languages. He was reared during a major transition period when all young Cajuns across the state experienced indoctrination into the English language. "Well, you didn't want to be left out, so you joined in the crowd," he said. Interestingly, he said that the young people of his generation identified with being Cajun, but not so much their parents. "I think they didn't realize they was Cajun."[45]

The Cajuns who traveled to and served in the Pacific found every opportunity available to use common traits learned in their upbringing, including speaking their native language. These young service members, who had been ridiculed for speaking French growing up, made a connection with other Cajuns and other francophone people in the Pacific theater. As in other campaigns around the world, military commanders soon discovered the value of these Cajuns as interpreters and as skilled backwoodsmen who could handle their own in the dense tropical jungle environment. The experience in the Pacific, far removed from their close-knit communities on the bayou, demonstrated to these young Cajuns that no matter where they went, their French language and culture would follow and aid them, even in the jungles halfway around the world.

CHAPTER 5

FORGING AN IDENTITY

"From my recent experiences you can understand why I'm more than just proud to be called a Cajun."

—Harold Pastor, France, 1944

Prior to World War II, the term "Cajun" often carried with it a negative undertone. The prevailing thought at the time stereotyped Cajun people as an uneducated underclass, determined to maintain their easy-going rural way of life, regardless of the rapid socioeconomic changes unfolding around them. Few Cajuns interviewed for or represented in this study, however, fit that description. While a large segment of Cajuns of the World War II generation did not graduate from high school, many of them did, and several attended college prior to the war. The vast majority spoke French *and* English—although individual levels of English proficiency (by modern standards) would have varied depending on where they lived and other factors. They volunteered for the military in droves. And while they upheld traditional American values and longed to be a part of the American experience, they also actively pursued their own group identity formation and maintenance, all while wearing the uniform. Yet most writers of the time, and even modern scholars, would agree that the negative ascription and social stigma attached to Cajun people at the end of the nineteenth century persisted in the 1940s and well into the post-war era. Despite whatever misgivings the Cajuns who served in the war may have had about their perceived cultural burdens, their experiences overseas, especially in French-speaking regions, changed their perspective. The worldly travels of thousands of Cajuns initiated a powerful final blow to their geographical and social isolation, and they came to realize and embrace the value of their distinct cultural differences. In the process, they forged a new identity, one that bore a striking resemblance to the modern Cajun culture celebrated the world over for its rich heritage.

Beyond Bayou Country

The vast majority of Cajuns who joined the war effort had never traveled far beyond their small communities. Some attended college in Baton Rouge and Lafayette; a few had ventured to other parts of the state with the Civilian Conservation Corps as teenagers during the Great Depression. A select group of National Guardsmen and early volunteers did participate in the Louisiana Maneuvers near Alexandria prior to the country's entry into the war. Within a year or two of the Pearl Harbor attack, however, an entire generation of Cajuns—several thousand—left the Bayou Country for parts unknown. These young adults—on average between the ages of seventeen and twenty-one—who grew up speaking French as their first language had never been among different cultures outside of their own enclaves. Encounters with new people and new places across the United States and abroad opened their eyes to a world completely different from their own—and yet, oddly familiar in some ways. The war broadened their horizons and educated them about different customs, lifestyles, and geography. Their English improved; some refined their French dialect and others even learned new languages. For example, Ned Guidroz, a tank driver from Lafayette, spent almost three years overseas and served as a French interpreter for his unit during the Mediterranean Campaign: "When I came back, I could speak French, Italian, Arabic, and a little bit of English," he said years later.[1] This worldly experience made them realize the significance of their own culture and the benefits of growing up Cajun.

Before joining the Women's Army Corps, Houma native Katharine Daspit had never seen snow or mountains or frozen rivers: "Believe me I have been discovering America," she wrote with enthusiasm. "The things that I have seen in just these last few days have brought home to me just what a wonderful land this is."[2] In two years, the army sent her to four different states. Harry Periou from St. Martinville wrote his sister with delight from the Blue Ridge Mountains in Maryland: "You should see this place! *C'est un paradis terrestre*!"[3] James Melancon, writing from officer training school, said "I have been here for a little over a month and I have learned quite a few things of value, not only from the school itself, but from merely associating and studying with men from practically all over the U.S., including the Philippines and Puerto Ricans; men who, like myself, have had at least a year or more of training behind them, and the exchange of ideas is very interesting."[4]

Traveling abroad through military service gave the Cajun GIs a real-world education. "When you left home for the war," Benny Granger from Loreauville said, "in ninety days, you were a man."[5] From Montana, J. C. Broussard wrote to his former teacher: "I have already realized some benefit [of traveling from home]; for now, I am no longer a student of classroom geography, but one of the geography of travel."[6] Through military schools and training, these Cajuns acquired all sorts of new skills: radio operation, mechanics, supply logistics, to name a few. The army sent George Champagne to the Harvard College of Astronomy for navigation courses. He wrote, "I have attended a few schools and feel that perhaps in time the Army will make an educated man of me."[7] Hewitt Theriot, a pint-sized Cajun from lower Terrebonne Parish, barely made the height and weight requirements to be a naval officer. He spent several weeks in Boston training in communications at Harvard University, where he struggled with his speech. "I was handicapped because of my accent," he said.[8] In spite of his shortcomings, Theriot became second in command to the fleet leader of a Landing Craft Infantry (LCI) flotilla that participated in the invasion of Peleliu in the Pacific in 1944.

Notwithstanding their worldly travels, these young Cajuns came to appreciate more—not less—of their cultural distinctiveness. Tom Ducrest, writing from Ireland, said that the country, although nice in its own way, "will never be like home, and the people will never be anything like the Cajun."[9] Jerome Domengeaux described the beautiful hula girls he encountered in Hawaii, but wrote, "As yet, I'm unable to find beauty of the feminine type that can cope with our own Cajun Belles."[10] For two years, he bounced around from one island in the Pacific to the next, noting that "it's an opportunity for countless experiences and when I get back to my dear old Cajun Country it'll take six months to relate all I've seen and done."[11] While in England, John Marchand compared his kind to the introverted English people: "They are quiet and reserved and not hasty to become friendly which are certainly not traits of the Louisiana Frenchman, who is nearly always ready to invite you in to have a cup of coffee with him."[12] Harold Durio wrote about his ability to communicate with people from France: "Being of French descent and able to speak the language has been a great help to me. Rattling away in French reminds me of the good old days in Breaux Bridge. I never realized then that being a Frenchman could mean so much to me in so short a period of time."[13]

Serving with other Americans—in training camps, on foreign soil, or sailing the open seas—Cajun soldiers greatly improved their English and began speaking more of it. For a generation that discovered early on the importance of speaking English (often forcibly in early primary school), the constant associating and communicating with English-speaking people during wartime was a tremendous benefit to them, especially for those few who never learned English at all. When he left the farm in lower Vermilion Parish for the navy in 1943, Willis Granger, who was twenty-one-years-old, could not speak a word of English. "I never went to school, not a day," he said in 2019.[14] While in basic training in California, he simply mimicked other recruits, so as not to call attention to himself. "I see the other one do it, I do it."[15] By the time he completed basic training and went off to sea, he could at least carry on a conversation in English. Granger kept a low profile, until the invasion of southern France, when he was called upon to serve as an interpreter between his commanders and officers of the French Navy.

One Cajun National Guardsman who spoke only French before the war desperately wanted to get reassigned to a new outfit because, "I knew if I went back with the fellows from home, I would never learn English," he told the local newspaper in 1945.[16] Staff Sergeant Don Marx, head cook for a mess hall in England and later France, talked to wartime reporters about his kitchen crew from south Louisiana who learned English in the military. "Most of these men are Cajun French," he said, "and hardly any of them could speak English when they enlisted. Now, most of them speak it well."[17]

For some, especially those sailors who remained at sea for months or years, the opportunities to speak to other francophones or share in face-to-face cultural exchange were few and far between. Navy man J. S. Angelle, writing from Australia in 1943, recognized the potential loss of his cultural ways through extended overseas deployment. "According to *L'Echo du Teche* the boys from home are scattered just about all over the world," he wrote. "I've seen more of the world than I ever dreamed of seeing. . . . I better run into somebody from back home quickly before I forget my French completely. I thought that guys that went away and when they came back, they had forgotten their French were putting on, but unless you have someone to speak to, you forget most of it."[18] While stationed in California, Elmo Hebert met a priest from France. "I surely enjoy speaking French," he wrote. "If it wouldn't be for [the priest], I would have to speak to myself."[19] Cecil Guidry, serving on the West Coast, concurred. "I have been stationed here for six

France
October 9, 1944

Dear Pres. Fletcher,

A copy of the "Vermillion" came in today and, believe you me, it was plenty welcome. Since leaving the States my APO has changed constantly, and I did not notify you because I realized that as I moved toward the front it would continue changing.

As Ordnance Liaison Officer I have been able to see very much of France and my "Cajun" French has been very handy; in fact, my French is more correct than most of the dialects I heard in Normandy and Brittany. You have to actually hear these people to realize how well Mrs. Zeigler and the other people of Lafayette speak French. Of mayble I am just prejudiced in favor of S.L.I.

In Paris you hear dozens of dialects. Some are good, some bad--all of them are "flowered" with colloquial terms I have never heard before.

I have never in my life seen so many beautiful girls, hairdresses, complexions, window displays, and fine clothes as they have in Paris. Every soldier is a king there and the G. I.'s love it.

Please note the new APO--and I will be waiting patiently and hopefully for the new Vermillion.

Very sincerely,

T. D. Doiron

Lt. Thomas D. Doiron
847th Ord. Depot Co.
APO #574, c/o Postmaster
New York, N. Y.

Thomas Doiron letter, 1944, Joel Fletcher Papers, UL Lafayette Special Collections

months, and it's about time to change," he said. "There are so many English-speaking fellows here that you become used to speaking only English. Don't mistake me, however; I haven't forgotten how to speak French."[20] Serving in the Pacific, James Cormier hoped to run into his Cajun buddies from back home. "I read in *L'Echo* about some of the Breaux Bridge boys here in Hawaii," he said. "I sure wish I had the good fortune to run into some. I'm anxious for a chance to speak French."[21]

Those who had the fortunate opportunity to speak to other French people around the world had no problem blending in, even though the dialect may have been a bit different from their own. Lazard Landry, a member of a military police company in France, wrote about the French people: "They think a great deal of us and because we can speak their language and understand them, we often get a great deal of helpful information from them, and they are glad to oblige."[22] James Begnaud added, "Only one who understands their language can fully appreciate their suffering."[23] Cajun soldiers discovered that the French taught to them as kids and spoken in their community was not inferior or useless. It was, in fact, a version of an ancient dialect still used in the rural areas of the French-speaking world, especially in Normandy and Brittany in northwestern France.

In 1947, veteran and newspaper man Alden Sonnier, older brother of Vernon Sonnier and future cultural advocate, wrote a piece that addressed the comparison of the Cajun French dialect to that heard in parts of France. He spent several months in France during the war as a captain in the Air Transport Command and visited several areas of the country. As a French-speaking Cajun, he had plenty of opportunity to try his brand of French on the locals. He talked with policemen, French soldiers, storekeepers, domestic workers, bartenders, waiters, government officers, printers, business men, and many other classes of people. "At no time did we have any difficulty whatsoever in making ourselves understood," he acknowledged, "and at no time did we have any difficulty in understanding these people. We know many other Louisiana lads who will tell the same story. In fact, on more than one occasion we were told that our brand of French is an old and dignified form of French, which was referred to as 'le Français poli,' or 'the polite French.' This is the natural result of this country having been separated for so long from direct contact with France and the influence this contact would have had to keep the language changing and up to date. . . . Also, there are some French accents and dialects that are difficult for the beginner to comprehend, just as a Southerner might have difficulty in getting on to the New England twang or the close-clipped jargon of an East Side New Yorker."[24]

The Cajun accent delighted locals, who took great pleasure in welcoming the soldiers into their villages and homes. It's no wonder so many wrote about befriending other francophones and being frequent guests at their homes. Some Cajun GIs developed lifelong relationships with these families. These experiences made them appreciate their Cajun French in its true, spoken form. "We all too often think of linguistic diversity—language difference—as a problem," said Barry Ancelet, noted expert on the Cajun French language. "It's not a problem; it's an opportunity. It's a treasure."[25]

Wiltz Segura, a Cajun from New Iberia, recognized the relevance of his French throughout his worldly tours during and after the war. His storied military career began with the famed Chennault "Flying Tigers" in the China-Burma-India theater in 1943. "[Knowing French] was a tremendous asset to me after I got in the military and got assigned to foreign countries because if you could speak French, you could communicate with many of the educated people in foreign countries," he said. "France, at one time, was the seat of education for foreigners who wanted to educate their children away from their own country. I was in China in World War II, and [it] was very difficult to learn to speak that language. But most of the educated Chinese could speak French because they had been sent to France to school and had learned the language. So, it was very important, especially in a combat situation where you may be thrown in with some people that you can't understand, and you need to communicate with them."[26]

Jefferson DeBlanc, another legendary pilot from south Louisiana who flew combat missions over the South Pacific, noticed how language diversity opened doors for him. "Nouméa reminded me of Louisiana," he wrote in his autobiography. "I felt at home on its streets. The voices speaking French were pleasant sounds as I could understand it all and read the street signs. . . . It's funny how the thin veneer of society's culture breaks down among strangers when one speaks the language."[27]

Through these travels and exposure to other people, the Cajun soldiers of World War II became more worldly, more culturally aware, and yet very much in tune with their own group identity.

Cajun Pride

As Cajuns were once again "scattered to the wind," this time in service to their country, their attitudes about their homeland and self-image reached new heights. They celebrated their heritage, a sentiment practically unthinkable for a generation that suffered such discrimination in their youth. "Cajun" suddenly had a positive ring to it. With this outpouring of self-worth, the Cajuns of World War II walked with heads held high. They came to view the "Cajun/Frenchie" title as a sign of respect and admiration. As they traveled to new places and ran into other Cajuns here and there, they embraced their common cultural traits. Harris Hebert with the Seabees wrote from New Caledonia: "Most of the few people on the island are French and really appreciate having someone talk to them in French. Only 4 boys in our outfit are able to do so. . . . By the way, the only name I'm known by in this outfit is Cajun, believe it or not."[28] Hebert mentioned that two other boys from Abbeville had arrived on the island. They all shared copies of the *Abbeville Meridional* that traveled thousands of miles to reach them. "Keep the Meridional coming," he pleaded, "for every issue is greatly appreciated." He signed the letter "Just another one of the many 'Frenchies' in the service."[29] Frank Summers from Abbeville, who served as a naval officer in the Pacific and was assigned to supervise fifty Indigenous laborers in New Guinea wrote, "I still love the Cajun country."[30]

This newfound affirmation of their identity stands out in the letters of and interviews with those who served; it is particularly pervasive with those who had the opportunity to use their language skills in some capacity.

Cajun Queen *B-29, cir. 1945,*
courtesy of Shane K. Bernard Collection, New Iberia, LA

"From my recent experiences you can understand why I'm more than just proud to be called a Cajun," wrote Harold Pastor from Lafayette, who served as a weather radio operator in France. "My French is still rusty after staying away from the dialect in the past 2 ½ years of service, but it's amazing how the tongue is returning. As baffled Americans would say who do not understand the French tongue. I'm just about in my own backyard except my own dear relatives aren't around to make it all the nicer."[31] From North Africa, Andrew Angelle wrote, "I ask the French people questions in English . . . then before leaving them I start rattling my old Cajun stuff, and they just stand there gapping as if to say, well [how is] it impossible that I can talk French so well. . . . Let me tell you that I am prouder of my French now than I have ever been."[32] Writing to SLI President Fletcher from the Marianas Islands in the Pacific, Jim Brignac stated, "I'm another 'cajun' as you can tell by my name. Proud of it too."[33]

Growing up in south Louisiana, Roy Armentor had been ridiculed for speaking French in school, yet he found retribution in the ranks of the elite Special Forces assigned to work with the French underground behind enemy lines. "We were looked down on because we were from Louisiana; [others] thought they were better than us," he explained. "But I was always proud of being able to speak French."[34] Robert LeBlanc, who's legendary military career began with his assignment to the OSS in France, felt the same way. At the start of the war, Cajuns were thought to be disadvantaged because of their language and culture. As LeBlanc explained, it didn't take long for those attitudes to change:

> I feel that the fact that we were prohibited from speaking French on the school grounds encouraged us to speak it off the school ground, maintain the language and maintain the ability to speak to our grandparents—who many of them could not speak English—enable us, when we were overseas, whether you were in French Indochina, whether you were in France, or wherever the French language was spoken, was to be of extreme value to the United States of America, the ability to speak a foreign language, which was not available in the general Army Air Force or Navy personnel who were available at the start of the war. . . . Even in the drafting of the draftees, the only draftees that could speak French were primarily those, not only, but the majority of them who could speak French came from Louisiana or came from Maine, New Hampshire, in that area up there that's close

> to the Canadian border. So, it was a valuable treasure that the United States had in the linguistic ability of these native Americans who had been born here, but who had followed the culture and followed the language of their ancestors, to be able to provide this technical expertise through the Army commands throughout the world. . . . So, we began to feel that we were not the back-hindquarter boys, that our self-evaluation of ourselves came to the point that we thought we were as good as anybody else, and a lot of the Louisiana boys who went into the service developed the attitude that they could do anything anybody else could do, and they proved it. And that's basically what I gained throughout my tour on active duty in World War II, that when a Frenchman put his mind to doing something, a Cajun Frenchman, he gets it accomplished.[35]

Throughout their collective war experience, Cajuns sought others with whom to share in cultural exchange. In countless stories, when Cajun service members ran into others from south Louisiana, they instinctively reverted back to speaking their native language—a sure sign of actively maintaining that illusive ethnic boundary. Another Cajun stationed in California met a soldier from Abbeville and wrote, "How we went to town with our Cajun lingo."[36] Joseph Guidry wrote about the benefits of having another local boy in his squadron: "It surely is nice because at every opportunity we get together and dish out our good old Cajun talk."[37] Dalton Usie from Henderson was stationed in India. "I am here with several boys from Louisiana," he wrote. "We enjoy Cajun talk every time we meet. I have been very busy, but not too busy to go to church every Sunday."[38] David Pellerin met three "Frenchmen" while stationed in California. "They are strictly Cajuns and very fine ones," he wrote. "We always stick together, and talk about the nice times we had when we were home. When we're out in the field we sleep in the same tents, and believe me, three Cajuns in the same tent can make plenty noise! Probably we'll be separated if this keeps up."[39] Pharmacist's Mate Carl Guillory ran into an old friend from Mamou while aboard a repair ship: "We had a long Cajun talk and I found out he could cook rice and make sauce piquant, so I guess you know I insisted that he prepare this old favorite dish of mine—and did I eat."[40] While in South Carolina, James Orgeron noted that he and former school chum Buddy Henry from Rayne were stationed together. "We are the only 'Cajuns' on this post but we get along just as though we were back in cajun country."[41]

The Cajun people have always been highly adaptive. This generation discovered that they had the skills, knowledge, and attributes to meet the challenges and transitions brought on by the Second World War. Their expertise in linguistics in particular became known throughout the country and throughout the military. It set them apart. As Lee Bernard, a tank driver in France, stated (in French) in Pat Mire's film, *Mon Cher Camarade*: "I don't think there was a day that officers didn't come get me to speak French. Oh, I'm still proud of my French!"[42] No longer seen as the marginalized country folk from the backwoods who spoke a corrupt patois, Cajun soldiers gladly accepted the role as specialists—the "Frenchies"—and welcomed every opportunity to perpetuate the habits that came naturally to them. They came home from the war invigorated, confident, and eager to get on with the rapidly advancing American post-war society and industrial economy. "While we still were Cajuns in our heart, we just got it in with the beat of the world and it carried on from there," said Benny Granger, veteran of the US Merchant Marines.[43] The Second World War finally legitimized the Cajuns in the eyes of their skeptics—and their own.

Seeds Planted

Cajun soldiers, like the millions of other American veterans who returned home after the war, didn't waste much time getting on with their new post-war lives. Within a year or two, many got married and started having children. Some moved back to country life and continued the traditional farming of their ancestors, which had, in short order, evolved to a highly mechanized vocation. The majority, however, moved to neighborhoods in urban centers and eventually found well-paying blue-collar jobs in various industrial sectors, especially the burgeoning oil and gas industry. Many of the returning Cajuns participated in and benefited from the GI Bill, which provided free college tuition and vocational training, along with low-interest home loans, to all veterans. They went about their normal lives, working full-time and raising young families, and when the opportunity arose, they took part in cultural events, festivals, and traditions that continued their communal bond, like family gatherings, cooking, church, and Cajun music. They still spoke French among themselves and with their spouses (those who could speak French), but they did not, for the most part, raise their children to speak French as a first language. The reasons for this are complicated and varied among individual families and communities, with socioeconomics and social acceptance playing a dominant role. That fateful decision among a broad spectrum of the World War II generation to raise their children in a predominately English-speaking home and community would have far-reaching generational consequences.

Cajun music gave the returning GIs an important outlet for cultural expression. The veterans immersed themselves in their own culture once home; they wanted to hear Cajun music sung in French and played with traditional instruments. Although the style of music had been infused with western sounds and English lyrics from the 1930s forward, Cajun musicians returned to the traditional accordion- and fiddle-based French songs to tap into the renewed interest of the young adult audience.[44] Musicians like the Hackberry Ramblers, Happy Fats, Harry Choates (who, in 1947, recorded the mega hit "Jole Blon"), Julius "Papa Cairo" Lamperez (who was an interpreter in France during the war), and Iry LeJeune made records and did live appearances on radio and on stage with set lists that featured traditional French songs and sounds.[45] As Barry Ancelet noted, in the early post-war years, "dance halls throughout South Louisiana once again blared the familiar sounds of home-made Cajun music."[46]

Festivals where Cajun music took center stage offered opportunities for cultural expression for returning veterans and musical performers. Beginning in 1946, the annual Crowley International Rice Festival added a "Cajun Music Jamboree" that showcased several Cajun-style bands on stage. Tens of thousands of attendees were expected for the two-day event. One of the highlights included an old-fashioned "fais do-do" contest of dance and song—featuring the traditional fiddle, accordion, and triangle—a throwback to the Acadian balls of past generations. Festivalgoers also got to experience Cajun storytelling and cooking—popular folkways that would have been discounted just a decade before.[47]

This interest in Cajun music and all things Acadian was in part influenced by a culture-wide obsession with Longfellow's epic story of Evangeline. In 1947, events across southwestern Louisiana celebrated the centennial of the famous poem and featured performances of genuine Acadian traditions of folk music, customs, dress, and dance. Throughout the late 1940s, these types of cultural events gave locals an opportunity to talk about their Acadian/Cajun heritage and to remind those in the region of their common threads and shared history.[48] "Hidden in the hearts of some there is that tend [*sic*] to slide away into another culture into almost another way of life, to lose our 'Cajun' identity and become just Americans of French descent," the *Abbeville Meridional* opined. "As hard as it is to believe, there are those who are ashamed of the fact that they are descendants of Evangeline, Gabriel and their fellow journeyers. . . . [W]e should strive to retain our identity, to remain Acadians, or Cajuns as some would call us—because our Acadian heritage is one of the most priceless that exist."[49]

A growing post-war trend to glorify the nostalgia of a previous era pervaded in film and media. As before the war, these outside influencers still viewed Cajuns as a peculiar group with exotic habits, still living in picturesque though noncivilized landscapes. The critically acclaimed 1948 documentary, *Louisiana Story*, directed by Robert Flaherty, brought much attention to the region's unique people and environs. The film, funded by Standard Oil of New Jersey, depicts how a French-speaking Cajun family, living in the preverbal moss-draped, alligator-infested swamp (the marshes near Avery Island), came to experience modernity through the lens of oil exploration and production operations in their watery "backyard." While there still remained some small pockets of Cajuns who lived year-round in these coastal wetland communities in the late 1940s, the region and the broader Cajun population had already started its rapid transition to a modern, industrial economy. Cajun war veterans did spend considerable time in the marshes and swamps, but primarily for recreational purposes and some commercial fishing.

Travel writers, still intrigued by the Cajuns in the post-war years, noted the many pleasantries of the people and their traditional way of life. "The 'Cajuns,' thoroughly Americanized, still form a distinctive element of the population, retaining many of their customs, much of their language and music," wrote one northern journalist. "They are a genial folk, proud of their heritage and apparently unaffected by good-natured imitations of them by later settlers for the entertainment of visitors."[50] A travel series on Louisiana featured in the *Boston Globe* "captured all the beauty and romance of the bayous and the Cajuns who live there."[51] The area of Vermilion Parish, another outsider admired, "is the friendliest community one can imagine. . . . These are the 'Cajuns,' though we must smile when we use that term. They call themselves 'Cajuns' and like for their friends to do so. They speak deliberately, with soft, musical tones."[52]

The practice of speaking Cajun French persisted among the returning veterans and of course the older generation. Yet as modernity took its course during the initial post-war years, fewer parents taught their children French. A local reporter spotted this disturbing trend while at a sporting event in August 1945: "We personally feel it is a shame that more French-speaking mothers and fathers do not teach their children the French language. And the only way to perpetuate the speaking of French in this great country of French descent is to talk and teach French to the youngsters as they are growing up. So many of our children with French-speaking parents cannot speak the language at all. The French influence is distinctive of this section and we should not let the great language fall to the wayside as a means of communication. We are strictly in favor of French classes in our public schools. Every child should know two spoken languages."[53] Some returning war veterans would have agreed with that observation, but the collective society made the conscious decision to prioritize the teaching and speaking of English in the home and in the community, much to the detriment of their own native tongue.

Sam Broussard saw this coming even before his return home. In a wartime letter, written shortly after his arrival in France in 1944, Broussard made some rather poignant remarks about the future of the French language in his native Louisiana. "My French gets plenty of practice and people say it is good, but that's to make me feel good," he wrote. "Have improved very much and getting finer points of the beautiful French language. It's just too bad the good people of La had to let a beautiful language as that slip between their fingers. It was just a lack of study and proper application. It is like my prayers in French. I would say regularly but didn't know what I was saying. Am afraid Louisiana is getting completely away from it."[54]

In retrospect, several veterans interviewed over the years spoke about the challenges of teaching French to their kids in the late 1940s and early 1950s. Otis Courville's kids learned it, but only because he took the time to teach them while on weekend getaways at the fishing camp in the Atchafalaya Basin near home. "When we'd leave and take off from here at Catahoula to go to [Lake] Fausse Pointe up there, an hour and something drive in a boat, when we'd get in a boat, no more English talking until we come back [on Sundays]." Jonas Perrin, from lower Vermilion Parish, taught his kids as well. "They just learn it. And some people, they didn't want the kids to speak French. We weren't like that."[55] Nevertheless, the vast majority of returning Cajun veterans, especially those who lived in urban environments, chose not to raise their children in a French-speaking home.

Why? The answer to that question has plagued scholars, teachers, cultural advocates, and Cajun society in general for more than half a century.

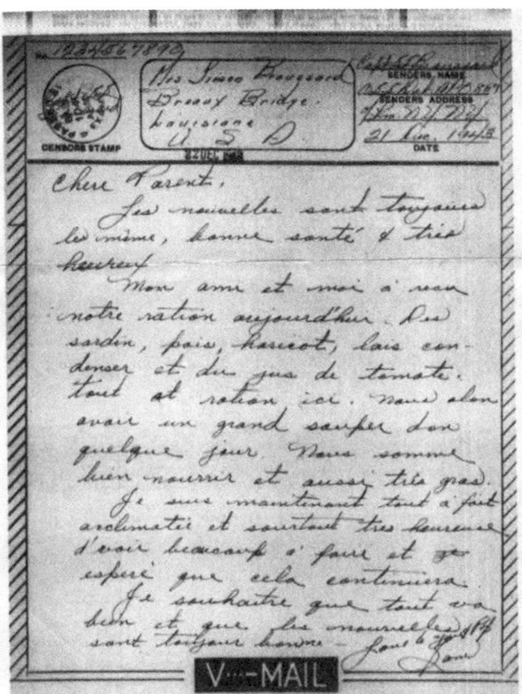

CENSORS STAMP

Mrs Simon Broussard
Breaux Bridge.
Louisiana
U S A.

SENDERS NAME

SENDERS ADDRESS

21 Nov. 1943
DATE

Chere Parent,
Les nouvelles sont toujours les même, bonne santé & très heureux.
Mon ami et moi a reçu notre ration aujourd'hui. Des sardin, pois, haricot, lais condenser et du jus de tomate. tout et ration ici. Nous alon avoir un grand souper dan quelque jour. Nous somme bien nourrir et aussi très gras.
Je suis maintenant tout à fait acclimatée et surtout très heureuse d'avoir beaucoup à faire et je esperé que cela continuera.
Je souhaite que tout va bien et que les nouvelles sont toujours bonne –
Sam

V-MAIL

V-mail (or "Victory mail") from Sam Broussard written in French, cir. 1943-1944, courtesy of the Broussard family

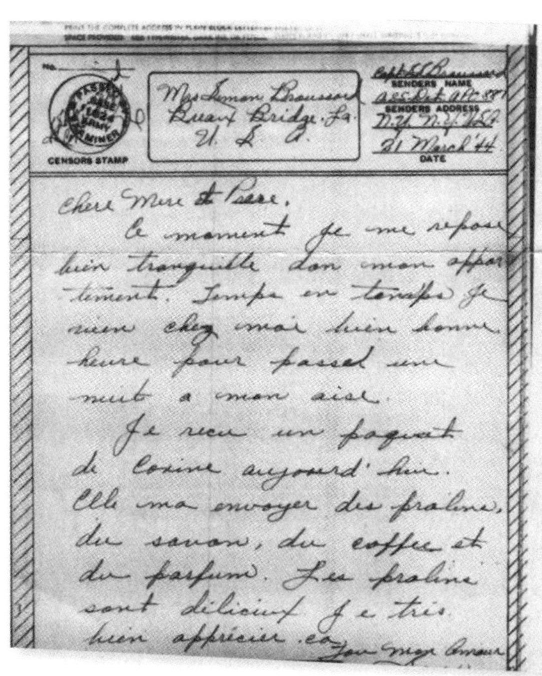

CENSORS STAMP

Mrs Simon Broussard
Breaux Bridge. La.
U. S. A.

SENDERS NAME

SENDERS ADDRESS

21 March '44
DATE

Chere Mere et Pere,
Ce moment je me repose bien tranquille dan mon appartement. Temps en temps je suis chez moi bien bonne heure pour passer une nuit a mon aise.
Je recu un paquet de Cosine aujourd'hui. Elle ma envoyer des praline, du savon, du coffee et du parfum. Les praline sont délicieux. Je très bien apprécier .ça
Tou mon amour

The reasons are multifaceted and complex. Those veterans, many of whom remembered the struggles and sacrifices of their families during the Depression and war, returned home in the wake of a growing post-war economic boom and unprecedented prosperity. Parents wanted their children to have a better opportunity in a modern, educated, American society. Speaking and writing English well was seen as a prerequisite for that. It was key to acceptance in the rapidly advancing, upwardly mobile middle class. "The French-speaking people wanted to make progress," navy veteran Harry Jackson said. "Certainly, the better jobs . . . you had to know how to read and write [in English] in order to advance in the coming world."[56] With improvements in transportation, education, communication, and commercialization—all requiring proficiency in English—many parents from that great generation felt that French would not be that useful to their children. As Curney Dronet from Abbeville simply stated, "the desire for Americanization curtailed our French speakers."[57]

Of course, many did not want their kids to experience the same level of discrimination or prejudice that they had endured in school in the 1920s and 1930s. The *honte*—French for shame—and the social liability that stigmatized Cajuns earlier in life still prevailed in many circles and among many families in south Louisiana. They did not want to pass that burden onto their children, and so many parents of that generation simply abandoned French in the home.

Some Cajuns, as Pacific War veteran Chester Cheramie noted, returned from the war speaking only English. Many of them married Anglo wives, and so consequently, their children spoke only English. "I think that's where we missed the boat," Cheramie expressed.[58] Ned Arceneaux, who grew up in the country but raised his family in Lafayette, agreed: "My children, they understand but they can't carry on a conversation," he confessed decades later. "That was our mistake."[59]

Army veteran Norris Morvant and his wife Bernice, a Guillot who grew up on a plantation in Thibodaux, struggled with teaching their two boys—both born shortly after the war—French and English at the same time. "Teaching the kids French was not easy because there's so much to teach French all total," he explained. "As you can imagine, French is sort of backwards from English. So, we had to teach them how to think French at the same time as using English as a background." Even though both he and his wife grew up steeped in the language on plantations in Lafourche Parish, they gradually spoke less and less of it at home after the war with their kids and with each other. "We were using the English language more than the French. But we reserved the French language for all our contacts such as families and friends that we knew that we talked in French and all. . . . English meant that we were advancing in the world. . . . Being that the world wanted us to speak English, we felt that it wasn't necessary to talk French. So, it was kind of limited on that part." As a result, their sons only learned a modicum of their parents' native language. "We wanted them to grow up in the world as it was progressing, so that they could keep up with the world," he said. "Sometimes it was a bad decision not to speak French with them. So, we lost out on that, that's for sure."[60]

The offspring of the World War II generation, the baby boomers, learned bits of French here and there from their grandparents, out in the fields, and working as teenagers at the local stores and gas stations. Whatever French they picked up on gradually diminished as they matured. Still, their parents continued to practice their native language and promote the culture in their own ways. They spoke among themselves, often in hush tones, so as to maintain a private line of communication with their spouse. "When we wanted to say something that we didn't want the kids to know, we'd talk in French," said Lee Bernard, one of many veterans who admitted to this logical, though unfortunate, practice.[61] They listened to French programs on the radio. These included the "Cousin Dud" show, hosted on KVOL in Lafayette by the politician-salesman Dudley J. LeBlanc, a leading culture advocate of his day.[62] The KLFT radio station in Golden Meadow, with disc jockey Dudley Bernard, an interpreter during World War II, carried Cajun music and French programs to the delight of the war veterans hungry for traditional waltzes, ballads, and squeeze-box sounds. They raised their children in the Catholic Church, cooked the traditional meals, attended the festivals, danced, drank, congregated in large family gatherings, and enjoyed Sportsman's Paradise—all the customs and folkways associated with the Cajun way of the life—with joie de vivre so pronounced and celebrated in the late twentieth century.

And so, the language survived, or some version of it, as did the culture, with the building blocks to set in motion a concerted effort by various groups to preserve, perpetuate, and promote traditional Cajun customs and identity, which included the Cajun French patois. The founding of the Council for the Development of French in Louisiana in 1968, with the support from political and civic leaders behind it, fostered a renewed interest in speaking, teaching, and learning generic French. While not necessarily designed to preserve

Cajun French, the efforts of state and community leaders in the late 1960s opened the doorway for a grassroots cultural renaissance that erupted in the 1970s. Working behind the scenes to promote the French language and culture in their communities were a number of World War II veterans, including Burton Angelle, Roy Theriot, James Domengeaux, J. B. Broussard, Allen Gremillion, Robert J. Angers Jr., George Bertrand, George Francis Dupuis Sr., Alden Sonnier, and Sam Broussard, among others. "For years and years we were ashamed of our French language," wrote Sam Broussard, president of the Iberia Parish CODOFIL chapter, in 1971. "All schools tried to discourage French and get us to speak English. We are just now realizing that instead of feeling sorry for ourselves as descendants of French people we are now that much further advanced, knowing English and still have our French background. Those of us who have that knowledge feel proud of the fact."[63] The recognition of "Cajun pride" that galvanized Louisiana's newly established "Acadiana" region in the 1970s can be traced back to the Cajuns of World War II and the formation of their own group identity decades before.

Cajun culture survived the World War II experience and in some ways flourished because of it. The young men and women who traveled the high seas, walked across foreign lands, and liberated the oppressed emerged from the war years as loyal Americans *and yet* distinctly Cajun. This group did not personify the stereotypes crafted by others. Indeed, the accounts told here by the veterans themselves tell a different story. They were not handicapped, inferior, or lacking abilities because of their culture. On the contrary, they were motivated, in constant demand, and well equipped. For the first time in the groups' long history, their Cajun French language became not one of ridicule but one of need. As Robert LeBlanc, one of the last of the living legends, once said, "The world travels that we were required to do throughout World War II really called to our attention what we had here in South Louisiana was a very distinct culture from the rest of the United States and that it was something that we needed to preserve."[64]

ACADIANS OF WORLD WAR II

"Language was there and made its way, not only in peacetime, but in wartime, where it was so important to have this unit gel together and come and recognize together, because little Acadian French-speaking boys were able to go in the same uniform."

—Camille LeBlanc, Acadian WWII veteran

Not all the French-speaking people expelled from Acadie in the eighteenth century migrated to Louisiana and became Cajuns. Several thousand Acadians either remained in their native homeland or resettled there some years after the expulsion. Yet despite their geographic distances, the Cajuns and Acadians share a distinct experience during the Second World War. They collectively represented North America's largest bilingual francophone group to serve the Allied cause.[1] As such, their shared experiences before, during, and after the war were unique and deserving of a succinct historical comparison. As a minority ethnic group, reared in poor farming and fishing communities with limited access to education, the Acadians from Nova Scotia and New Brunswick were marginalized for much of the group's history.[2] Most Acadians who joined the military during the early 1940s were illiterate and could speak, at best, only broken English. Even though they made up a sizable segment of the Canadian Maritime population—between 30 and 40 percent—the Canadian government did not organize special French-speaking infantry units for overseas deployment. For those thousands of young Acadians who joined the war effort, learning English was imperative. Like the Cajuns, they too were discriminated against because of their cultural differences, especially their French dialect. But once overseas, the Acadians found value in their bilingual abilities as they could interpret on the fly, not only with the French people, but also for their monolingual Québécois comrades. In the war's aftermath, the Acadians too fostered a renewed interest in their cultural heritage and shepherded a French-language preservation movement that continued well into the twentieth century.

Despite being separated by nearly three centuries—and thousands of miles—the Acadians and Cajuns have been culturally aligned in more ways than one. Their language, folkways, and close ties to the land and Catholic religion represented common bonds among the two groups. Their French dialects were as old as their Acadian surnames and distinct among the Allied soldiers who fought in Europe during World War II. These unique cultural circumstances captured the attention of travel writers who, throughout the first half of the twentieth century, often viewed the two groups through the prism of Longfellow's epic Evangeline story. Writing in 1944, a Canadian journalist identified some of the mutual ties among the Acadians and their Cajun cousins from the Bayou Country:

> To visit these people is to find another and different, yet much the same, part of Canada tucked away in the deep south of America. . . . They are a simple living folk, and they speak a strange dialect of French. It isn't quite like that of what remains of the backwoodsy element among the Acadians of the Maritimes in Canada, but it has much in common. Anyone who understood the one would have little trouble with the other. . . . They do not speak the French of Quebec or of modern France either in the old Acadia or the Acadia of the south. Though it is difficult these days to live far from the influences of the present-day world, there are still a few of the Acadians in New Brunswick and parts of Nova Scotia who live unto themselves, and in much the same way as the Cajuns of Louisiana. . . . The happy simplicity of the lives of the peoples is their greatest bond of relationship. Others may think them under-privileged, deprived of the material benefits and advantages of our mechanical world, but they don't think themselves lacking in anything and they ask no sympathy for their lot. They are to be envied and they have some good reasons to think so.[3]

Approximately 24,000 Acadians of military age served as volunteers during World War II. Perhaps as many as 10,000 saw combat overseas. Most fought in Italy, France, Belgium, and the Netherlands. These Acadians had grown up amid the Great Depression, so joining the military was an economic choice for most. The armed services offered them a small paycheck and an opportunity for a better future after the war. "Acadians served like everyone else, and it wasn't for patriotic reasons for most of them," said Ron Cormier, who authored a series of books on the Acadians of World War II. "Most of them, at least, they admitted it, unlike other people, 'Oh, we did it for king and country.' No, they didn't do it for king and country. They didn't owe anything to England and didn't owe anything to France. They had been conquered by the British and abandoned by the French, so they didn't owe anyone anything. Most joined to get a decent salary. It was strictly for economic reasons that they joined."[4]

Cormier, a New Brunswick author, has documented the stories of the Acadians in wartime. He conducted dozens of interviews with veterans from the Maritime region and recounted their stories of hardships and heroics during the European theater. "Contrary to most of their fellow New Brunswickers, Acadians had to learn English to serve their country, which was different. . . . Maybe a quarter could speak English. The rest did not know a word of English except 'yes' or 'no.'"[5]

Cormier brothers (left to right) *Norman, André, Laurie from Moncton, New Brunswick, courtesy of Ron Cormier*

Unlike in the First World War, the Acadians did not have their own unit, but they served alongside other French-speaking brethren. They were dispersed throughout nearly every branch of the Canadian Armed Forces, and while their English was not great, they became fully bilingual by the end of the war. Some of the Acadians received training at camps in Ontario, Quebec, and New Brunswick that included bilingual recruits. Many served in units outside of the Maritime Provinces with English-speaking soldiers and officers. While the Canadian Army accommodated French-speaking soldiers among the ranks, the Royal Canadian Navy forbade the speaking of French on its bases.

The Acadians, because of their desire to learn English for upward mobility and their acceptance of Anglo culture, had an advantage over Canada's dominant French-speaking ethnic group, the Québécois. "The Acadians are a different type from Quebec French-speaking citizens," noted the *Windsor Star*. "They have had a high rate of enlistment. Some of the trends which cause trouble in Quebec are completely absent from the Acadians, who generally get along well with the English-speaking population of New Brunswick and are content to do so."[6] A political candidate in Quebec, who advocated for Québécois rights, appropriated the Acadian diaspora in order to score political points: "The dispersal of the Acadians by the British early in Canada's history was being repeated at an accelerated rate by military movements today. Under the present dispersal, Quebec youths were being sent in a body to military training camps made up exclusively of English-speaking soldiers, where they are not allowed to speak anything but English."[7]

Interestingly, the first signs of the Acadian's bilingual advantage came when the Canadian military arrived in England to prepare for the Allied invasion of Europe. Some Acadians were purposely transferred into Québécois units to assist with *English* translation among the English speakers and the francophones, who could not communicate otherwise. "That was a common thing to do when in England," noted Cyr LeBlanc, a local historian from Nova Scotia, "recognizing that a lot of the Quebec were unilingual French, not understanding of English, so it was decided, in England, that because they didn't speak English, that they needed somebody to help them translate, to help them along in England and then with the English regiments. . . . I doubt whether there was a policy, but it was something that was adapted on the fly."[8]

Acadians served in every Canadian regiment that participated in the invasion of Normandy in June 1944. Several hundred Acadians came ashore at

Juno Beach with the North Shore Regiment, the Nova Scotia Highlanders, and Le Régiment de la Chaudière from Quebec. "There were Acadians in all regiments," said Ron Cormier. "Everything was standard English in those regiments, even though in the North Shore Regiment, about a third of the soldiers were Acadians. So they came in handy when D-Day arrived, because at first [when] they landed in France, they could talk to the people. They had a similar accent to the people living in Normandy, so they'd tell them, '*N'y allez pas. Il y a une mine.*' 'Don't go there. There's a mine.' 'Don't go there. There's Germans or the Germans are hidden in the woods there.' People around those villages knew where the Germans were, so the Acadian soldiers would go to their officers or their platoon commanders, or whoever it was, and tell them, 'Okay, the Germans are there. We know that because they told us they were there.' So they came in very handy. I understand that something similar happened with the American forces that landed in France."[9]

A Canadian newspaper picked up on this unique historical circumstance: "New Brunswick and Nova Scotia have a historical link with the scene of invasion fighting in France. A large part of the population of the two provinces are descendants of the Acadians, immigrants from the ancient cities of Bayeux and Caen and other parts of Normandy."[10]

Zoel LeBlanc of Moncton, New Brunswick, volunteered for the army in April 1944. He arrived in England soon thereafter and joined the North Shore Regiment as a replacement. "I hadn't spoken much French since I had enlisted," he said in an interview. "At the training centre in Fredericton, everything was in English. There weren't too many who spoke French there but when I joined the North Shore I could speak French with others that became friends."[11] After landing in Normandy, his unit came across a French café named "LeBlanc." The guys yelled, "look ZP, it's your cousin." The café's owner came over and gave LeBlanc a large bottle of liquor and LeBlanc gave him whatever money he had in return."He was a LeBlanc like myself." The store owner invited LeBlanc and his comrades to his home as guests for a few days.[12]

Fidele Landry was an Acadian from Grande-Anse on the northern coast of New Brunswick and landed at Saint-Aubin at Juno Beach with a French-speaking company of the North Shore Regiment. "I couldn't speak English very well at the time and found it hard," he said. "I didn't understand half of what they were saying. I had asked to go with an English-Canadian unit to learn to speak English."[13] Landry was joined by Acadian Joseph LeBouthillier from Bas-Caraquet, another small town in northern New Brunswick. He oversaw ten soldiers—all English-speaking. His unit captured a small railway station near Juno Beach before running into a minefield disguised as a hay pasture. "A Frenchman came to tell us that they had been one of those who had put the mines in the field under the threat of bayonets," he said. "He had the plans of the whole minefield. . . . It was a great help."[14] Havelyn Chiasson, a radio operator, recalled his first encounter with a Frenchman near Juno Beach: "One of the first Frenchman we met, he said, '*Mon dieu, canada soldat est parler français!*' They couldn't get over it. You know, there was Canadian soldiers here, and they speak French. Isn't that something?"[15]

Alphonse Vautour of Shediac, New Brunswick, landed in Normandy as part of an armored unit with the North Shore Regiment. He drove a Bren Gun carrier, a small track-wheeled vehicle with a mounted machine gun, onto Juno Beach in the first wave on D-Day. His birthplace, famous for its lobster fishing fleet, was predominantly populated by French-speaking Acadians. The young Acadians of his generation did not speak much English before the war, but they caught on fast. By Vautour's account, they learned to be conversational in a manner of weeks. "There were about fifteen of us from Shediac," he said. "We took a train to Moncton and told them we wanted to join the army because we had no money. . . . They were from a battered area—well, mostly French. It didn't take long that I learned English enough. . . . In the North Shore Regiment, there were still a lot of French people there. It was mixed up." The regiment had both French- and English-speaking officers, and the soldiers found ways to work together considering the language gap. "The important thing was that we understood each other," he said.[16]

Charlie Muise, a native of Hubbards Point village in Yarmouth County in southwestern Nova Scotia, joined the Princess Louise Fusiliers in the early stages of the war. He served in Italy, France, and the Netherlands. He too was a poor Acadian who joined the army to make a few bucks. In 1941, he and several others hopped on a train to Halifax that stopped along the way and picked up a few dozen more young Acadians men from various villages—all headed in the same direction: the army recruit station. He spoke just enough English to get by. "I can speak French, speak English not too bad," he said in a 2022 interview. "The schools were all French. We had what they called French grammar, French reader, but you learned English also. The old people had a hard time with English, but all the young people, I mean of my time, pretty well could get by in English. They were maybe not actually the best, but they could make themself understood."[17]

Following a tour in Italy as a member of a heavy mortar combat unit, he went through France and spent a year in the Netherlands, where his French came in handy with the locals, many of whom spoke French. For a time, he was assigned to transport a recreational unit that provided music and entertainment to the troops in rear echelon areas. Muise drove the band around to perform for the troops and the locals. "Oh, the French, they thought a lot of the Canadians. Oh, God almighty, yes, they did," he said. "But I think that Holland was the most appreciative, all told, because they were the last ones—they were starving, and I was there when they had permission to come in with Allies' planes to drop food to the people in Holland."[18]

At 102 years old, Charlie Muise was the last living Acadian World War II veteran from the Yarmouth region, and he accepted that recognition with great humility and pride: "Yep, I'm the last one. I'm the last one; yes, we consider ourselves Acadians because we are Acadians."[19]

Basil LeBlanc, an Acadian from the nearby region of Argyle, served in the Canadian Army and left a memoir of his experiences. He joined the Canadian Grenadier Guards and fought in the Battle of Normandy.

Charlie Muise and Jason Theriot, Tusket, Nova Scotia, 2022

Like other francophones, he got along well with the French locals and made friends. He met a local woman in Normandy and, as he said, "in my imperfect French," asked if he could trade canned goods for some fresh eggs. He went back a second night for dinner and met the priest for a seven-course meal, including wine. He wrote, "We had never seen the likes, even in better times." After dinner, the locals broke out a bottle of Armagnac, a close cousin of cognac, and he said that the Frenchman had buried that bottle for four years so the Germans could not find it. This gift from the French priest was a token of appreciation for his country's liberation. "For a brief moment, life had seemed sane again and had gained a degree of normalcy," he wrote.[20]

Once in Belgium, LeBlanc served as a translator for members of a small Belgian Resistance unit. He wrote about meeting the small band of French-speaking underground fighters in a dimly lit room. His job was to give instructions on the use of Canadian automatic weapons. He wrote, "There I was, a 19-year-old kid with fuzz for a beard, among those veterans of guerrilla warfare. They were smoking, and the room was full of tobacco smoke, the room barely lit, probably by candles, and the guys all talking in French. I felt like a character in a clandestine movie about spies."[21]

On the southern coast of the Yarmouth region lays the tranquil, seaside fishing community of Wedgeport, best known for its seafood industry and lobster fleet. When the Acadians returned to this area in the late eighteenth century, following Le Grand Dérangement and the seizing of their fertile farmland, many of those vanquished families turned to fishing as a means of survival. Generations later, Acadian fishermen and boatbuilders, like the LeBlancs and the Theriaults, pioneered the modern commercial lobster industry on the Bay of Fundy in southwestern Nova Scotia. On a casual drive along the "French Coast" in the neighboring region of Clare, one comes across a large shipyard with the name A. F. Theriault—a third-generation lobster-boat builder—along with many homes and businesses that don the Acadian flag. This is indeed the Acadian heartland.

One of those pioneering Acadian boatbuilders, Harold LeBlanc, served in France in World War II and wrote a series of wartime letters, which his family has preserved. In addition to crafting hulls, LeBlanc was a prolific storyteller. The family also uncovered an old interview with LeBlanc from a local radio station in which he described his wartime experience as a French-speaking Acadian in France. He served with Le Régiment de Maisonneuve, a unit from Quebec, and likely improved his English by translating for the

Québécois and other Canadian and British troops. The family noticed from the dozens of letters that he wrote to his mother that his spelling in English greatly improved over time because he was being taught English. His bilingual skills were put to good use in a French hospital, where he was used as a translator, and as a company runner to send messages across the line in both French and English.

His son, Kevin LeBlanc, explained the significance of these testimonials:

> My father, locally, as a young man would speak our Acadian French here. Probably his English was not the greatest when he first went in the army, and as the letters that we've read, the first letters are very hard to read because of his writing and spelling, but the last letters are pretty good, because they were being taught in English, so he probably learned more English at war than he done at home. So he learned his English, many times as being in a Quebec regiment, they learned a lot of the Quebec French by being with Quebec people, and after a while, they probably lost their dialect, but he told us many times that he had to translate for people. Especially when he worked in the hospital and he had to translate from patient to doctor, or from doctor to patient, because they couldn't understand each other. . . . He took the job of what they call a "company runner," and one of the reasons that they did put him in company runner is because he could speak two languages. . . . The people from France could not understand the Quebec people, or vice versa, so they had a better way of communicating with them than the Quebecers.[22]

Cyr LeBlanc, the local historian mentioned previously who has researched the Acadians of World War II for many years, is also a relative of Harold LeBlanc. He described the historical and linguistic circumstances by which the Acadians of that generation maintained a distinct, ancient dialect, which the Cajun Frenchies also found immensely valuable in parts of France. "We were so isolated in this area that we kept the old French," he said.

> So the standardization of French wasn't taught in the schools, and so some of the old words we just kept within the people. Like we count in Acadian French, it's "*septante*" instead of "*soixante-dix*" in standard French, and that's seventy. And we still count that way. I mean, we

> kept that for three hundred years. And there are quite a few other expressions like that. The problem now is that a lot of English words are mixed into our French, but at that time, in Harold's time, it was a pure French. Like I remember my grandparents, I wouldn't hear any English words from them, or very, very seldom. They were all speaking always totally in French, so Harold was the same way. Then when they spoke to French people from France, the French people from France knew a lot of these old words we were still using, even if they didn't speak the words, but in some areas, even in other parts of Europe, they still count the old way. So we kept the old French, and the French people, as I say, they understood us because they knew from their parents.[23]

"Up the line," as they say, and across the bay in neighboring New Brunswick, Roger Babineau struggled with English in the military and was singled out because of it. But it ultimately became a major benefit to his military career while stationed in France immediately after the war. Raised in the French-speaking community of Shediac River in Eastern New Brunswick, he did not learn to speak English until he joined the service. "I joined the service in 1941, age eighteen. That's when I left the nest. During the war, we were not treated the same. If there was any dirty job, I mean, I was one of them, those three, four of us, they was always picking on us, but that's normal, I guess." He lived and worked in France for four years after the war as a service member working at an Air Force base for the North Atlantic Treaty Organization (NATO). His ability to speak French played a key role in this unique opportunity to continue to serve his country and its francophone allies abroad. "NATO was the force after the war that took over Europe. I was part of NATO. We were sent all over the place. I lived in France for four years and I was in the French city of Metz. My boss didn't speak a word of French, so when he wanted something, I had to translate for him."[24]

When the Acadians returned home after the war, there were few parades to welcome them. Many felt that their sacrifice was unappreciated. Most had a hard time finding work after the war, but they persisted and fought for equal economic opportunities. Beginning in the 1950s, with the bicentennial observance of the Acadian expulsion of 1755, the inklings of a cultural awakening began to take shape across the Acadian Maritimes. "Acadians generally are working towards a rebirth of their racial group instead of crying over what has happened in the past," Roger Comeau, a genealogist at the public archives in Ottawa, noted in 1954.[25] By the 1960s, with the election of the first Acadian, Louis Robichaud, as the premier of New Brunswick (similar to the role of a state governor), the Acadian populous experienced a resurgence of ethnic pride and progress. Camille LeBlanc, an Acadian veteran and cultural advocate in the post-war era, shared his words of wisdom about this historical transformation and what it meant for the broader community of Acadia:

> *Je suis né d'une famille Acadians ici au Nouveau Brunswick. J'ai participé à plusieurs le diverse Acadians et aussi pour la promotion de l'éducation des Acadians au Nouveau Brunswick.* I was born in Memramcook, New Brunswick, and right now I'm a hundred years old. That's where the life of French Acadians started, because Memramcook was a swamp hole of the Acadian people and of course the Acadian history of the *dispersion des Acadians*. So, there was the stronghold, New Brunswick, and, of course, all these other villages, too, and going up as far as Hamilton [Mountain], New Brunswick, and towards Saint John, New Brunswick. So there was lots of, each one of those groups, around the province, there was activity, towards the idea of making Acadia a place for home, a place that would progress, a place where we could tell people, "This is our land! Let's look at it!" Of course, we're proud of it. We're proud of any noise we might have made. . . . Again, language was there [in the military] and made its way, not only in peacetime, but in wartime, where it was so important to have this unit gel together and come and recognize together, because little Acadian French-speaking boys were able to go in the same uniform. . . . We took advantage of the opportunity to express ourselves in French and to ask the English community to understand why we're doing this, avoid any malice or anything like that, but it was an understanding that we respected the English-speaking people and their language, don't forget, oh, yes, you know, because there was an advantage. There was an advantage for us as well. The English-speaking understood that. . . . So progress was made.[26]

The Acadians, like the Cajuns, indeed made progress after the war with respect to their ethnic self-awareness and entrenched efforts at preserving their culture and language. With the motto "*Surge Acadia*!" or "Rise,

Acadia!" a national movement to advance social and political recognition of Acadian heritage gripped the province of New Brunswick throughout the 1960s and spilled over into neighboring regions. The pride in being an Acadian reached a crescendo in 1969, following the creation of the official dual-language system in New Brunswick. Keeping that language and culture intact throughout the Maritime provinces remains a constant battle for this proud francophone group, which has proven that knowledge of two languages carries a distinct advantage.

ENDNOTES

PREFACE

1. Paul Surette, *Atlas of the Acadian Settlements of the Beaubassin, 1660–1755* (Sackville: Tantramar Heritage Trust, 2005).

INTRODUCTION

1. Stephen E. Ambrose, *D-Day, June 6, 1944: The Climactic Battle of World War II* (New York: Simon & Schuster, 1994), 104. The signals translate, respectively, to "It is hot in Suez" and "The dice are on the carpet."

2. *Cajun* is the Anglo derivative of the word *Cadien*, a French name traditionally associated with people of Acadian descent—those exiled from the modern-day Canadian maritime provinces of New Brunswick, Prince Edward Island, and Nova Scotia by the British in 1755. The word "Cajun" apparently originated in Louisiana in the mid-nineteenth century by English-speaking people and—supported by upper-class landowning Acadians—came to represent in most cases a lower class of peasant farmers and fisherfolk living in rural south Louisiana.

3. Interview with Robert LeBlanc by Jason P. Theriot, 2006. All interviews by Jason P. Theriot are part of the Jason P. Theriot Oral History Collection archived at the Center for Louisiana Studies, University of Louisiana at Lafayette.

4. For a historical treatment on Cajuns on the home front, see Jason P. Theriot, "Cajun Country During World War II," *Journal of the Louisiana Historical Society* 51, no. 2 (Spring 2010): 133–70. It is important to note that, on occasion, primary source documents will substitute the term "Creole" for "Cajun" and vice versa, especially in the pre-World War II era. Throughout Louisiana history, particularly the earlier period, "Creole" was associated with native-born people of the state; therefore, "Cajun" can be considered a form of Creole or a subset of the broader Creole native people, in that Cajuns are primarily south Louisiana natives of French-speaking, Roman Catholic heritage.

5. The definitive historical work on this topic is Carl Brasseaux, *Acadian to Cajun: Transformation of a People, 1803–1877* (Jackson: University Press of Mississippi, 1992).

6. Interview with Jefferson DeBlanc by Jason P. Theriot, 2006.

7. "Capt. Mouton Will Travel Bayous to Recruit Fighters for Marines," *Daily Advertiser*, January 1, 1942, 3.

8. Interview with Harry Jackson by Jason P. Theriot, 2006.

9. "Never Hit a Child with a Broom; It Will Make Him Stupid—Or So Many in Evangeline Area Believe," *Shreveport Times*, June 4, 1939, 19.

10. "Swamp 'Grapevine' Hums and Cajuns' Troop in to Register Houston," *Houston Chronicle*, October 17, 1940, 16.

11. "Evangeline Life in Swamp Told by Cajun," *Atlanta Constitution,* March 7, 1941, 5.

12. William Faulkner Rushton, *The Cajuns: From Acadia to Louisiana* (New York: Farrar Straus Giroux, 1979), 5.

13. "Cajuns Cherish Outdoor Oven," *Democrat and Chronicle*, June 1, 1941, 70.

14. "Louisiana Cajuns," *Atlanta Constitution*, February 11, 1940, 58.

15. "A Tip on Calling Them Cajuns," *Times-Picayune* (New Orleans, LA), October 25, 1942, 34.

16. Harnett T. Kane, *The Bayous of Louisiana* (New York: William Morrow & Company, 1943), 17.

17. "Harnett Kane Addresses Rotary, Kiwanis Club," *Town Talk* (Alexandria, LA), November 23, 1943, 10.

18. "Thirty-Two Grounded Airmen Owe Lives to Cajun Swamp Guardians," *Dallas Morning News*, December 14, 1943, 11.

19. The term "coonass" is a derogatory ethnic slur originally attached to the Cajuns by non-Cajuns in the early twentieth century, but later became a popular label among Cajuns themselves in the 1970s and 1980s.

20. Interview with Robert LeBlanc by Jason P. Theriot, 2003.

21. Shane K. Bernard, *The Cajuns: Americanization of a People* (Jackson: University Press of Mississippi, 2003), 11.

22. James H. Dorman, *The People Called Cajuns: An Introduction to an* Ethnohistory (Lafayette: The Center for Louisiana Studies, 1983), 70–71.

23. Dorman, *The People Called Cajuns*, 70.

24. Dorman, *The People Called Cajuns*, 74.

25. Dorman, *The People Called Cajuns*, 73.

26. Jacques M. Henry and Carl L. Bankston, III, *Blue Collar Bayou: Louisiana Cajuns in the New Economy of Ethnicity* (Connecticut: Praeger Publishers, 2002), 13–14.

27. In the early 2000s, local researcher Kenneth Delcambre compiled excerpts from the wartime letters in a multivolume series, *L'Echo du Teche Revisited.* The excerpts, often short and to the point, are numerous and revealing.

28. Kenneth P. Delcambre, *L'Echo du Teche Revisited*, January 1943 to November 1943 (Breaux Bridge, Louisiana: self-pub., 2003), 109.

29. Delcambre, *L'Echo du Teche Revisited*, 1943, 154.

30. Delcambre, *L'Echo du Teche Revisited*, 1943, 268.

31. Kenneth P. Delcambre, *L'Echo du Teche Revisited*, January 1944 to June 1944 (Breaux Bridge, Louisiana: self-pub., 2003), 15.

32. Kenneth P. Delcambre, *L'Echo du Teche Revisited*, March 1942 to December 1942 (Breaux Bridge, Louisiana: self-pub., 2003), 296.

33. Delcambre, *L'Echo du Teche Revisited*, 1944, 110.

34. It is interesting to note that several letters reference the term "Cajun," but in lowercased or in quotations. This suggests that young Cajuns of that period—and society at large—had yet to recognize the Cajuns as an official ethnic group with the appropriate capitalized proper noun.

35. "Letters and News from Our Boys," *Daily World* (Opelousas, LA) February 3, 1944, 3.

36. Letter from Murphy Fontenot to Joel Fletcher, Sept. 1944, Joel L. Fletcher Presidential Papers, Archives and Special Collections, University of Louisiana at Lafayette, Coll. A03, Box 63, Folder 1 [hereafter Fletcher Papers]. For reference, the letters are arranged alphabetically by last name.

37. Harry Baudoin letter, Fletcher Papers, 62-3.

38. "Proper Position asked for France," *Times-Picayune* (New Orleans, LA), September 20, 1944, 8.

39. "Lights at Sea," *Daily Advertiser* (Lafayette, LA), November 28, 2000, 46.

40. "Misses Cajun Food," *Abbeville Meridional*, September 4, 1943, 7.

41. "This and That," *Teche News* (St. Martinville, LA), March 2, 1945, 1.

42. "Personals," *Eunice News*, January 17, 1945, 2.

43. "Teaches French," *Clarion-News* (Opelousas, LA), January 18, 1945, 8.

44. "Receives Bronze Start Medal," *Town Talk* (Alexandria, LA), May 30, 1945, 4.

45. "In Uniform," *Jennings Daily News*, July 17, 1945, 3.

46. "Wounded Grand Coteau Soldier is Recovering," *Daily Advertiser* (Lafayette, LA), November 24, 1944, 2.

47. Quote from Pat Mire's *Mon Cher Camarade*, 2008, Louisiana Public Broadcasting.

48. Donald A. Richie, *Doing Oral History: A Practical Guide* (New York: Oxford University Press, 2003), 46, 57.

49. Robin Meche Kube, "Cajun Soldiers During WWII: Reflection on Louisiana's French Language and People," *Louisiana History* 35, no. 3 (Summer 1994): 345–49.

50. I. Bruce Turner, "Dear Southwesterners: World War II, Southwestern Louisiana Institute, and Joel L. Fletcher's Newsletter," *Le Chêne*, (Spring 1998), University Archives and Acadiana Manuscripts Collection, University of Louisiana at Lafayette.

51. Bernard, *The Cajuns*, 6.

52. Robert LeBlanc interview, 2006.

Chapter One

1. "President's National Guard Plan," *New York Times*, July 30, 1940, 11.

2. *Initial Rosters: Organizations and Units of the Louisiana National Guard*, Office of the Adjutant General, Jackson Barracks, New Orleans, 1 October 1941, Jackson Barracks Library Archives, New Orleans, Louisiana [hereafter Jackson Barracks Archives].

3. Interview with Homer Comeaux by Jason P. Theriot, 2003.

4. Interview with Addy Melancon by Jason P. Theriot, 2020.

5. Ernest Broussard wartime diary, copy in author's possession.

6. Bender Scarpero, "Breaux Bridge: The Gentle Bond of a Common Country," *National Guardsman* (March 1951): 9, Jackson Barracks Archives.

7. "Signal Callers," *American Press* (Lake Charles, LA), August 19, 1940, 12.

8. Interview with Ed Broussard by Jason P. Theriot, 2004.

9. Wilfred Sellers letter, Fletcher Papers, 30-8.

10. James Melancon letter, Fletcher Papers, 30-9.

11. For details on the Louisiana Maneuvers, see G. Patrick Murray, "The Louisiana Maneuvers: Practice for War," *Louisiana History* 13 (1972): 117–38; Michael Depp, "Battlefield Louisiana," *Louisiana Life* (Winter 2001/02): 46–51.

12. Addy Melancon interview.

13. Addy Melancon interview.

14. Addy Melancon interview.

15. Homer Comeaux interview.

16. Addy Melancon interview.

17. Addy Melancon interview.

18. Addy Melancon interview.

19. "New England and Louisiana French Meet," *Boston Globe*, March 20, 1941, 26.

20. "New England and Louisiana," 26.

21. Interview with Alonzo "Al" Nugent by Jason P. Theriot, 2004.

22. Scarpero, "Breaux Bridge," 10.

23. Delcambre, *L'Echo du Teche Revisited*, 1942, 194.

24. "The Washington Merry-Go Round," *American Press* (Lake Charles, LA), October 2, 1941, 8.

25. "Medium French," *The Dixie* (Official Newspaper of the Dixie 31st Division), April 25, 1941, 4.

26. Homer Comeaux interview.

27. Ernest Broussard diary.

28. All three served in combat in France as officers of infantry units; Oswald Ronsonet was killed in action in 1944; Mestayer and Broussard were both wounded and received Silver Stars for heroism.

29. Interview with Lennard Martin by Jason P. Theriot, 2006.

30. Lazard Landry letter, Fletcher Papers, 30-11.

31. "Colorful, French-speaking Louisiana Soldiers are Here," *Charleston News and Courier*, January 17, 1942, 12.

32. In this case, the reporter from the *Charleston News* mistakenly substituted the term Creole for Cajun in referencing the national guard troops from Louisiana.

33. "Colorful, French-speaking," 12.

34. Lennard Martin interview.

35. Ed Broussard interview.

36. Addy Melancon interview.

37. Homer Comeaux interview.

38. Lennard Martin interview.

39. Shelby L. Stanton, *World War II Order of Battle* (New York: Galahad Books, 1984), 227.

40. Lennard Martin interview.

41. Delcambre, *L'Echo du Teche Revisited*, 1943, 68, 92.

42. Delcambre, *L'Echo du Teche Revisited*, 1943, 143–44.

43. Delcambre, *L'Echo du Teche Revisited*, 1943, 177.

44. "Where Court is Conducted in French Columbus," *Dallas Dispatch*, February 15, 1943, 11.

45. Delcambre, *L'Echo du Teche Revisited*, 1943, 42.

46. "News of Our Men and Women in Uniform," *Rayne Acadian-Tribune*, October 29, 1943, 7.

47. Delcambre, *L' Echo du Teche Revisited,* 1943, 74.

48. Delcambre, *L' Echo du Teche Revisited,* 1943, 134.

49. Interview with Percy Johnson by Jason P. Theriot, 2001.

50. "J. Pellessier is Crew Chief of Bomb Group," *Daily Advertiser* (Lafayette, LA), June 27, 1944, 7.

51. Interview with Lloyd "Pete" Rogers by Andrew Gardner, January 16, 2002, Offshore Oil and Gas History Project (OOGHP), 2002, a study funded by the US Department of the Interior, Minerals Management Service.

52. World War II oral history interview collection by Robin Meche Kube, 1991, archived at the Center for Louisiana Studies, University of Louisiana at Lafayette. [Hereafter Kube interviews.]

53. Interview with Bernice LeJeune by Jason P. Theriot, 2001.

54. Kube interviews.

55. "Takes Voluntary Demotion by Army to Rejoin Tank Unit," *Times-Picayune* (New Orleans, LA), June 24, 1944, 11.

56. "Patton-Swell ... LeBlanc Informs Rotary," *Abbeville Meridional*, June 24, 1944, 1.

57. Delcambre, *L'Echo du Teche Revisited*, 1943, 137.

58. Delcambre, *L'Echo du Teche Revisited*, 1943, 310.

59. Delcambre, *L'Echo du Teche Revisited*, 1943, 109.

60. Delcambre, *L'Echo du Teche Revisited*, 1943, 244.

61. Delcambre, *L'Echo du Teche Revisited*, 1943, 170. Translation provided by Zachary Fuselier.

62. W. V. Dupre letter, Fletcher Papers, 62-6.

63. "They're in the Service," *Advocate* (Baton Rouge, LA), February 2, 1943, 5.

64. "Communications Man Upbraids Italy Climate," *Daily Advertiser* (Lafayette, LA) February 26, 1945, 2.

65. Kenneth Delcambre, *L'Echo du Teche Revisited*, January 1944 to January 1946, 117.

66. Interview with Sam Delcambre by Jason P. Theriot, 2003.

67. Interview with Emery Toups by Jason P. Theriot, 2006.

68. "Interpreter Helps Save B-26," *Barksdale's Bark* (LA), October 28, 1944, 8.

69. Louis Courtade family personal papers, copy in author's possession.

70. Delcambre, *L'Echo du Teche Revisited*, 1943, 306.

71. Delcambre, *L'Echo du Teche Revisited*, 1943, 283, 306.

72. Delcambre, *L'Echo du Teche Revisited*, 1943, 283.

73. Delcambre, *L'Echo du Teche Revisited*, 1943, 33.

74. Delcambre, *L'Echo du Teche Revisited*, 1944, 107.

75. Delcambre, *L'Echo du Teche Revisited*, 1944, 77.

76. "Uncle Sam's Nephews, Nieces," *American Press* (Lake Charles, LA), June 2, 1944, 24.

77. Delcambre, *L'Echo du Teche Revisited*, 1944, 25.

78. Delcambre, *L'Echo du Teche Revisited*, 1945, 39.

79. Interview with Robert Gerami by Jason P. Theriot, 2001.

80. Homer Comeaux interview.

81. Interview with Alfred Zeringue by Jason P. Theriot, 2001.

82. Pierre Laiche personal papers, copy in author's possession.

83. Laiche personal papers.

84. "Sgt. Louis Cormier of Crowley Is Back Home," *Acadian-Signal* (Crowley, LA), May 17, 1945, 4.

85. Louis Cormier personal papers, copy in author's possession.

86. Interview with Wallace Thibodeaux by Jason P. Theriot, 2001.

87. Interview with Warren Hebert by Jason P. Theriot, 2001.

Chapter Two

1. "They help keep the colors flying," *Weekly News* (Marksville, LA), August 5, 1944, 2.

2. Rodney Young letter, Fletcher Papers, 64-7.

3. "Parents Received Delayed Letter," *Bunkie (LA) Record*, July 7, 1944, 8.

4. "Sailor's French Comes in Handy," *Times-Picayune* (New Orleans, LA), September 4, 1944, 16.

5. Interview with Jim Lanclos by Jason P. Theriot, 2005.

6. Interview with Charles Ducote Sr. by his granddaughter, no date, archived at the Center for Louisiana Studies, University of Louisiana at Lafayette.

7. "Pfc. Clifford Borel Awarded Purple Heart," *Teche News* (St. Martinville, LA), July 21, 1944, 1.

8. "Lafayette Man Saves Day by Talking French," *Daily Advertiser* (Lafayette, LA), August 19, 1944, 7.

9. "Livonia Sergeant Called One of the Best Soldiers on the Western Front," *State-Times* (Livonia, LA), April 17, 1945, 8-B.

10. Interview with Ned Arceneaux by Jason P. Theriot, 2006.

11. Ned Arceneaux interview.

12. Ned Arceneaux interview.

13. "Marion McGee of Eunice Writes He Was in Battle of Cherbourg," *Eunice News*, August 9, 1944, 4.

14. "Mademoiselle of Bar-le-Duc is Gone," *Daily News* (New York City), August 9, 1944, 45.

15. "Letters to SLI's President," *Abbeville Meridional*, September 19, 1944, 4.

16. "A Remembrance: Army Days of P. F. C. Curtis Myers," prepared by his granddaughter, Michelle Longman Dugas, copy in author's possession.

17. Robert LeBlanc interview, 2003.

18. Robert LeBlanc interview, 2003.

19. "Leo Thomas Writes to SLI President," *Teche News* (St. Martinville, LA), November 10, 1944, 2.

20. Interview with Carroll Mestayer by Jason P. Theriot, 2006.

21. Carroll Mestayer interview.

22. Carroll Mestayer interview.

23. Carroll Mestayer interview.

24. "Lack of French leads to Delay," *Times-Picayune* (New Orleans, LA), September 24, 1944, 23.

25. Lee Arceneaux letter, Fletcher Papers, 62-2.

26. A. J. Resweber letter, Fletcher Papers, 64-3.

27. Delcambre, *L'Echo du Teche Revisited*, 1944, 61.

28. "Service News," *Morgan City Review*, June 30, 1944, 6.

29. Delcambre, *L'Echo du Teche Revisited*, 1944, 34.

30. "Pvt. H. Vidrine is Interpreter," *Ville Platte Gazette*, July 13, 1944, 1.

31. "Sez Eye," *Bunkie (LA) Record*, July 14, 1944, 1.

32. Homer Doucet letter, Fletcher Papers, 62-6.

33. Thomas Clement letter, Fletcher Papers, 62-5.

34. Thomas Doiron letter, Fletcher Papers, 62-6.

35. Rita Merle Durand letter, Fletcher Papers, 62-2.

36. Sam Broussard personal papers, copy in author's possession.

37. Harold Pastor letter, Fletcher Papers, 64-2.

38. "Life in War-Torn France is Described by Army Officer," *Daily World* (Opelousas, LA), September 17, 1944, 10.

39. "Letters from Overseas," *Abbeville Meridional*, September 30, 1944, 20.

40. Interview with Lloyd Berard by Jason P. Theriot, 2006.

41. Interview with Sidney Vincent by Jason P. Theriot, 2005.

42. Quote from Pat Mire's *Mon Cher Camarade*, 2008, Louisiana Public Broadcasting.

43. Kube interviews.

44. C. G. "Buddy" Simon, Jr. letter, Fletcher Papers, 64-4.

45. Kube interviews.

46. Kube interviews.

47. Kube interviews.

48. Interview with Norris Morvant by Jason P. Theriot, 2020.

49. Norris Morvant interview.

50. Norris Morvant interview.

51. Norris Morvant interview.

52. Norris Morvant interview.

53. Norris Morvant interview.

54. Therese Bienvenue, a native of Normandy, France, who married a Cajun GI, taught French in Iberia Parish for many years.

55. Delcambre, *L'Echo du Teche Revisited*, 1945, 14.

56. Ed Broussard interview.

57. Lucien Laborde interview, the National WWII Museum, 2015, https://www.ww2online.org/view/lucien-laborde#ve-day-a-popular-officer-and-relationships-with-locals.

58. Lucien Laborde interview

59. Delcambre, *L'Echo du Teche Revisited*, 1945, 43.

60. Delcambre, *L'Echo du Teche Revisited*, 1945, 46.

61. Delcambre, *L'Echo du Teche Revisited*, 1945, 67.

62. Delcambre, *L'Echo du Teche Revisited*, 1944, 89.

63. Delcambre, *L'Echo du Teche Revisited*, 1944, 117.

64. "Stationed in France," *Abbeville Meridional*, August 12, 1944, 3.

65. Interview with Ambroise "A. J." Champagne by Jason P. Theriot, 2002.

66. Mansel Mayeux personal memoir, copy in author's possession.

67. Mansel Mayeux personal papers, copy in author's possession. French translation provided by David Marcantel.

68. Joseph Delcambre personal papers, copy in author's possession. French translation provided by David Cheramie.

69. Delcambre, *L'Echo du Teche Revisited,* 1944, 118.

70. "Leo Thomas writes from France," *Teche News* (St. Martinville, LA), December 1, 1944, 2.

71. The FFI stood for the French Forces of the Interior, the broader network of organized resistance groups operating throughout the country during the battle for France.

72. Interview with Dennis Neal by Jason P. Theriot, 2006.

73. "Paris to Point au Chein," *Houma Times*, November 16, 1946, 1.

74. "French War Bride of Sgt. Stutes, Rayne GI Arrives in America," *Clarion-News*, May 30, 1946, 3.

75. "French War Bride Arrives to Join Iberia Husband," *New Iberia Enterprise*, May 3, 1946, 1.

76. Interview with Reaux Meaux by Jason P. Theriot, 2006.

77. "Says French War Bride," *Weekly News* (Marksville, LA), April 26, 1947, 10.

78. Interview with Lee Bernard by Jason P. Theriot, 2020.

79. Lee Bernard interview.

80. Lee Bernard interview.

81. Lee Bernard interview.

82. Lee Bernard interview.

83. Quote from Pat Mire's *Mon Cher Camarade*, 2008, Louisiana Public Broadcasting.

84. Lee Bernard interview.

85. Lee Bernard interview.

86. Lee Bernard interview.

87. Lee Bernard interview.

88. Alton "Ton" Girouard personal papers, copy in author's possession.

89. Alton Girouard personal papers.

90. Isadore Labbe story, written by Joan Boudreaux, copy in author's possession.

91. Lionel Abshire personal memoir, copy in author's possession.

92. Lionel Abshire personal memoir.

93. Addy Melancon interview.

94. Addy Melancon interview.

95. Addy Melancon interview.

96. Addy Melancon interview.

97. Addy Melancon interview.

98. Lester Armand letter, Fletcher Papers, 62-2.

99. Damas Romero family personal papers, copy in author's possession.

100. "Crowley Infantryman," *Crowley Daily Signal,* July 13, 1945, 5.

101. Interview with Prigeon Fontenot by Jason P. Theriot, 2021.

102. Prigeon Fontenot interview.

103. Interview with Sidney Hardy by Jason P. Theriot, 2021.

104. Sidney Hardy interview.

105. Sidney Hardy interview.

106. Interview with Meus "Pie" Hebert by Keith Leger, accessed June 13, 2024, YouTube: https://www.youtube.com/watch?v=RDXOiKKFzow&t=477s.

107. Interview with Shirley Guidry by Jason P. Theriot, 2021.

108. Shirley Guidry interview.

109. Shirley Guidry interview.

110. Lester J. Guillory papers, newspaper articles (no date), copy in author's possession.

111. "Back in Mufti Crowley," *Daily Signal* (Crowley, LA), September 7, 1945, 1.

112. "Back in Mufti," 1.

113. Addy Melancon interview.

114. Addy Melancon interview.

115. "Speaking French was 'badge of honor' for last living veteran of original Louisiana guard unit," *Acadiana Advocate* (Lafayette, LA), September 27, 2021, 1.

116. Addy Melancon award ceremony, 2021, author's personal collection.

117. Addy Melancon award ceremony, 2021.

Chapter Three

1. Cory Ford, *Donovan of OSS* (New York: Little, Brown & Company, 1970), 135.

2. Stephen E. Ambrose, *Ike's Spies: Eisenhower and the Espionage Establishment* (Jackson: University Press of Mississippi, 1981),105.

3. Ambrose, *Ike's Spies* 108.

4. Sam Broussard personal papers, copy in author's possession.

5. Interview with Sam Broussard by the Smithsonian Institute, no date, Broussard family collection, copy in author's possession.

6. Sam Broussard, Smithsonian interview.

7. Sam Broussard's personal papers.

8. Sam Broussard's personal papers.

9. Sam Broussard's personal papers.

10. Sam Broussard's personal papers.

11. Sam Broussard's personal papers.

12. "Commandos in Action," *Spokesman-Review* (Spokane, WA), June 12, 1944, 12.

13. Sam Broussard's personal papers.

14. Sam Broussard's personal papers.

16. Sam Broussard's personal papers.

17. "Interview with Sam Broussard," hosted by James Fontenot, *En Français*, Louisiana Public Broadcasting, November 7, 1982.

18. Sam Broussard's personal papers.

19. "Interview with Sam Broussard," *En Français.*

20. Sam Broussard's personal papers.

21. Sam Broussard's personal papers.

22. Sam Broussard's personal papers.

23. Sam Broussard's personal papers.

24. Sam Broussard's personal papers.

25. Sam Broussard's personal papers.

26. "Jedburgh" was the code name for a secret international unit within OSS that parachuted into France on and after D-Day to train and lead Resistance forces and integrate their actions with other Allied units.

27. Paul Gaujac, *Special Forces in the Invasion of France* (Paris: Histoire & Collections, 1999), 99.

28. Ford, *Donovan of OSS*, 234.

29. Interview with Shirly Ray Trumps by Jason P. Theriot, 2005.

30. Shirly Ray Trumps interview.

31. Shirly Ray Trumps personal papers, copy in author's possession.

32. Shirly Ray Trumps personal papers.

33. Interview with Robert LeBlanc by Jason P. Theriot, 2019.

34. Interview with Robert LeBlanc by Jason P. Theriot, 2003.

35. Interview with Robert LeBlanc by Jason P. Theriot, 2006.

36. Robert LeBlanc interview, 2006.

37. Robert LeBlanc interview, 2006.

38. Robert LeBlanc interview, 2006.

39. Robert J. LeBlanc, *An Acadian Citizen Soldier and Public Servant* (self-pub., 2005).

40. Robert LeBlanc interview, 2003.

41. Robert LeBlanc interview, 2003.

42. Robert LeBlanc interview, 2003.

43. Robert LeBlanc interview, 2003.

44. LeBlanc, *An Acadian Citizen Soldier and Public Servant.*

45. Robert LeBlanc interview, 2003.

46. Robert LeBlanc interview, 2003.

47. Robert LeBlanc interview, 2019.

48. LeBlanc, *An Acadian Citizen Soldier and Public Servant.*

49. Interview with Roy Armentor by Jason P. Theriot, 2004.

50. Roy Armentor interview.

51. Gaujac, *Special Forces in the Invasion of France*, 106.

52. Roy Armentor interview.

53. Interview with Claude Galley by Jason P. Theriot, 2006.

54. Claude Galley interview.

55. Claude Galley interview.

56. Roy Armentor interview.

57. The word "coonie" is short for "coonass," which historically was viewed as a derogatory slur for a person of Cajun ethnicity. However, since the 1980s, many Cajuns have embraced the term "coonass" as a marker of ethnic pride.

58. Roy Armentor interview.

59. Claude Galley interview.

60. Roy Armentor interview.

61. Roy Armentor interview.

62. Claude Galley interview.

63. Claude Galley interview.

64. Roy Armentor personal papers, copy in author's possession. The compete story of the *Maquis Jean Robert et Faita* and Operational Group "Peg" can be found here: http://maquisftp-jeanrobert-faita.org/.

65. At this meeting, author Jason Theriot, alongside (retired) Brigadier General Robert LeBlanc, gave a three-hour presentation on "Cajun Espionage," with Armentor and Galley in attendance. The full video presentation can be seen at www.jasontheriot.com/media.

66. Interview with Orleans Pitre by Billy Pitre, 1991, Marco J. Picciola Papers, Archives and Special Collections, Nicholls State University, Thibodaux, Louisiana.

67. Orleans Pitre interview.

68. Orleans Pitre interview.

69. Orleans Pitre interview.

70. Orleans Pitre interview.

71. Robert LeBlanc interview, 2003.

72. Robert LeBlanc interview, 2006.

Chapter Four

1. Kenneth P. Delcambre, *L'Echo du Teche Revisited*, 1944 (Breaux Bridge, Louisiana: self-pub., 2003), 60.

2. Kenneth P. Delcambre, *L'Echo du Teche Revisited*, 1943 (Breaux Bridge, Louisiana: self-pub., 2003), 158.

3. "Sugar cane in the Pacific brings back memories for former Erath boy," *Abbeville Meridional* (11 March 1944), 7. Five months later, Lt. DeRouen died from wounds received in combat on Saipan.

4. Ray Broussard letter, Joel L. Fletcher Presidential Papers, Archives and Special Collections, University of Louisiana at Lafayette, Coll. A03, Box 62, Folder 3 [hereafter Fletcher Papers].

5. Delcambre, *L' Echo du Teche Revisited*, 1944, 84.

6. Jerome Domengeaux letter, Fletcher Papers, 62-6.

7. Delcambre, *L'Echo du Teche Revisited*, 1944, 84, 119.

8. Delcambre, *L'Echo du Teche Revisited*, 1943, 126.

9. Interview with Otis Courville by Jason P. Theriot, 2006.

10. Interview with Otis Courville.

11. Interview with Jefferson DeBlanc by Jason P. Theriot, 2006.

12. Jefferson J. DeBlanc, *The Guadalcanal Air War: Col. Jefferson DeBlanc's Story* (Gretna, LA: Pelican Publishing Company, 2008), 54.

13. Interview with Jefferson DeBlanc by Jason P. Theriot, 2005.

14. Coastwatchers served as Allied military intelligence operatives in the Pacific. They spied on Japanese military movements and helped rescue downed airmen.

15. Jefferson DeBlanc interview, 2006.

16. "Where are the Yanks?" *Advocate* (Baton Rouge, LA), March 19, 1944, 18.

17. "Benoit, in South Pacific Finds French Invaluable," *Abbeville (LA) Meridional*, June 17, 1944, 8.

18. "Soldier in Pacific War Area Missing His Gumbo, But Enjoying the Scenery," *Abbeville (LA) Meridional*, October 16, 1943, 2.

19. Eno Bares letter, Fletcher Papers, 62-4.

20. "Two Louisiana Navy Nurses Lived in Native Huts on New Caledonia," *Times-Picayune* (New Orleans), January 23, 1945, 22.

21. Joseph Porchiau personal papers, copy in author's possession.

22. Valex Doucet letter, Fletcher Papers, 62-6.

23. DeBlanc, *The Guadalcanal Air War*, 4.

24. "Letter from Rex Chauvin Interesting," *Teche News* (St. Martinville, LA), November 5, 1943, 1.

25. Harris Callahan personal papers, copy in author's possession, translated by David Cheramie.

26. "Farm Project Conducted by Lafayette Man," *Advocate* (Baton Rouge, LA), July 25, 1945, 16.

27. Ford Gremillion letter, Fletcher Papers, 63-2.

28. Ford Gremillion letter, Fletcher Papers, 63-2.

29. Ford Gremillion letter, Fletcher Papers, 63-2.

30. "They Help Keep the Colors Flying," *Weekly News* (Marksville, LA), July 21, 1945, 4.

31. Interview with Mike Trahan by Jude Trahan, no date, copy in author's possession.

32. Ernest Bullington letter, Fletcher Papers, 62-4.

33. Mina Curtiss, ed., *Letters Home* (Boston: Little, Brown and Company, 1944), 223.

34. Delcambre, *L'Echo du Teche Revisited*, 1943, 242.

35. Curtiss, *Letters Home*, 221.

36. Interview with Jonas Perrin by Jason P. Theriot, 2021.

37. Delcambre, *L'Echo du Teche Revisited*, 1943, 260.

38. J. A. "Blackie" Arceneaux letter, Fletcher Papers, 62-2.

39. Delcambre, *L'Echo du Teche Revisited*, 1944.

40. Declambre, *L'Echo du Teche Revisited*, 1944, 28-29. In modern context, "Creole French" is considered to be a separate Creole language of Louisiana called *Kreyòl* or *Kouri-Veni*. The respondent likely meant Cajun French or Louisiana French generally and not the modern interpretation.

41. Declambre, *L'Echo du Teche Revisited*, 1944, 53.

42. Delcambre, *L'Echo du Teche Revisited*, 1943, 213.

43. Delcambre, *L'Echo du Teche Revisited*, 1945, 143.

44. "Lafayette Boys in Philippines hold Gathering," *Daily Advertiser* (Lafayette, LA), August 20, 1945, 7.

45. Interview with Ovide Lancon by Jason P. Theriot, 2021.

Chapter Five

1. "Medals finally in veteran's hands," *Daily Advertiser*, August 21, 2008, 10.

2. Katharine Daspit letter, Joel L. Fletcher Presidential Papers, Archives and Special Collections, University of Louisiana at Lafayette, Coll. A03, Box 62, Folder 6 [hereafter Fletcher Papers].

3. Kenneth P. Delcambre, *L'Echo du Teche Revisited*, 1943 (Breaux Bridge, Louisiana: self-pub., 2003), 263.

4. Delcambre, *L'Echo du Teche Revisited*, 1943, 124.

5. Interview with Alfred "Benny" Granger by Jason P. Theriot, 2006.

6. Delcambre, *L'Echo du Teche Revisited*, 1943, 127.

7. Delcambre, *L'Echo du Teche Revisited*, 1943, 51.

8. Interview with Hewitt Theriot by Jason P. Theriot, 2001.

9. Tom Ducrest, Jr. letter, Fletcher Papers, 62-6.

10. Jerome Domengeaux letter, Fletcher Papers, 62-6.

11. Domengeaux letter.

12. John Marchand letter, Fletcher Papers, 63-8.

13. Kenneth P. Delcambre, *L'Echo du Teche Revisited*, 1944 (Breaux Bridge, Louisiana: self-pub., 2003), 61.

14. Interview with Willis Granger by Jason P. Theriot, 2019.

15. Willis Granger interview.

16. "Vermillion Soldier Learns to Speak English to Stay With Outfit that Went to the Pacific Area," *Abbeville (LA) Meridional*, September 8, 1945, 3.

17. "Cajun Cooks Prepare Meals at Headquarters in London," *News and Courier* (Charleston, SC), July 18, 1943, 17.

18. Delcambre, *L'Echo du Teche Revisited*, 1943, 77.

19. Delcambre, *L'Echo du Teche Revisited*, 1943, 266.

20. Delcambre, *L'Echo du Teche Revisited*, 1943, 157.

21. Delcambre, *L'Echo du Teche Revisited*, 1944, 34.

22. Lazard Landry letter, Fletcher Papers, 63-7

23. Delcambre, *L'Echo du Teche Revisited*, 1944, 21.

24. Alden Sonnier, "The Little Signal," *Crowley (LA) Daily Signal*, March 10, 1947, 4.

25. Quote from Pat Mire's *Mon Cher Camarade*, 2008, Louisiana Public Broadcasting.

26. Janet Barnwell, ed., *Louisiana Voices: Remembering World War II* (Baton Rouge: T. Harry Williams Center for Oral History, 1998), 99.

27. Jefferson J. DeBlanc, *The Guadalcanal Air War: Col. Jefferson DeBlanc's Story* (Gretna, LA: Pelican Publishing Company, 2008), 4.

28. "Letters from Overseas," *Abbeville (LA) Meridional*, April 15, 1944, 7.

29. "Letters from Overseas," *Abbeville (LA) Meridional*, September 16, 1944, 3

30. Frank Summer letter, Fletcher Papers, 64-1.

31. "Letters to S.L.I.'s President" *Abbeville (LA) Meridional*, July 19, 1944, 2.

32. Delcambre, *L'Echo du Teche Revisited*, 1943, 144.

33. Jim Brignac letter, Fletcher Papers, 62-3.

34. Roy Armentor interview.

35. Interview with Robert Leblanc by Jason P. Theriot, 2006.

36. Delcambre, *L'Echo du Teche,* 1943, 95.

37. Delcambre, *L'Echo du Teche,* 1943, 171.

38. Delcambre, *L'Echo du Teche*, 1944, 16.

39. Delcambre, *L'Echo du Teche*, 1944, 81.

40. "Musings About This and That State," *State Times Advocate* (Baton Rouge, LA), March 24, 1945, 8.

41. James Orgeron letter, Fletcher Papers, 64-1

42. Quote from Pat Mire's *Mon Cher Camarade*, 2008, Louisiana Public Broadcasting.

43. Alfred "Benny" Granger interview.

44. Barry Jean Ancelet and Elemore Morgan Jr., *The Makers of Cajun Music/ Musiciens cadiens et créoles* (Austin: University of Texas Press, 1984), 27; See also

Ryan A. Brasseaux and Kevin S. Fontenot, ed., *Accordions, Fiddles, Two Step and Swing: A Cajun Music Reader* (Lafayette: Center for Louisiana Studies, 2006), 114.

45. "Lamperez shares WWII memories," *Crowley (LA) Post-Signal*, May 26, 1996, 1.

46. Barry Jean Ancelet, "A Perspective on Teaching the 'Problem Language' in Louisiana," *The French Review* 61, no. 3 (February 1988), 345. Iry LeJeune led the revival of traditional Cajun-style music after the war, and others such as Austin Pitre, Lawrence Walker, and Nathan Abshire, followed suite. See also Ancelet and Morgan, *The Makers of Cajun Music*, 27.

47. "Fais Do Do Champs to be Named at Festival Contest," *Crowley (LA) Daily Signal*, September 12, 1946, 3; "Acadian Dance Expected to Prove Popular With Festival Goers," *Crowley (LA) Signal-Post,* October 22, 1947, 1.

48. "Evangeline Pag will be shown at Abbeville High," *Gueydan (LA) News*, November 27, 1948, 8.

49. "Editorials: Preserve the Acadian Culture," *Abbeville (LA) Meridional*, February 26, 1949, 4.

50. "Excursion into Louisiana One Embracing Colorful Sights and Hospitable People," *Cincinnati Enquirer*, April 10, 1949, 118.

51. "Globe's deLue on Trip to Cajun Bayous," *Boston Globe*, November 18, 1949, 24.

52. "Colorful, Kindly Cajun Country," *Atlanta Constitution*, October 4, 1950, 13.

53. "Speaking French," *Acadian-Signal* (Rayne, LA), September 2, 1945, 4.

54. Sam Broussard personal papers, copy in author's possession.

55. Interview with Jonas Perrin by Jason P. Theriot, 2021.

56. Interview with Harry Jackson by Jason P. Theriot, 2006.

57. Interview with Curney Dronet Sr., by Jason P. Theriot, 2006.

58. Interview with Chester Cheramie, 2004, Offshore Oil and Gas History Project (OOGHP), 2002, a study funded by the U.S. Department of the Interior, Minerals Management Service.

59. Interview with Ned Arceneaux by Jason P. Theriot, 2006.

60. Telephone interview with Norris Morvant by Jason P. Theriot, 2023.

61. Interview with Lee Bernard by Jason P. Theriot, 2020.

62. See Dudley J. LeBlanc, *The Acadian Miracle* (Lafayette, LA: Evangeline Publishing Co., 1966).

63. "How Far Should We Go In Developing French Language," *Mamou (LA) Acadian Press*, December 2, 1971, 2.

64. Robert LeBlanc interview, 2006.

Appendix

1. French Acadians from Maine and from other pockets of the New England states also served in the US military in the war, along with thousands of Québécois, who were unilingual French.

2. The province of Prince Edward Island is part of the Acadian Maritime region.

3. "Acadians in Canada, Louisiana," *Windsor Star* (Ontario, Canada), February 12, 1944, 25.

4. Interview with Ron Cormier by Jason P. Theriot, 2022.

5. Ron Cormier interview.

6. "Acadians Different from Quebec French," *Windsor Star* (Ontario, Canada), May 26, 1945, 16.

7. "Acadian Dispersal Seen as Repeated," *Windsor Star* (Ontario, Canada), July 18, 1944, 2.

8. Interview with Cyr LeBlanc by Jason P. Theriot, 2022.

9. Ron Cormier interview.

10. "Nazis still confused," *Windsor Star* (Ontario, Canada), June 8, 1944, 27.

11. Ronald Cormier, *Forgotten Soldiers: Stories of Acadian Veterans of the Second World War* (Fredericton, New Brunswick: New Ireland Press, 1992), 82.

12. Cormier, *Forgotten Soldiers*, 83.

13. Cormier, *Forgotten Soldiers*, 65.

14. Cormier, *Forgotten Soldiers*, 89-91.

15. Interview with Havelyn Chiasson, Juno Beach Memorial; https://www.junobeach.org/legacy-of-honour/havelyn-chiasson/.

16. Interview with Alphonse Vautour by Jean-Robert Frigault, 2021.

17. Interview with Charles Muise by Jason P. Theriot, 2022. Muise passed away in January 2024.

18. Charles Muise interview.

19. Charles Muise interview.

20. Basil LeBlanc memoir, Argyle Township Courthouse and Archives, Tusket, Nova Scotia.

21. Basil LeBlanc memoir.

22. Interview with Kevin LeBlanc and Cyr LeBlanc by Jason P. Theriot, 2022.

23. Kevin LeBlanc and Cyr LeBlanc interview.

24. Interview with Roger Babineau by Jason P. Theriot, 2022.

25. "Expulsion of Acadians Now is Thorny Question in Canadian History," *Sun Times* (Owen Sound, Canada), September 4, 1954, 19.

26. Interview with J. Camille LeBlanc by Jason P. Theriot, 2022.

INDEX

D

E

F

M

N

O

P

W

Y

Z

ABOUT THE AUTHOR

Jason P. Theriot, PhD, is an author, historian, and consultant. He earned a doctorate in history from the University of Houston and a degree in journalism from Louisiana State University. Additionally, he is a former Energy Policy Fellow at Harvard University's Kennedy School of Government. Dr. Theriot specializes in family memoirs, biographies, and company histories. He published his first book on World War II in 2002.